ANANDA

MEDITATION AND MANTRAS

Swami Vishnudevananda (1927–1993), a disciple of Swami Sivananda, was the founder of the International Sivananda Yoga Vedanta Centres. He established the Sivananda Yoga Teachers' Training Course, a unique program that allowed the trainees to incorporate the teachings of yoga into their daily lives. His book *The Complete Illustrated Book of Yoga* is considered to be the bible for yoga practitioners.

Swami Vishnudevananda was a Karma Yogi and a peace activist who flew on several 'peace missions' over places of conflict, bombarding war-torn areas with flowers and pamphlets while repeating the peace Mantra: *Om Namo Narayanaya*. He created the Om Namo Narayanaya bank in the Himalayas, hoping to bring positive vibrations to the whole world. Although he left his body on 9 November 1993, his legacy and energy still shine throughout the organization, the centres and ashrams of which have spread all over the world, training over 30,000 teachers.

SWAMI
VISHNUDEVANANDA

MEDITATION & MANTRAS

PENGUIN
ANANDA

PENGUIN ANANDA

USA | Canada | UK | Ireland | Australia
New Zealand | India | South Africa | China

Penguin Ananda is part of the Penguin Random House group of companies whose addresses can be found at global.penguinrandomhouse.com

Published by Penguin Random House India Pvt. Ltd
7th Floor, Infinity Tower C, DLF Cyber City,
Gurgaon 122 002, Haryana, India

Penguin Random House India

First published in the US by OM Lotus Publishing Company, New York 1978
Second edition, 1981; Third edition, 1995
First published in India in Penguin Ananda by Penguin Books India 2014

ISBN 9780143430940

Typeset in Adobe Garamond by Eleven Arts, Delhi
Printed at Repro Knowledgecast Limited, India

www.penguin.co.in

Dedicated to
My Revered Master
H.H. SRI SWAMI SIVANANDA MAHARAJ

And His Chief Disciples
MY VENERABLE GURUBHAIS

Swami Paramananda
Swami Swarupananda
Swami Atmananda
Swami Narayanananda
Swami Chidananda
Swami Krishnananda
Swami Saswadananda
Swami Poorna Bhodh
Swami Visweswarananda
Swami Chinmayananda
Swami Satyananda
Swami Satchidananda (I)
Swami Sahajananda
Swami Purushottamananda
Swami Brahmananda
Swami Vasudevananda
Swami Nijabodhananda
Swami Satchidananda (II)
Swami Nirmalananda
Swami Omkarananda
Swami Harisarananananda
Swami Govindananda
Swami Madhavananda
Swami Sivananda Hridayananda
Swami Vidyananda
Swami Nadabrahmananda
Swami Venkatesananda
Swami Sivapremananda
Swami Chaitanyananda
Swami Dayananda
Swami Nityananda
Swami Saradananda
Swami Sadasivananda
Swami Tejomayananda
Swami Pranavananda
Swami Sadananda
Swami Jñanananda
Swami Raghavananda
Swami Ramananda
Swami Hari Omananda
Swami Premananda (Senior)
Swami Mounananda
Swami Sudhananda
Swami Sraddhananda
Swami Jyotirmayananda

And to my revered poorvashram mother and father,
SWAMI SIVASARANANANDA (P. Devaki Amma)
and P. CHATHU PANIKKER

Contents

Preface to the Second Edition xi
About the Author xv

1. Why Meditate? 1
   Mechanics of the Mind
   Thought Power
   The Self
   Karma and Reincarnation
   What Does Yoga Have to Do with It?

2. The Basics of Meditation 11
   Guide to Meditation
   Health for Meditation
   A Peaceful Diet
   Karma Yoga

3. Concentration: Theory 23
   Power of Concentration
   Pleasure and the Mind
   Best Friend: Worst Enemy

4. Concentration: Practice 31
The Eight Steps
Attention
Establishing the Practice

5. Meditation 39
Mind: Master or Servant?
From the Unreal to the Real
Wild Horses
Advanced Meditation

6. Japa Meditation: Theory 54
The Yoga of Physics
Sound: The Seed of All Matter
Sound as Energy
Using Sound Vibrations for Meditation
Initiation into a Mantra

7. Japa Meditation: Practice 68
Saguna Mantras
Mantras for Japa
Gayatri Mantra
Gayatris of Different Deities
Nirguna Mantras
Abstract Mantras
Bija Mantras, Mystic Seed Letters
Meditation with the Mantra

8. Hatha Yoga Meditation: Kundalini 92
Kundalini Shakti
The Chakras

9. Jnana Yoga Meditation: Vedantic Theory 107
Vedanta
The Veils of Illusion
Who Is This 'I'?
Adhyaropa
Nyayas

10. Jnana Yoga Meditation: Vedantic Practice 127
Neti Neti: Not This, Not This
Sakshi Bhav: Witness State
Abheda Bodha Vakya: Eliminating Name and Form
Laya Chintana: Absorption
Panchikarana: Doctrine of Quintuplication
Mahavakyas or The Great Proclamations
Bhagatyaga Lakshana

11. Bhakti Yoga Meditation 145
Converting the Emotions
Forms of Devotion

12. Raja Yoga Sutras: Theory 152
Chapter One: The Road to Samadhi

13. Raja Yoga Sutras: Practice 183
Chapter Two: Yoga Sadhana
Chapter Three: Divine Manifestations of Power
Chapter Four: Liberation

14. Electronic Meditation 226
What Is Biofeedback?
Beyond Relaxation
Externals vs Internals

15. Obstacles to Meditation 238
Cessation of Practice
Health and Diet
Laziness and Sleep
Complications of Daily Life
Useless Conversation
Uprooting the Ego
The Emotions
Discouragement
Loss of the Vital Energy
The Mind Itself
Obstacles for the Experienced Meditator

16. Experiences in Meditation 258
Various Experiences in Meditation
Anahata Sounds
Lights in Meditation
Mystic Experiences of Sadhakas
In the Hours of Meditation
Vision of God
Feeling of Separation
Cosmic Consciousness
Blissful Experiences
Mind Moves
Bhuta-Ganas
Glimpses of the Self
Jyotirmaya Darshan

International Sivananda Yoga Vedanta Centres 294

Preface to the Second Edition

This volume is intended to dispel the cloud of confusion that has accumulated around the subject of meditation. Those who are looking for secret shortcuts, novel innovations, exciting new trends and fads in the area of self-development may be disappointed. The methods presented here stem from the classic—four paths of Raja Yoga, Karma Yoga, Jnana Yoga and Bhakti Yoga. These are given in their uncorrupted form, yet with consideration for the Western mind and scientific tradition.

Meditation is a universal tradition which traces its origin thousands of years before the advent of today's civilisation. The science of meditation has survived uninterrupted and exhaustive testing as it has passed from generation to generation. It has endured in its original form because the outstanding and fundamental appeals of Yoga have been Tolerance, Universality, and Simplicity. Within its simple framework are contained the principal teachings and approaches which make up the substance of all known philosophies, religions, and disciplines. If one understands the four paths to meditation, it is possible to unravel the trappings and mysterious elements of any religious or philosophical system.

The shelves of bookstores are overloaded with numerous 'new developments' and streamlined approaches to meditation. But many are by the blind leading the blind, with little or no experience to back the methods they tout. There are one-sided fanatics, Mantra hucksters, and outright charlatans. Some promise rapid development of psychic powers. Others are modern spiritual propagandists and conmen. Even the Madison Avenue contingent is well represented. There are only a handful of selfless Masters teaching true spiritual disciplines of meditation.

Real meditation is liberation from the clutches of the senses and lower mind. By definition it is transcendental, the word not being used as an advertising slogan, but to convey the beauty of meditation, in which all fears, desires, longings and negative emotions are transcended. The meditator reaches the superconscious state in which he or she is able to identify with the all-blissful Self. In this transcendental state there is no awareness of body, mind, or duality, and the knower becomes one with the knowledge and the known.

There is no need for mystery or secrecy about Mantras or any other accessory to meditation. There are no spiritual injunctions against discussing one's Mantra. A Mantra is a mystical energy encased in a sound structure. Its vibrations directly affect the *chakras*, of energy centers of the body. It steadies the mind and leads to the stillness of meditation. Those Mantras which are suitable for meditation are included in this book.

Many concoctions of syllables which are currently being peddled in the West as Mantras are obviously bogus. These 'Mantras' can lead to deep relaxation but nothing more. So can the repetition of any word or meaningless phrase. One can even slow the pulse and breathing as well as lower the blood pressure by sitting still and concentration on a ticking clock or dripping water tap.

Life in the West has become computerised, compartmentalised and oriented toward instant results. But the tradition from which the four yogic paths stem is a holistic one. In this system science, religion, philosophy, psychology, and health are all integrated. In the same way, the various classical meditation techniques that have been in use over the ages are based on solid discipline and regular practice. Proper breathing, proper exercise, proper relaxation, proper diet, and positive thinking are the necessary groundwork for successful meditation. These are covered to some extent in the first chapters, although for a comprehensive view on these and other aspects of Hatha and Raja Yoga, you may want to refer to my previous book, *The Complete Illustrated Book of Yoga.*

If this book clarifies the methods and aim of meditation, it will have served its purpose. The spiritual quest is a thorny path that ultimately must be walked alone. My own path has been blessed by the firm, compassionate, and boundless wisdom of my Master, India's late great saint and sage, H.H. Sri Swami Sivananada Maharaj. If, through me as his instrument, the echo of his words and insight can guide the footsteps of seekers in the Western world, I shall have achieved my earthly purpose.

Finally, I wish to gratefully acknowledge the following people whose contributions helped to make this book possible: Dr. Fritjof Capra, for permission to reprint excerpts from his speech 'The Yoga of Physics' and the photomontage of dancing Siva in particle tracks taken from his book *The Tao of Physics*; Nicholas and June Regush, for permission to reprint from their book *Mind Search*; Silamata Karuna, for her extensive research and editorial expertise; Silvio Paladini, for the Kundalini Chakra illustrations; and the many disciples and students of the Sivananda Yoga mission for invaluable aid in artwork, editing, proofreading, and typing.

Swami Vishnudevananda
Val Morin, Quebec, Canada
28 February 1981

The third edition of *Meditation and Mantras* was brought out to commemorate the second anniversary of Swami Vishnudevananda's Mahasamadhi. Swamiji Maharaj left his body on 9 November 1993.

About the Author

In 1957 Swami Vishnudevananda set out from the foothills of the Himalayas to carry out the bidding of his Guru, H.H. Sri Swami Sivanandaji Maharaj. His instructions were: 'Spread the seeds of Yoga in the West.' For thirty-seven years, Swami Vishnu worked tirelessly as an active and dedicated spiritual teacher. He traveled around the world many times teaching Yoga and establishing Centers and Ashrams where his Master's work could be carried out.

Swami Vishnudevananda was born in the south Indian state of Kerala on 31 December 1927. After completing school he entered the Engineering Corps of the Indian Army. It was while he was in the army that he first met his Guru, Swami Sivananda, one of the great saints of modern times. After being discharged from the army, Swamy Kuttan Nair, as he was then known, taught in a school in his native Kerala for a short while, before entering the Sivananda Ashram in Rishikesh in 1947. Within a year, he had renounced all things of the world and embraced a life of Sannyas on the auspicious night of MahaSivaratri. At that time he was given the name of Swami Vishnudevananda.

Remaining at the Ashram for ten years, Swami Vishnu was the first professor of Hatha Yoga at the Yoga Vedanta Forest Academy. He held a number of other positions at the Ashram, including acting as personal secretary to his Master, Swami Sivananda.

Upon leaving India for the West, Swami Vishnudevananda spent a year traveling, lecturing and teaching Yoga in Sri Lanka, Singapore, Hong Kong, Indonesia, Australia and Hawaii. Arriving in San Fancisco in 1957, Swamiji taught himself to drive and spent the next year driving throughout North America, studying the lifestyles of its people.

It soon became apparent that westerners were so caught up in the whirlwind of their lives that they neither knew how to relax nor how to lead healthy lives. Swamiji devised the concept of the Yoga Vacation and set about establishing places where people could have a complete rest of body, mind and spirit. Several Sivananda Ashrams were established based on the five principles of Yoga:

- Proper Exercise (Asanas)
- Proper Breathing (Pranayama)
- Proper Relaxation (Savasan)
- Proper Diet (Vegetarian)
- Positive Thinking and Meditation (Vedanta and Dhyana)

Within a few years, the Sivananda Yoga Vedanta Centers and Ashrams had been established. This is now an international network located in major cities around the world and six Ashrams, or retreat places, where people can find peace and quiet away from the tensions and anxieties of everyday life.

In 1969 the True World Order was established. It grew from a vision which Swamiji had. He 'saw' hundreds and thousands of people tearing down the walls and boundaries that separate nation from nation, and man from man. The purpose of this organisation is to establish unity and understanding between peoples of the world. A unique Yoga Teachers' Training Course is offered with the aim of bringing harmony in the world by training its future leaders in the basics of Yoga discipline. Over the years, thousands of people from around the world have taken the course.

In 1971 Swami Vishnudevananda made headlines by flying around the world in his Piper Apache plane, painted by the American artist Peter Max. He 'bombed' the trouble spots with flowers and leaflets of peace. At that time he braved a flight from Tel Aviv to Cairo, flying directly over the Suez Canal (which was closed). Although he and his Jewish co-pilot were almost shot down, they made the effort in the name of peace.

Swami Vishnudevananda marched through the streets of Belfast with actor Peter Sellars, chanting and praying for peace. In 1983 he flew an ultralight plane over the Berlin Wall in a bid to call the attention of Mankind to the need to break down all man-made boundaries. He sponsored numerous festivals, conferences, symposiums and world tours—all calling for peace and understanding.

In addition to being a tireless worker for world peace and an inspiring teacher, Swami Vishnudevananda is well known for his outstanding work *The Complete Illustrated Book of Yoga*, often referred to as the 'Bible of the Yogis.' Swami Vishnudevananda attained Mahasamadhi on 9 November 1993.

1

Why Meditate?

Without the help of meditation, you cannot attain Knowledge of the Self. Without its aid, you cannot grow into the divine state. Without it, you cannot liberate yourself from the trammels of the mind and attain immortality.

Meditation is the only royal road to the attainment of freedom. It is a mysterious ladder which reaches from earth to heaven, from error to truth, from darkness to light, from pain to bliss, from restlessness to abiding peace, from ignorance to knowledge. From mortality to immortality.

—Swami Sivananda
Bliss Divine

Who am I? What is my purpose in life? Why do some people seem to have an easier time in life than others? Where did I come from and where am I going?

These are the classic questions that almost everyone muses over at some time in life. Some struggle their entire lives to find the answers. Some give up looking, or put the questions aside as they get caught up in the routines and details of daily life. Others discover the answers, and their lives are full and contented.

The meaning of life is found by diving deep, deep within. But ever distracted by the business of living, people seldom stop, even for a moment in their busy days, to observe what is going on inside. It is hardly noticed that the mind is being constantly stimulated by the bombardment of perceptions from the senses. Very often, it is not until a person reaches a point of great distress that he realises it is time to stop and take stock of what is happening in his life. Meditation is the practice by which there is constant observation of the mind. It involves setting aside a regular time and place for the specific purpose of discovering that infinite well of wisdom which lies within. The chapters that follow give a comprehensive introduction to the philosophy and techniques of meditation. First, however, it is best to explore some of the background psychology and terminology that help to explain the purpose of meditation.

Mechanics of the Mind

In our search for happiness, we invariably turn to external objects and events for satisfaction. We think, 'If I can just have that car,' or 'If I were just able to get that job,' or 'If I only lived in Arizona, then I would be happy.' The mind may be stilled and at peace for a short time on attaining the desired object, but eventually it tires of its new toy, and seeks pleasure elsewhere. External objects fail to bring happiness. One may acquire new material possessions, a position with more responsibility, and a home in the country, but there always remains the same mind. Contentment is derived from the approach and attitude toward the external world, not from the objects themselves. Every person passes through easier and more difficult periods in his life. When the obstacles in life are confronted with a serene mind, then one lives more happily.

The challenge, then, is to gain control of the internal world. The mind is constantly conversing with itself—replaying past events, rearranging them into a better drama, planning for the future, discussing the pros and cons of this and that. By methodically slowing down its continuous ramblings, the internal dialogue, and focussing on positive and uplifting objects, it is possible to begin to understand the mechanics of the psyche and bring about a more effective life.

But the mind is an elusive animal to tame. So many theories exist as to how it works, yet the human mental process remains intangible. Why does one so often find himself caught in the same frustrations, the same problems? Free will does exist, but only when it is used to break out of the bad habits that have been developed in life. It is said that this is a free society, but in truth, it is each person's own desires and emotions that bind him. Consider the friend who smokes cigarettes, daily disclaiming them, determined to stop 'tomorrow.' How many years has he been caught in this charade? He may truly want to be free of the habit, but lacks the necessary control of his own mind.

In a sense, the mind is like a phonograph record. It contains grooves, or impressions, called *samskaras* in Sanskrit. These *samskaras* are formed when certain thought waves, or *vrittis*, become habitual. For example, a man passes a bakery and sees a chocolate eclair in the window. The *vritti* arises in his mind, 'How delicious; I will buy that eclair.' If he ignores that *vritti*, and turns his mind to something else, no pattern is formed. But, if he identifies with the thought, he gives life to it. He buys the eclair, looking forward to enjoying it as dessert that evening. Now, suppose he finds he must pass that same bakery every Tuesday and Thursday. Each time he goes by, he recalls that wonderful eclair, and purchases another. What was originally just a flash in the mind has become a force in his life, and a *samskara* has been formed.

Samskaras are not necessarily negative. There can be grooves in the mind which are uplifting and those which bring one down. It is the express purpose of meditation to create new, positive channels in the mind, and to eradicate those which are destructive. It is an absolutely scientific process, but at the same time, the goal is spiritual. It is not sufficient to eliminate the negative. There must be a striving to develop love, compassion, a sense of service, cheerfulness, kindness, and the many other qualities which not only make one's own life happy, but which radiate to others.

Everyone wants to do his best. Each person would like to think that he is perfect. Yet despite repeated resolutions, every person finds himself so many times being less than what he would like to be. The cause of this predicament is the *ahamkara*, or ego. Sri Sankara, one of the wisest men of all times, stated in the *Vivekachudamani*, 'Calamity is due to being subject to ego, bad agonies are due to ego, desire is due to subjection to ego; there is no greater enemy than ego.' This *ahamkara* is the cause of all bondage and is the chief barrier to the experience of inner Reality.

Ego is the self-arrogating aspect of the mind. It is the ego which separates the individual from unity with others and within himself, for the ego asserts 'I-ness.' *Ahamkara* is the greatest obstacle to tranquility, for it is that which occupies the mind with whether we are better or worse, possess more or less, and have greater or lesser power than others. It is attended by desire, pride, anger, delusion, greed, jealousy, lust and hatred. The ego is the most difficult aspect of the mind to control, for its nature is such that it deludes even while one is striving to overcome it. It is that very part of the being that would not be controlled.

Through meditation, the play of the mind is witnessed. In the early stages nothing more can be done than to gain understanding as the ego is observed constantly asserting itself. But in time its games become familiar, and one begins to prefer the peace of contentment. When the ego is subdued, energies can then be utilised constructively for personal growth and the service of others.

Thought Power

Every person projects some kind of vibration. Some people are a pleasure to be with. They seem to have a certain *prana*, or energy, that they share with others. Then there are those who are negative and depressed; they seem to actually draw *prana* out of others. The reason for this is that there is a power contained in thought. It is very subtle, yet it does exist and is extremely powerful. Whether a person is aware of it or not, he is constantly transmitting and receiving thoughts. This is why people have experiences of ESP from time to time. Some wish to call these experiences coincidence, but they are not. The ability to communicate and perceive thought is developed to a higher degree in those who are said to be psychic, or to have great intuitive abilities.

Every thought has weight, shape, size, form, colour, quality, and power. An experienced meditator can see this directly with his inner eye. For example, a spiritual thought has a yellow color, while a thought charged with anger and hatred is dark red. A thought is like an object. Just as an apple can be given to your friend, or taken back, so also it is possible to give a useful, powerful thought to someone and take it back.

Good and evil, friend and enemy, are in the mind only. Each person creates a world of virtue and vice, pleasure and pain, out of his own imagination. These qualities do not proceed from the objects themselves; they belong to the attitude of the mind. One person's joy is another's sorrow. Thoughts control our lives, mold our characters, shape destiny, and affect other people. When the potential contained in the power of thought is realised, it is the beginning of great spiritual growth in the individual; a great step forward for all of humanity.

The Self

What is spirituality? The past few decades have been called an age of alienation. Old traditions and religions were rejected. Thousands of 'New Age' seekers began to experiment with a myriad of chemicals and philosophies. There was a pervasive current of feeling that the Truth was someplace close at hand—but where was it? Somehow it seemed necessary to broaden perspectives a little.

In each society, the organised religion contains cultural practices and techniques which are handed down from generation to generation. It is when the means becomes confused with the end that its members begin to search elsewhere. They look for inspiration that is alive, that has a practical and observable effect in their daily lives. Whether a person lives a spiritual life on his own, or is part of an organised tradition, the goal—the same: the attainment of perfection, purity, and peace of mind, or Self-Realisation.

There is a Power, an Energy, which each person can tap into if he knows it is available. This Force inspires, encourages, reinforces, and gives strength to those who seek to grow in a positive direction. Many, however, are unaware of this resource, or they have misconceptions about it. They are like the farmer who moved to a house in the city, and lived in darkness because he did not know what those strange boxes in the wall were. The Light is there and available to all; we need only to connect ourselves with the current.

This source of wisdom is the Self. The Self is not the individual body or mind, but that aspect deep inside each person that knows the Truth. It exists in each being, and yet it exists independently also. Some call it God. Others call it Jehovah, Allah, Brahman, Cosmic Consciousness, *Atman*, Holy Spirit, or the Universal

Mind. The names and paths are many, but there is one Essence which pervades all beings.

The Self is impossible to understand with the limited senses and intellect. The human mind cannot fathom the Infinite and the Eternal. Therefore a visualisation is sometimes used to help one focus on the Supreme. Christians may meditate on the image of a cross, or the form of Jesus Christ. Hindus may picture Lord Siva (that Energy which destroys the old in preparation for renewal) as a very beautiful eternally youthful ascetic meditating atop the Himalayas. Those who conceive of the Absolute in more abstract terms may concentrate on a candle flame, a *chakra* (energy center of the body), or the sound of OM. But these are only partial impressions of the Truth.

A highly advanced scientist may know the theory and mathematics of how large space is. He may have studied how minute an atom is, or what the difference is between life and death. He can explain them in detail and at great length. But this is only theoretical knowledge; he can never really grasp the essence of these things. There is no way to intellectually define or describe that which is limitless. It is only through direct experience that Absolute Knowledge can be attained. Through the protracted practice of meditation it becomes possible to still the outgoing mind, develop intuitive abilities, and touch that part of the Supreme that lies within all.

Karma and Reincarnation

Meditation unleashes immense potential. We gain mastery of the mind by bringing a halt to its incessant chatter and teaching it to focus in a concentrated manner. Awareness of thought patterns helps to give the power to project thoughts to others. Yet one must be very careful always to send only vibrant, positive, loving and healing energy. For a complete understanding of why this is so, consider the subjects of Karma and reincarnation.

There is a law in physics that states, 'For every action there is an equal and opposite reaction.' Jesus taught, 'Do unto others as you would have them do unto you.' These are all expressions of the law of Karma, of cause and effect. It works something like a boomerang. Whatever thought or deed comes from a person will return to him. It may not come in the same form, but sooner or later each will confront the results of his own actions. A joyous and giving person draws a response of warmth and love. If a person is hateful, he will be disliked until this negative quality is removed. This is the Law.

Karmic reactions are not always experienced immediately. Sometimes lessons are not easily learned, and negative patterns may continue for many years. A single lifetime usually is not sufficient for anyone to attain Perfection. So each person reincarnates again and again. This is the reason for the apparent inequality between people. One is poor and another rich, one is healthy and another crippled, one is cheerful and another depressed. It is neither cruel fate nor a distant and unconcerned God that sets the stage for these situations, but one's own Karma.

Don't be fooled by those quick-realisation gurus who sell magic mantras and instant insight. You will be disappointed. Ultimately we must reckon with the effects of our own deeds. Each person's life is his own responsibility. To blame difficulties on unfortunate circumstances or parents who weren't well enough versed in psychology is to beg the question. Only when we realise that we are caught in our own web and begin to spiritualise our lives, do we break out of the wheel of births and deaths, and find peace and union in the Self.

Reincarnation is not an exclusively Eastern precept. It is contained in some form in almost every major religion and mystical philosophy. Research indicates that it was an accepted doctrine, at least in some quarters, at the time of Christ, and is still an integral part of some sects of the Jewish tradition. The Bible contains no condemnation of the principle of reincarnation—and in fact, when Christ was asked when Elijah would return, he answered that Elijah had returned, referring to John the Baptist. Origen, of the early Christian Greek Church, wrote extensively regarding the pre-existence of the soul. This concept was basically accepted in the Church until the fourth century AD. More recently, Pope Pius XII named Origen a Doctor of the Universal Church, indicating a tolerance if not an actual embracing of his teachings.

But reincarnation is not merely an abstract principle. Each of us has experienced recollections from past lives at some time or another. It is called déjà' vu. It is not unusual to meet someone for the first time, yet experience an uncanny sense of familiarity. This is because that person was known in previous lives. Occasionally there may be a place or scene that stirs memories deep inside. It will seem as if you have been there before, and in fact, that may be the case. At times we awaken from a dream that is strangely familiar, even though it bears no relationship to the present life and environment; it is a segment of an earlier lifetime that has surfaced in order to help work out present Karma.

What Does Yoga Have to Do with It?

There are many methods for eliminating these Karmic debts. Through meditation one learns to understand how the mind operates and thus is able to begin the growth process. Exactly what techniques are used depends on the nature of the individual. In Yoga, there are four main paths. Raja Yoga is the scientific psychological approach focussing on concentration and meditation. Karma Yoga is the path of eliminating the ego and attachments through selfless service. Jnana Yoga is the method by which the intellect is used to negate bondage to the material world. Bhakti Yoga sublimates the emotions into devotion.

There are a number of other forms of Yoga. Hatha Yoga is actually an aspect of Raja Yoga. It starts with the physical body and goes on to work with the energies of the astral body In Kundalini Yoga the meditator concentrates on a specific Sanskrit phrase for the purpose of stifling the mind and evoking positive energy.

It is said that the paths are many but the Truth is One. Each person must travel his own road to union with the Source. It should be borne in mind, however, that by placing all of one's energies into only one form of Yoga, there is a danger of imbalance, even fanaticism. For stable and consistent progress, the meditator should choose a preferred path, but always draw from the techniques and wisdom of the other methods. Through a synthesis of Yogas an equilibrium is maintained.

Through meditating regularly, the mind becomes clearer and motives more pure. The subconscious releases hidden knowledge that allows better understanding. The ego is slowly eradicated. Ultimately the superconscious, or intuitive forces, are released, leading to a life of wisdom and peace.

2

The Basics of Meditation

O aspirants! Struggle hard. Make sincere efforts. Meditate regularly and systematically. Never miss a day in meditation. There will be a great loss if you lose even a day.

No more words! Enough of discussions and heated debates. Retire into a solitary room. Close your eyes. Have deep silent meditation. Destroy the imaginations, thoughts, whims, fancies and desires when they arise from beneath the surface of the mind. Withdraw the wandering mind and fix it on the Supreme. Now meditation will become deep and intense. Do not open your eyes. Do not stir from the seat. Dire deep into the recesses of the heart. Enjoy the silence now.

—Swami Sivananda
Concentration and Meditation

Much has been said and written about meditation, yet it takes years to understand its nature. It cannot be taught, just as sleep cannot be taught. One may have a king-sized posturepedic mattress, an air-conditioned room, and the absence of all disturbances, but sleep may not come. Sleep itself is not in anyone's hands. One falls into it. In the same way, meditation comes by itself. To still the mind and enter into the silence requires daily practice. Yet there are certain steps that can be taken to establish a foundation and insure success.

Before beginning, have a proper environment and attitude. Your place of meditation, schedule, physical health, and mental state should all reflect a readiness to turn inward. Many difficult obstacles are removed by creating a setting which is conducive to meditation.

Guide to Meditation

The following are practical points regarding the basic techniques and stages of meditation. They are primarily intended for the beginner, although even the most experienced meditator will find a review of them useful.

1. Regularity of time, place and practice are the most important. Regularity conditions the mind to slow down its activities with a minimum of delay. It is difficult to focus the mind, which wants to jump about as soon as you sit for concentration. Just as a conditioned reflex is a response to established external stimuli, so the mind will settle down more quickly when time and place are established.
2. The most effective times are dawn and dusk, when the atmosphere is charged with special spiritual force. The preferred time is *brahmamuhurta*, the hours between four and six a.m. In these quiet hours after sleep, the mind is clear and unruffled by activities of the day. Refreshed and free of worldly concerns, it can be molded more easily; concentration will come without effort. If it is not feasible to sit for meditation at this time, choose an hour when you are not involved with daily activities and the mind is apt to be calm. Regularity is the most important consideration.

3. Try to have a separate room for meditation. If this is impossible, screen off a portion of a room; do not allow others to enter it. The area should be used only for meditation, and should be kept free from other vibrations and associations. Incense should be burned morning and evening. The focal point of room should be a picture or image of the chosen deity or inspirational figure, with the meditation mat placed before it. As meditation is repeated, the powerful vibrations set up will be lodged in the room. In six months the peace and purity of the atmosphere will be felt; it will have a magnetic aura. In times of stress you can sit in the room, do repetition of Mantra for half an hour, and experience comfort and relief.
4. When sitting, face north or east in order to take advantage of favorable magnetic vibrations. Sit in a comfortable steady posture, with spine and neck held erect but not tense. This helps to steady the mind and encourages concentration. The psychic current must be able to travel unimpeded from the base of the spine to the top of the head. It is not necessary to place the legs in *padmasana*, the classic lotus posture. Any comfortable cross-legged posture provides a firm base for the body. It makes a triangular path for the flow of energy, which must be contained rather than dispersed in all directions. Metabolism, brain waves and breathing will slow down as concentration deepens.
5. Before beginning, command the mind to be quiet for a specific length of time. Forget the past, present and future.
6. Consciously, regulate the breath. Begin with five minutes of deep abdominal breathing to bring oxygen to the brain. Then slow it to an imperceptible rate.
7. Keep the breathing rhythmic. Inhale for three seconds and exhale for three seconds. Regulation of breath also regulates the flow of *prana*, the vital energy. If a Mantra is being used, it should be coordinated with the breathing.

8. Allow the mind to wander at first. It will jump around, but will eventually become concentrated, along with the concentration of *prana*.
9. Do not force the mind to be still. This would set into motion additional brain waves, hindering meditation. If the mind persists in wandering, simply disassociate from it, and watch it, objectively, as though you were watching a movie. It will gradually slow down.
10. Select a focal point on which the mind may rest. For those who are predominantly intellectual, the object of focus should be visualised in the space between the eyebrows. For those who are more emotional, it should be visualised in the heart plexus. Never change this focal point.
11. Focus on a neutral or uplifting object or symbol, holding the image to the place of concentration. If using a Mantra, repeat it mentally, and coordinate the repetition with the breathing. If you do not have a personal Mantra, OM may be used. Those who prefer a personalised deity may refer to the chapter on Mantras. Although mental repetition is stronger, the Mantra may be repeated aloud if one becomes drowsy. Never change the Mantra.
12. Repetition will lead to pure thought, in which sound vibration merges with thought vibration, and there is no awareness of meaning. Vocal repetition progresses through mental repetition to telepathic language, and from there to pure thought. This is a subtle state of transcendental bliss with duality, where there remains awareness of subject and object.
13. With practice, duality disappears and *samadhi*, the superconscious state, is reached. Do not become impatient, as this takes a long time.
14. In *samadhi* one rests in a state of bliss in which the Knower, Knowledge and Known become One. This is the superconscious state reached by mystics of all faiths and persuasions.

15. Begin the practice of meditation with twenty-minute periods and increase to one hour. If the body is overcome by jerking or tremors control them and keep the energy internalised.

Health for Meditation

A healthy body is essential to the development of one's full potential. If the physical machinery is not in optimum condition, it will not be a fit instrument for daily work, meditation, and service to others. Some think a yogi should be emaciated in the name of self-discipline. But in fact, excessive physical austerities indicate an over-concern with body. Others believe that those on the spiritual path need not concern themselves with matters of the body as their energies are directed toward loftier things. These are extreme points of view. In Yoga, it is important to keep a balance in life. Moderation in all things is recommended.

Proper exercise, proper breathing, proper relaxation, proper diet, and positive thinking are the requisite attendants of meditation. In order to remove distractions from the mind, a healthy body and psyche are necessary. When there are disturbances of a physical or emotional nature, meditation is not possible.

Proper exercise is not muscle building, nor is it a short set of strenuous calisthenics for the purpose of reducing one portion of the body which has taken on extra weight due to poor living habits. The entire physical system, internal and external, should be kept in tune. This is the purpose of Yoga exercises, or asanas, which involve systematically stretching muscles rather than contracting them. The effect is to tone the body, release tension, and insure excellent circulation, digestion, assimilation and elimination. The body is kept supple; at the same time concentration and serenity are developed.

Yogic breathing is called *pranayama*, which actually means control of the vital energy. You can live without food, water, sunlight, and sleep for fairly extended periods of time, but the body cannot survive without oxygen beyond several minutes. *Prana*, the vital force, makes the difference between life and death. Its primary source is the breath. The quality and quantity of air,and the timing of the breath have a direct effect upon the brain and its function. This is an area which Western scientists are just beginning to investigate. There are certain *pranayamas* or breathing exercises that increase the amount of energy in the body, cleanse the lungs, reduce the amount of sleep needed, calm the nerves, still the mind, heat or cool the physical system and even help raise the kundalini, or spiritual energies of the body.

Proper relaxation is also needed to maintain mental, spiritual, and physical health. Yogic asanas and *pranayama* include special techniques for relaxation. These techniques also emphasise the conservation and efficient use of the energies contained in the body. Many think that relaxation involves leaving home or some exotic place where the mind and body are ceaselessly pumped with stimulants and depressants and a full range of other damaging delights. It is no wonder one hears so often 'I just couldn't wait to get home from my vacation so I could relax!' True relaxation comes from removing the stimuli—visual edible and otherwise—and tuning into the inner awareness.

Like a piece of sturdy machinery, our physical and mental bodies can take quite a bit of abuse before giving signs of protest. Unfortunately it has become a practice to ignore the basic rules of health. We think that a pill which relieves symptoms will actually bring about well-being. Quite the opposite is true. Pain in the body is a warning, like a red light on the instrument panel of a car. Taking this or that compound of chemicals to remove the symptoms is the same as taking a hammer and breaking the red light. It does nothing to solve the problem, and in fact may make it worse, while only giving the appearance of helping. Many of the chemicals ingested are not useful to the body, cannot be eliminated, and are therefore stored. These medicines accumulate, along with the food additives that are eaten in such abundance (on the average of 25 pounds per person, per year). They combine with each other to literally poison the system, although the effects may not be felt for many years.

We are just beginning to be aware of the collection of illnesses that are partner to a technologically advanced society. While this is not to say that there is no need for modern medicine, too often doctors are considered to have some form of absolute knowledge. Many people substitute frequent visits to the local GP, specialist, or psychologist for living a healthy life. Most of the diseases of the mind and body can be eliminated by following the five basic points.

1) Proper exercise, 2) proper breathing, and 3) proper relaxation all come under the realm of Hatha Yoga, and are covered extensively in my first book, *The Complete Illustrated Book of Yoga*. We will now take a closer look at the other two points, 4) proper diet and 5) positive thinking and meditation.

A Peaceful Diet

What is consumed by the human body correlates directly to the efficiency with which the brain functions. Recent studies show that certain red food coloring creates hyperactivity in children, and that refined sugar can cause emotional instability. These are just two examples of substances that are often heedlessly consumed without understanding their effect on the body and mind. A person who meditates regularly must be particularly aware of these substances, for even on a day-by-day basis, diet affects the quality of meditation.

The optimum diet for a meditator is a simple one. This is not to say that meals should not be appetising, but there should be an absence of those foods which negatively affect the mind. Hot and pungent spices, garlic, onions, salt, coffee, black tea, and meat agitate the mind, and hence control of the thoughts becomes difficult. Then there are those foods which dull the mind, rendering a state of sleepiness instead of concentration. These include all pre-cooked and overripe foods, as well as the obvious, alcohol. Marijuana and cigarettes, though not taken as foods, also fit into this category.

Of course the above items are on most people's list of favorite indulgences. It is not expected that every person will make an immediate radical change in diet, but those who are sincerely interested in meditation may begin by phasing out meat and cigarettes. (Asanas/*Pranayama* will make this much easier.) Many detrimental habits will fall away of themselves simply due to the change of consciousness that occurs in meditation. Start by shopping and cooking with a greater degree of awareness. Buy fresh fruits and vegetables. Avoid additives, processed foods, and canned goods wherever possible. Buy a few good books on nutrition and vegetarian diet. Within a few months a great change will take place.

Several years ago vegetarianism was, in a sense, an underground practice. A person who refrained from eating meat was viewed with a certain amount of curiosity, if not suspicion. Today it is quite a different story. Health food stores and vegetarian restaurants are prevalent. There is a growing awareness that our health is directly affected by what we eat. Many diseases can be cured by a change in diet or a short period of fasting, with no medications at all. This is true not only of physical disorders, but of many mental difficulties as well. It is particularly important that pregnant women have this awareness; too often they do not realise the effect of their diet on the developing foetus.

Contrary to the popular concept, vegetarians do get enough protein. It is meat-eaters who take in an excess of protein. Animal protein contains a high concentration of uric acid, which is a nitrogen compound similar to ammonia. It is not water soluble and cannot be broken down by the liver. Thus, though a certain amount is eliminated, the greater portion of uric acid is deposited in the joints. The result is often arthritis.

Hardening of the arteries and heart disease are two of the most common maladies in the West, where the greatest amount of meat is consumed. The culprit is cholesterol, which cannot be eliminated from the body. It forms fatty deposits along the walls of the heart and arteries, gradually thickening until they are clogged and inflexible. Some think that merely switching from butter to margarine will solve the problem, but in fact any oil that has been hydrogenated is equally as harmful. The major source of cholesterol, however, does not come from occasional butter on your toast in the morning but from the hundreds of pounds of meat and its fats that most people consume each year.

Of all most common infirmities, the one that strikes fear into most hearts is cancer. Many substances have been found to create cancer in animals, but results of most studies seem to indicate that the amount consumed by the average person is insufficient. What is not revealed is that the accumulation of these poisons over a period of years does create cancer.

Innumerable chemicals are fed and injected into animals; these increase weight to yield more money per animal. Nitrites, food coloring, artificial hormones, and even arsenic are among the chemicals contained in animal flesh by the time it goes on the supermarket shelf. These, plus the many other additives consumed by members of an industrialised society, collect in the body and are stored in the tissues. Cancer occurs when the cells react to these excessive toxins by mutating into cells which reproduce uncontrollably.

There are other physical and spiritual reasons for not eating meat. One is that four times as much grain is used when fed to animals than if a person consumed the grain directly. This raises a moral question in regard to sharing of the world's resources. Plants are the original source of energy for all living things, as they store the energy of the sun through photosynthesis. Vegetarians take their nourishment from the original source; their diet is more economical with regard to personal cost and the best utilisation of available land.

It is also noteworthy that our digestive system is not one of a carnivore. Our teeth are designed for biting and mashing vegetables, not tearing flesh; we must age, tenderise, and cook meat. The human liver is proportionally smaller than that of a meat-eating animal and is not built to handle the filtering of animal poisons. Also the alimentary canal, which is short in carnivorous animals to speed poisons through the body quickly, is quite long in humans, as it is in any vegetarian animal.

For a yogi, though, the main consideration in not eating meat is the basic principle of ahimsa, or non-injury. 'Thou shalt not kill.' Animals have feelings and a consciousness, just as humans do. The mass breeding and slaughter are as much cruelty as throwing stones at the neighbour's dog. In India, a cow is regarded with great respect for the service it renders to man. It tills the fields, provides milk and its by-products for nourishment, and its dung is used for fuel and building houses. An Indian farmer would never think of cooking his cow for dinner.

There is no doubt that, 'You are what you eat.' A subtle part of what is consumed becomes the consciousness. Those who have changed from a meat to vegetarian diet notice a corresponding change in consciousness. There is a certain grossness that disappears, and the awareness becomes finely tuned. This is, of course, extremely conducive to meditation. The purer the diet, the more easily the mind is controlled. Then, with time and practice, success in meditation is assured.

Karma Yoga

Meditation means a continuous de-hypnotising from identification with body, mind, name and form. It must start in everyday life. If you cannot, be detached from the day-to-day activities, it will be difficult to enter into meditation. If there is continuous identification with your actions, then those same activities will go on even when the body is sitting still. The eyes may be closed, hands clasped and feet crossed, but the mind will not be checked. There remains the identification with the mental play. Activity or inactivity makes no difference. The mind plays its part in all conditions, and in order to sit for meditation, the mind must be detached—withdrawn from day-to-day concerns. The means for achieving this is Karma Yoga, or selfless service. It is the fundamental step on which meditation is built; no meditation is possible without it. Through service to others without thought of personal gain, positive thinking is also practiced in daily life.

A true Karma Yogi is continuously meditating. When he helps others his attitude is 'Lord, I am working, worshipping and serving You through this particular person. Thank you for giving me this opportunity.' He also detaches himself from the effect of the action, whether good or bad. Whether working in the kitchen, worshipping in the temple, or mowing the lawn, the Karma Yogi knows that he is different from the work, and that the work is only a way of achieving the Supreme.

Detachment may be learned through service. Until it is acquired and one is able to renounce emotional ties to one's labour, no meditation is possible. As the detachment increases, it becomes easier and easier to disassociate from activities. Then, when the eyes are closed, the mind will remain unperturbed; it has been trained to focus inwardly at all times. Others may see a Karma Yogi and think he is just another person working; they will not know the secret of his inner peace.

A true meditator is circumspect. Outwardly he appears to be an ordinary person, but inside he is a fathomless ocean. He has touched infinite peace; nothing can change him. Karma Yoga leads to that peace which, once tasted, can never be described. Time and patience are necessary to reach it.

Detachment from action does not mean shirking responsibilities. A haphazard life is not yogic, for it engenders no steadiness of mind. When a yogi takes on a job, he finishes it. His mind does not waver; that is the secret of his success. If he assumes a responsibility, his mind is focussed steadily on it until completion. Because it can be focussed at all times, the yogic mind is powerful. The average person does a little here and there, keeping several projects going and finishing nothing. There is no meditative state of mind.

A person who meditates can turn out more work in less time. He has peace within. His actions are all on a pure level, and those who come in contact with him are uplifted. In his dynamic presence people find strength and encouragement. They are inspired to perform actions that they could not otherwise do. Lethargy vanishes in the presence of a true yogi.

Through Karma Yoga, the path of selfless service, you can learn detachment in everyday life. This is the first essential step of meditation. Do not be misled by promises of instant meditation. It is a long and disciplined path. The goal, however, can be reached if you make a determined effort.

3

Concentration: Theory

In man's struggle to achieve any desired end, there is no necessity for him to turn to external forces. He contains within himself vast resources of inherent power lying untapped or only partially used. Because he has scattered his faculties on a hundred different things, he fails to achieve anything substantial, despite inherent potentialities. If he intelligently regulates and applies them, concrete results are ensured. To use his existing forces rationally and effectively, he need not wait for the invention of new methods for guidance. Nature itself abounds in instructive lessons.

—Swami Sivananda
Concentration and Meditation

The world is the materialisation of the thought forms of Divine Intelligence. It exists as vibration. Just as there are waves of heat, light, electricity and energy, there are also thought waves. Thought has tremendous power. Everybody experiences it to some degree. It could be used a thousand times more effectively if one had a comprehensive understanding of the workings of thought vibration, the techniques for controlling them, and the method of transmitting them to others at a distance.

Hidden psychic and occult powers are awakened by understanding and realising the powers of the mind. You can see distant objects, hear distant sounds, send messages to any part of the universe, heal people thousands of miles away, and move to distant places in no time. There is no limit to the power of the human mind which has learned to merge with the Cosmic Mind.

Power of Concentration

When flowing loosely over a wide area, every force in nature moves more slowly and with less power than if gathered in one mass and directed through a single restricted outlet. Dammed and accumulated, the once sluggish and leisurely flow of a river rushes out with amazing force through the sluice. The warm rays of the sun focussed through a magnifying glass become hot enough to burn objects. Such is the power generated by the concentration of force.

This natural law is also applicable to all branches of human activities. Mental concentration is the fixing of the mind for an extended period of time on one external or internal point. There can be no concentration without something on which the gathered rays of the mind can rest. It must be a single object or idea.

People sometimes pride themselves on being able to think of two things at once. The mind does not work in this way; its oscillating waves are merely bouncing back and forth with lightning velocity between the two ideas. Mind can do only one thing at a time. Those who imagine that a mundane chore such as dish-washing goes faster if they are thinking of palm trees and a sunny beach are fooling themselves. Their mental waves are moving between the daydream and the task at hand. The attention actually given to the work is slowed down because of the constant interruptions, and the hands slow down too. How much better to keep the mind one-pointed and finish the job in half the time.

If you are deeply engrossed in a book or television show, you hear no outside noises, not even your own name being called. If somebody approaches, you do not see him. Nor do you smell the fragrance of the roses on the table by your side. This is concentration or one-pointedness of mind fixed firmly on one thing.

Everybody possesses the ability to concentrate to some degree. Conscious practice of this innate ability strengthens the thought currents, clarifies ideas and utilises some of the immense latent power of the mind. What was once cloudy and hazy becomes clear and definite. What was difficult, complex and confusing becomes easy. One is able to work with greater efficiency, to turn out more work in less time, and to increase one's earning capacity.

Concentration can also prevent or minimise the problems of senility. After the age of thirty, man's brain cells die off at the rate of 100,000 per day and are not replaced. It is vital to strengthen and make the best use of one's waning capacity. He who practices concentration retains clear mental vision.

With utmost concentrated attention the surgeon operates on his patient. Deepest absorption marks the state of the technician, engineer, architect or painter engaged in drawing the minute details of a plan, in which accuracy is of the highest importance. The same concentration is necessary on the spiritual path, where the aspirant must deal with the internal forces. For progress to be made, it must be developed to a very high degree. Practice demands patience, will, untiring persistence and regularity. There are no shortcuts along the spiritual path.

In Yoga, as in other spiritual disciplines, concentration is the first stage of meditation, which in turn leads ultimately to experience of God. What most people think of as meditation is, in fact, concentration. The focussing power of the mind is brought to bear on one abstract or uplifting symbol. When all extraneous waves are stilled, one goes straight to the Source like a truly shot arrow. There are many streets leading to the heart of a city. You reach it by following one of them, not by wandering from route to route.

All of creation is God, according to Advaita, or monistic Vedanta. Intense concentration on any symbol can, therefore, eventually lead to God-Realisation. Abstract symbols, because they are not emotional, uplift the mind and are more effective than those that are emotionally colored and drag the mind downward.

Although the mind is controlled during concentration, the point at which it becomes meditation cannot be controlled. One falls into meditation much as one falls into sleep. Meditation is the continuous flow of one thought of the Supreme. It is the identification of the individual with God, and is experienced like a constant flow of oil from one vessel to another.

Pleasure and the Mind

It usually takes years before this shift in consciousness occurs during practice. This is because most people are ruled by the senses. When the mind is distracted by passion and desires, it is difficult to concentrate on anything. Sense objects and desires are externalising forces. They encourage the mind's natural tendency to run outward. When it is externalised, it engages itself with the unending rush of fleeting events. The mental rays scatter and energy is dissipated. To concentrate, these mental rays must be gathered and turned toward the Self. When they are concentrated, illumination begins.

Proper application of the senses can help internalise the mind. Of the various methods employed to curtail the innate oscillatory tendency of the mind, those using sight and sound are the most effective. These two senses are the strongest. They are able to capture the attention and still the thought waves.

The hypnotist subdues the subject's mind by capturing his gaze and repeating suggestions in a rhythmic, monotonous way. The teacher's sudden 'Look here!' when he wants special attention to what he is saying is significant. By fixing the student's gaze, he also fixes the attention of their minds upon his teaching.

Similarly, in the course of spiritual discipline the methods of developing concentration rely on sight and sound. One may gaze steadily at an abstract symbol, the image of a favorite deity (covered in the sections on Japa Meditation), the sky, a rose or any concrete object. As an alternative to visual concentration, one may repeat a Mantra, the Lord's name, OM or certain chants with regular rhythm and intonation. By these means the mind gradually becomes focussed inward. As the inward state deepens, one slowly looses awareness of material surroundings. The next step is meditation, in which body awareness is also lost. When perfected, meditation brings about *samadhi*, the ultimate state of Self-awareness or God-Realisation.

Worldly pleasures intensify the desire for greater and greater enjoyment. The mind can never be satisfied, no matter how many pleasures it is fed. The more it possesses, the more it wants. Without knowing it, people are exceedingly plagued by the insatiability of their own minds. In order to remove this sort of trouble, the craving for sensory stimulation must be removed. Once the mind has been stilled and concentrated, it no longer presses one to seek further pleasures.

When the senses are controlled and the outgoing tendencies stopped, the mind will no longer pose a threat to successful meditation. During the times of meditation, the mind must be introspective, turning inward to explore its own mysteries. The senses can be controlled through reduction of wants and activities. Dietary discipline is essential. Further, one should avoid undesirable company as well as stimulants and depressants. Television, cinemas and newspapers, which agitate the mind, should be reduced and replaced with periods of sitting in silence and solitude. By witnessing and tempering desires and emotions, the qualities of egoism, anger, greed, lust and hatred are eradicated.

For trained yogis, distinctions between withdrawal of the senses (*pratyahara*), concentration (*dharana*), meditation (*dhyana*) and the beginning of the superconscious state (*samadhi*) are blurred. When they sit to meditate, all the processes occur almost simultaneously, and they reach the meditative state very quickly.

Neophytes first experience withdrawal of the senses. Then concentration begins. Only after that does true meditation slowly come. Before the superconscious state manifests itself, the mind usually becomes impatient and tired, for it has not been trained to bear the strain of prolonged attention and wants to give up. Success in achieving *samadhi* depends on constant and intense practice, knowledge of the workings of the mind, awareness of the pitfalls, and willingness to make sacrifices to overcome the obstacles.

Best Friend: Worst Enemy

The mind is its own worst enemy as well as its own best friend. According to yogic thought, the mind has five different types of behavior. In the *kshipta* state, it is fragmented, distracted and scattered on various objects. It is restless and jumps from one thing to another. In the *mudha* state it is dull and forgetful. *Vikshipta* is the gathering mind. It is occasionally steady and at other times distracted. This is its condition during practice as it struggles to become focussed. In the *ekagrata* or one-pointed state there is only one idea present. In the *niruddha* state full control is achieved.

The greatest impediment to concentration is restlessness and tossing of the mind. When a beginner sits for practice, the thoughts, unaccustomed to this new game and freed from their usual grooves, leap about in an uncontrolled way. To remove tossing and other obstacles to one-pointedness, adamantly fix the mind on one object alone. When it runs away, as it naturally will, pull it back again and again. It will want to create hundreds of alternate thought forms. But if not disciplined no progress can be made.

It is necessary to introspect and watch the mind carefully. Bubbling thoughts must be silenced and emotions calmed; the purpose of concentration is the stilling of mental waves. One should not allow the mind to dissipate energy uselessly—on vain thoughts, worries, imagination and fears. Through constant practice it will hold to one thought form for half an hour, and then it is possible to increase the time to several hours. When the mental vibrations are collected and focussed in concentration, one experiences Bliss from within.

The mind is attracted to pleasing or favorite ideas. Therefore, concentrate on something that is appealing. Because of its natural externalising bent, in the beginning concentrate on gross objects. A flame, the moon or a concrete spiritual symbol can be concentrated upon with open eyes. Later use subtle objects and abstract ideas. With the eyes closed, the aspirant concentrates on the space between the eyebrows, the heart, or any of the *chakras*, or centers of spiritual energy.

By manipulating the mind, one is able to bring it under control and compel it to concentrate. However, don't wrestle with it. Struggle only sets more mental waves into motion. Many beginners commit this grave error in their impatience to succeed. They may develop headaches or sometimes feel the need to urinate, because of irritation set up in the spinal cord. As a clever cook notes which foods are most enjoyed and makes a point of serving those foods, so the aspirant notes the conditions that encourage progress in the attainment of the goal. In duplicating and fulfilling those conditions, he moves forward along the path.

Sometimes spiritual aspirants leave off the practice of concentration, as they find it difficult. They make a great mistake. In the initial struggle to overcome body consciousness, practice may well be troublesome. There is physical restlessness attended by an overabundance of emotions and thoughts. In due time, often only after many years, the mind becomes cool, pure and strong, and immense joy is derived from it.

The sum total of all the pleasures in the world is nothing compared to the bliss derived from meditation. Do not give up the practice at any cost. Have an attitude of patience, cheerfulness, and tenacity. Success will eventually come. By serious introspection, it is possible to discover the various impediments to concentration. They may be removed with patience and effort. They can be nipped in the bud through discrimination, right inquiry and meditation.

The more concentrated the mind is, the more power is brought to bear on one point. The purpose of life is to fix the mind on the Absolute. When it is so fixed, one becomes calm, serene, steady and strong. In concentration the senses cease to function, and there is no longer awareness of the body and surroundings. As it deepens, one experiences great joy and spiritual intoxication. Concentration opens the inner chambers of love and, as it leads to meditation, is the sole key to the realm of Eternity.

4

Concentration: Practice

It is difficult for Man to establish a control over his own mind. For gaining mastery over his own mind, he has to know what the mind is, how it works, how it deceives him at every turn and by which methods it can be subdued. As long as the mind restlessly wanders about amidst objects, ever fluctuating, excited, agitated and uncontrolled, the true joy of the Self cannot be realised and enjoyed. To control the restless mind and bring all thoughts and cravings to a stillness and sublimation is the greatest problem of Man. If he has subjugated the mind, he may be said to be, in his subjective freedom and power, the Emperor of emperors.

—Swami Sivananda
Conquest of Mind

Scientists estimate that the average person has conscious control of about 10% of his mental power while the rest lies hidden like the bulk of an iceberg floating beneath the surface. There are vast resources lying untapped below the surface of the conscious mind. The practice of concentration opens the gates of these latent resources and releases them for use. A proper foundation must be laid before the practice of concentration can be taken up in earnest, for the powers of the mind are elusive and unpredictable. This foundation is built of right conduct, a healthy body and steady posture, breath regulation and withdrawal of the senses. Only if it is firm will the superstructure of concentration and meditation be successful.

The Eight Steps

The blueprint for this base is found in the ashtanga, or eight limbs, of Raja Yoga. These eight progressive steps are *yama* (abstentions), *niyama* (observances), asanas (postures), *pranayama* (breath control), *pratyahara* (withdrawal of the senses), *dharana* (concentration), *dhyana* (meditation), and *samadhi* (superconscious state). The first five steps form the basis for concentration.

Yama is a series of injunctions similar to the Ten Commandments. They are non-injury to any living thing; truthfulness in thought, word and deed; non-stealing, which includes non-covetousness; and sublimation of sexual energy. *Niyama* is the cultivation of such virtues as cleanliness of body and environment, contentment, austerity or control of senses, study of spiritual books, and surrendering to the Divine Will. Together, the *yamas* and *niyamas* foster high moral character and ethical conduct. The mind is uplifted and purified for deep meditation.

A healthy and strong physical system is also essential. Steady mind presupposes steady posture. Concentration is impossible if one is plagued by aching knees, backache and other attendant woes of prolonged sitting. To attain one-pointedness of mind, one must be able to forget the body altogether. The nerves must be strong enough to withstand various mental phenomena and disorientations that can occur during practice. In the process of turning the mind inward, old negativities surface; on rare occasions they may even appear symbolically in the form of visions. A frail person may discontinue his practice of concentration rather than confront these aspects of his subconscious. Concentration is successful only when the body and mind are kept healthy. Asanas keep the body and nervous system strong and flexible, and help to ensure that the flow of vital energy is unimpeded.

Just as steady posture is mandatory, so also is breath control. Consider what happens when a person concentrates very hard to hear an indistinct whisper. The breath stops. The mind and breath are as inseparable as the two sides of a coin. When the mind is agitated, the breath becomes irregular. Similarly, when the breath is slow and regular, the mind responds by becoming calm. *Pranayama*, the yogic system of breath control, is designed to steady and prepare the mind for concentration.

To reduce the outward flow and waste of mental energies, the senses must be subjugated. One-fourth of our energy is diverted to the digestion of food, often eaten for the pleasure of the taste buds rather than for sustenance. Additional mental and physical energy is squandered in useless idle talking. Follow a wholesome, natural, vegetarian diet and eat frugally. Learn control of the tongue by observing silence for an hour or two a day. Our senses have been habitually overfed and geared to gluttony. Examine worldly habits and curtail them sharply.

Pratyahara, or withdrawal of the senses, is a kind of fasting for the mind. The thoughts are weaned from attachment to the many fleeting sensations that they feed upon. The senses do not convey experience without the cooperation of the mind. *Pratyahara* is not permitting the senses to come in contact with their objects. For example, if certain music or television programs are found to leave the mind in an agitated state, they should be eliminated. By withdrawing the mind, the senses are also withdrawn. *Pratyahara* in its most graphic form is symbolised by the *yoni mudra*, which itself is a concentration exercise. To execute it, the eyes, nose and mouth are closed with the fingers of both hands and the thumbs block the ears. Distractions are thus blocked out; the attention is freed to be fixed on the only thing that remains, the internal or *anahata* sounds.

When some degree of attainment has been reached in these five steps, one may proceed to the practice of concentration, which is the springboard for meditation and *samadhi*. Practice need not merely be confined to an hour or two in a quiet room. It can and should pervade all aspects of life.

Attention

The faculty of attention may be developed in everyday situations. Concentration itself is a narrowing of the field of attention. The entire attention is thrown into whatever is being done. The individual becomes lost in the job at hand. Learn to concentrate on the work and shut out all other thoughts, doing nothing haphazardly or hastily. In this way the mind becomes one-pointed.

Failure is a stranger to work done with perfect attention. When one sits for meditation, there should be no thought of office work. When doing office work, household chores never enter the mind. In training the mind to attend only to the work at hand, there will be a development of willpower and memory.

A person with good concentration can accomplish a task in half the time and with twice the accuracy of the average person. It is easy to pay attention to what is pleasant; the mind is naturally attracted to what pleases it. A more difficult but highly beneficial exercise is to fix the attention on unpleasant tasks. Under scrutiny, they become more interesting and interest reduces the unpleasantness. Similarly, the attention can be fixed on uninteresting objects and ideas. If they are held before the mind and examined, interest slowly manifests. Many mental weaknesses and blocks vanish. The mind and willpower become stronger.

As a preliminary exercise in concentration, retire to a quiet room and sit in a comfortable cross-legged position. Sitting on a pillow helps to bring the knees to the floor so that the body may relax properly. Close the eyes and notice what occurs when concentrating on an apple.

At first, there may be thoughts of its colour, shape, size and different parts such as stem, skin, pulp and seeds. Next, think of its effects on the digestive system and blood. Through the law of association, ideas of other fruits may also try to enter the mind. Soon, extraneous ideas pop in. The mind begins to wander about. It may think of meeting a friend at four p.m. It may think of buying a towel or a can of beans. It may review an embarrassing happening of the previous day.

The point of the exercise is to follow a definite line of thought, without any break in it. Extraneous thoughts, not connected with the object at hand, are to be banished. This demands persistence. The mind will try its best to run in the old familiar grooves. The attempt to concentrate is somewhat like going uphill, but each small success is greatly rewarding.

Just as laws of gravitation, cohesion, etc., operate in the physical world, so also do laws of thought, such as the law of continuity, operate on the mental plane. Those who practice concentration should thoroughly understand these laws. They must be aware that when the mind thinks of an object, it also thinks of its qualities and parts; when it thinks of a cause, it thinks of its effects. Awareness of the workings of the mind is developed by training it to concentrate on various subjects, gross and subtle, and of various sizes. In the course of time, a strong habit is formed.

A classic yogic exercise in concentration is *tratak*, or steady gazing. It can be done with a candle flame, an OM symbol, a picture of one's favorite deity, or any other suitable object or symbol. Sit in front of it. Concentrate on it with open eyes until tears come. Then close the eyes and visualise the object. Repeat and gradually increase the period of time for the gazing and visualisation. It should be possible to visualise the object of concentration very clearly, even in its absence. With practice comes the ability to conjure up the mental picture at a moment's notice.

Tratak and visualisation steady the wandering mind and help greatly in concentration. Practice the exercise for only one minute on the first day, gradually increasing the length of time each week. Do not strain the eyes. In some people who have weak capillaries, the eyes may become red. There is no cause to be alarmed, for the redness will pass quickly. An excellent preliminary concentration exercise, *tratak* should be practiced for six months. It is necessary to be regular and systematic about it. If there is a break in practice, the time should be made up. *Tratak* is effective in preventing or eliminating many ailments of the eye.

Tratak utilises the sense of sight. Sense, object and mind are captured in the gross concrete world and then internalised to the subtle plane. Sound also, when expressed on the subtle level, can draw the mind inward. But unlike the visualisation exercise, concentration on the *anahata*, internal, sounds begins and ends on the subtle plane.

Sit in a comfortable cross-legged posture. Close the eyes; close the ears with the thumbs, earplugs or cotton. Try to hear the inner mystic sounds. It may be possible to hear various kinds of sounds, such as flute, violin, kettledrum, thunder, conch, bells and the humming of bees. If several sounds are heard simultaneously, hold the mind to the loudest one. Generally they will be experienced in the right ear, sometimes in the left. Concentrate only on the sound in the right ear. This practice develops one-pointedness of the mind, which is achieved by focussing on sound vibrations.

Establishing the Practice

To establish a regular practice of concentration, the beginner should choose a pleasing object or symbol and stay with it. If he is on the spiritual path, he should fix the mind on the image or Mantra of his chosen deity. Sit in a comfortable cross-legged position, close the eyes and make the breathing regular. Three seconds' inhalation and three seconds' exhalation are recommended. Once the breathing pattern is established, withdraw the mind from it; the body will automatically carry on that rhythm. The object of focus is visualised in the space between the eyebrows (*ajna chakra*) or in the heart (*anahata chakra*). Generally speaking, the *ajna chakra* is best for those of an intellectual nature, while the heart area is better for emotional types. Once the center of concentration is chosen, it should not be changed.

Avoid tension anywhere in the body or mind. When the mind wanders, as it will, gently pull it back, but do not wrestle with it. If emotions cause disturbance during practice pay no attention. They will soon pass away. If there is an attempt to drive them away, more mental waves and strain are created. Keep an indifferent attitude. If emotions and mind-wandering fail to fade out of their own accord, do not identify with them. Detach and observe as a witness, as though watching a motion picture. The Self is neither body nor mind. in detaching from physical and mental activity, one experiences one's true nature.

The aim of concentration is to bring the mind to the same point or object again and again by limiting its movements in the beginning to a small circle. When meditating on an object, summon all thoughts connected with that object and dwell on those thoughts alone. Do not allow thoughts related to any other subject to enter the mind. There should be one line of thought. There may be several ideas connected with the one subject, but this does not matter. The number of ideas can eventually be reduced to one.

A time will come when the mind will stick to one point alone, like the continuous sound of a church bell. This is meditation, the fruit of constant and protracted practice of concentration. The joy will be indescribable. When this one idea also dies, the superconscious state, *samadhi*, is attained. With the fading out of the one idea, there is a stage of mental vacuity or thoughtlessness. Rising above this blank state, one identifies with the Supreme, the silent, motionless witness of everything. Then and then alone does one reach the highest goal of life.

The practice of concentration may seem tedious in the beginning, while new grooves are being formed in the mind. Yet after a period of practice, real interest develops. As the aspirant advances and realises some of the benefits, he finds he does not want to abandon the practice. If he neglects it even for a day, he becomes restless. Concentration brings supreme joy, inner spiritual strength and infinite eternal bliss. It plumbs the depths of profound knowledge and intuition, and leads to communion with God.

5

Meditation

Put a piece of iron-rod in the blazing furnace. It becomes red as fire. Remove it. It loses its red colour. If you want to keep it always red, you must always keep it in the fire. So also, if you want to keep the mind charged with the fire of Brahmic wisdom, you must keep it always in contact with the Brahmic fire of knowledge through constant and intense meditation. You must keep up an unceasing flow of the Brahmic consciousness. If you can meditate for half an hour, you will be able to engage yourself with peace and spiritual strength. Such is the beneficial result of meditation. As you have to move with different minds of peculiar nature in your daily life; get the strength and peace from meditation. Then you will have no trouble or worry.

—Swami Sivananda
Practice of Yoga

Meditation does not come easily. A beautiful tree grows slowly. We must wait for the blossom, the ripening of the fruit and the ultimate taste. So also with the blossom of meditation, an inexpressible peace that permeates the entire being.

Its fruit is the bliss of the superconscious state, and is indescribable because one becomes It, leaving no one to say anything about It. Wherever in the world you may wander, the mind is nowhere truly satisfied except within, when it withdraws from the world and touches the inner silence.

Mind: Master or Servant?

We rush about in search of unknown experience, but unfortunately, you always take the same mind with you. Only after years of continually withdrawing the mind from the external world can you attain a glimpse of ineffable peace. There is no easy way to reach it. It cannot be attained in ten easy lessons, as is often expected today.

Many modern scientists do not fully understand the theory of mind over matter. Too often they equate control of the mind with mental institutions; drugs, and biofeedback techniques. They do not realise that the soul stands above both mind and body, which it uses for its expression and evolution. Until the power of the soul over all animate and inanimate objects is understood, there will be more and more confusion in the scientific world. Both body and mind have to adapt and adjust the new environmental situations as well as new levels of awareness in order for man to evolve and achieve his final freedom.

In the Western tradition, behavior of the body is often related only to the accepted laws of physical nature. Such experiences as astral projection, seeing without eyes, hearing without ears, communicating telepathically, or bending a spoon with thought waves are commonly considered to be beyond the pale of rational acceptability. However, for the meditator who practices intunement with his intuitive faculties, these natural phenomena are occasionally experienced and are easily accepted. They are no more miraculous than the projection of sight and sound to distant places by means of radio or television waves. Voluntary control over the heart and 'involuntary' functions, as well as extrasensory perception, astral travel, the astral body and its *nadis*, *prana* and kundalini are commonly accepted facts in the Eastern way of living and thinking.

The mind is a hard taskmaster. It insists that we jump when it says jump, that we eat when it says eat. If it wants a cigarette, it convinces us to go out for one, however inconvenient it may be. Its desires are insatiable, and one fulfilled desire can spawn a hundred more.

There was once a monk who retired to a cave in the Himalayas. He had only two possessions—the loincloth that he was wearing and an extra one. Returning one day from a distant village where he had gone to beg food, he found that the spare loincloth had been chewed up by a rat. He got another cloth and the same thing happened. So he bought a cat to get rid of the rat. The cat disposed of the rat, but it had to have milk. It is difficult to buy milk in an Indian village, and as daily expeditions for it would have been too time-consuming, the monk bought a cow. It is also difficult to feed and milk a cow, look after its needs, tend to a cat and pursue intensive spiritual practice. Needing help, the renunciate got married, and everything that he had renounced came back to him.

You must always be wary. One desire can multiply and destroy the best intentions. The secret of conquering the tyranny of the mind is to not to play the game. By continuously controlling the thought waves, or by observing but not identifying with them, you can reduce and eventually stop them. When the thought waves are stilled during meditation, the true Self is revealed and you experience Cosmic Consciousness. The realisation of the Oneness of all existence, manifested and unmanifested, is the goal of human life.

Unity already exists. It is our true nature but has been forgotten through ignorance. Removal of the veil of ignorance, the idea that we are confined within body and mind, is the chief aim of any spiritual practice. If a lamp is brought into a dark room, the darkness is instantly dispelled, and the entire room is illuminated. If identification with body and mind is broken through constant meditation on the Self, ignorance is destroyed, and the supreme light of *Atman* is seen everywhere.

To realise unity, the idea of diversity must be given up. The idea of the self as all-pervading and all-powerful must constantly be nourished. In unity there is neither desire nor emotional attractions and repulsions; there is only steady, persistent, calm, eternal bliss. Spiritual liberation means attainment of this state of unity.

The desire for liberation in itself is meaningless because infinite freedom already exists as man's real essence. There can be no desire to gain that which is one's very nature. All desire for progeny, wealth and happiness in this world or in the next, and even the illusory desire for liberation itself, must eventually be abandoned whether in the present or in a future lifetime. By pure and disinterested will, all actions should be guided toward the goal. The fruits of meditation should not be pursued impatiently. It takes time before the mind is sufficiently ripened and purified to make any visible progress.

The constant attempt to feel that you are the All can and ought to be practiced in the midst of intense activity. Let the mind and body work, but feel that you are above them as their controlling witness. Do not identify with them. If the senses are under full control, perfect peace and solitude can be found even in the noisiest and most crowded city. If the senses are turbulent and you have not sufficient power to withdraw them, there will be no peace of mind even in a solitary cave in the Himalayas.

In the beginning one must consciously sit and meditate to experience the feeling of unity. Steadiness of posture and mind makes the effort comparatively easy. In the midst of activity it is more difficult. The practice, however, must be kept up at all times. Otherwise, progress is slow. A few hours spent meditating on identification with the All, while identifying with body and mind for the rest of the day does not bring about rapid or substantial progress.

From the Unreal to the Real

Meditation is an experience that cannot be described, just as colors cannot be described to a blind man. All ordinary experiences are limited by time, space, and the law of cause and effect. Normal awareness and understanding do not transcend these bounds. Finite experience cannot be transcendental, for it is measured in terms of past, present and future. These concepts of time are illusory, for they have no permanence. Immeasurably small and fleeting, the present cannot be grasped. Both past and future are non-existent in the present, and therefore are unreal. We live in illusion.

The meditative state transcends all such limitations. In it there is neither past nor future, but only the consciousness of I AM in the eternal NOW. This consciousness is only possible when all of the mental waves are stilled and there is no mind. The closest analogous state is deep sleep, in which there is neither time, space nor causation. Meditation differs from deep sleep, which embraces an experience of the void. Because meditation is a state of intense, pure awareness, it works profound changes in the psyche. For the same reasons, and because it operates on the superconscious rather than the subconscious level, it is not to be confused with a hypnotic state.

Meditation is the source of real rest. True deep sleep is a rare occurrence. During dreams the mind remains active, working subtly. There is little true rest during sleep. In meditation, when the mind is fully concentrated, far away from objects and near the *Atman*, the Self, a lasting, spiritual, blissful rest is experienced. Once meditation is achieved, the time normally devoted to sleep will gradually be reduced to as little as three or four hours.

On the purely physical level, meditation helps to prolong the body's anabolic process of growth and repair and to reduce the catabolic, decaying process. Ordinarily the anabolic process predominates until the age of eighteen. Between eighteen and thirty-five the catabolic process sets in. Meditation significantly reduces this decline because of the innate receptivity of body cells to its benign vibrations.

Only recently have scientists become aware of the relationship between mind and cells. Until a few years ago they would react with extreme skepticism to yogic demonstrations of mental control over such supposedly involuntary functions as heartbeat, respiration and circulation. They believed the autonomic nervous system to be independent of any conscious mental process. Biofeedback techniques now prove that most bodily functions can be controlled by concentration.

Modern research substantiates the fact that the mind can control the activity of a single cell, as well as groups of cells. Each of the body cells is governed by the instinctive, subconscious mind. Each has both individual and collective consciousness. When thoughts and desires pour into the body, the cells are activated, and the body obeys the group demand.

Meditation is a powerful tonic. During meditation there is generally a tremendous acceleration of energy to the individual cells. Just as negative thoughts can pollute them, positive thoughts rejuvenate them and retard decay. Penetrating all the cells, its vibrations can prevent and cure diseases. The soothing waves that arise also exercise a favorable effect on mind and nerves, resulting in a prolonged, positive state of mind. Thus the interior world takes direction from the mind and promotes physical health, mental acuity, and tranquility.

Every individual possesses inherent potentialities and capacities. From past incarnations he brings to this life a storehouse of power and knowledge. During meditation these unsuspected faculties emerge. New changes also take place in the brain and nervous system as new currents, channels, vibrations and cells are formed. In addition to new sensations and feelings, one acquires new modes of thinking, a new view of the universe, and the vision of unity. Negative tendencies vanish, and the mind becomes steady. One enjoys perfect harmony, undisturbed happiness and abiding peace.

With meditation comes freedom from fear of death. Most people think that death is the end of existence, but in fact, death means only the extinction of the present name and form. The greater the identification with name and form, the greater the fear. The practice of meditation induces detachment from name and form. It makes one aware of the ever-changing nature of the body and of all phenomenal existence. In recognising the ephemerality of it all, one realises the impossibility of holding on to anything, including one's cumbersome ego-identity. When this need to grasp disappears, when the fear of losing what one never has really possessed vanishes, immortality is within reach.

One who meditates regularly develops a magnetic and dynamic personality. Those who come into contact with him are influenced by his cheerfulness, powerful speech, lustrous eyes, healthy body and inexhaustible energy. Just as a grain of salt dropped into a basin of water dissolves and is distributed throughout the water, so the spiritual aura of the meditator infiltrates the minds of others. People draw joy, peace and strength from him. They are inspired by his words, and their minds are elevated by mere contact with him. The advanced yogi who meditates in a solitary cave in the Himalayas can help the world more than can somebody preaching fine words from a platform. Even as sound vibrations travel in space, so the indestructible spiritual vibrations of a meditator travel an infinite distance, bringing peace and strength to thousands.

Wild Horses

To achieve the meditative state takes time, for the mind is like a wild horse resisting all attempts at control. Discipline, order and specific techniques, as well as perseverance are necessary to insure progress. At first the mind will resort to tricks, dodges and rebellion, making progress slow and difficult. One should therefore have an understanding of its workings. As part of the progress of self-inquiry and control, preliminary practice can be done on the subconscious level.

One means of counteracting the many tricks of the mind is by training the subconscious mind, potentially your most obedient servant. This wonderful power can be utilised by everybody if the effort is only made. Because it cannot reason, it awaits training by command. Trust is the most important factor in developing it. Indeed, any doubts about the power of the subconscious mind will impede its effectiveness. This inherent power, which can be destroyed and polluted by drugs and alcohol, has generally gone unrecognised as a practical tool. Swami Sivananda realised its latent possibilities, and wrote in his book *Concentration and Meditation*:

> The subconscious mind never rests. Even during sleep it is sifting, analysing and comparing information, and carrying out commands. A great deal of the subconscious mind is bundles of submerged experiences, which can be drawn up to the surface of the conscious mind by means of concentration. It is the repository of memories, not only of this life but also of past lives. All that you have inherited, all that you have seen, heard, enjoyed, tasted, read or known in this life and past lives is hidden in it.

By mastering the technique of commanding the subconscious mind, all of this knowledge can be tapped and extracted.

When you are unable to solve a problem, whether personal, philosophical or scientific, tell your subconscious to do it for you. Approached with full trust and confidence it will provide the right answer. The command must be couched in very clear, explicit terms, with no ambiguity. If the solution is not elicited after a night's sleep, repeat the command at the same time each day, until the response is forthcoming.

As well as a source of knowledge, the subconscious mind can be a faithful servant. It can be trained to awaken you at a particular hour. It needs only a positive suggestion or clear command before you go to sleep. As a preliminary exercise, give it one of these simple tasks. By making further use of its potentialities, pressure will be taken off the conscious mind, which will then be freed of some of its customary clutter.

The practice of concentration and constant vigilance help to prepare and discipline the conscious mind for meditation. There are two basic modes of meditation—*saguna*, meaning with qualities, or concrete, and *nirguna*, without qualities, or abstract. Meditation on a picture or other external object is concrete. Meditation on an idea or concept, such as love or beauty, is abstract. Because it is easier to hold the mind to a concrete image than to an abstract idea, *saguna* meditation must be practiced for a long time before the mind is ready to handle an abstraction.

There is no problem in visualising a rose and considering its various aspects—its color, aroma, thorns, various uses, etc. The mind moves in a specific orbit. But to meditate on Divine Intelligence? One can exhaust the mental energy in wandering down a thousand byways.

Needless to say, beginners should practice concrete meditation. It does not ultimately matter what the object is. Meditation on a dot can lead to the same result as meditation on the Christian Cross, although it might take much longer. In either case the mind exhausts itself by thinking all possible thoughts about the object, or it may keep to one or two ideas about it and rigidly exclude all other ideas. What matters is not the object, but the stilling of the mind.

Because of this, however, the task is made easier if the object is neutral, with no emotional or mental connotations that might trigger additional mental waves. A dot on the wall is a preferable object to one's sweetheart; meditation on the latter would be like opening Pandora's box. Because it creates mental waves, an uplifting spiritual symbol, image or Mantra is beneficial and mandatory for spiritual aspirants. The vibrations of such a symbol do not excite the lower mind, but lift one up to the higher planes of consciousness. In concrete meditation the devotee considers himself to be separate from the object of meditation. He wants to experience it, just as one experiences the taste of honey. He holds back from actually merging with the object.

With practice and purification through *saguna* meditation, the mind becomes well trained and disciplined. One can then move on to abstract meditation, which is a natural progression from the concrete mode. In fixing on an abstract idea, the mind slowly melts, expands, loses its own consciousness and becomes one with the formless Absolute. Instead of just tasting the honey, the meditator merges and becomes the honey itself.

Evolving out of concentration, meditation is a continuous flow of perception or thought, like the flow of water in a river. During concentration a tight rein is kept on the mind; during meditation the rein is no longer necessary because the mind stays of its own accord on one single thought wave. For the spiritual aspirant, it is just keeping up an unceasing flow of God-consciousness. Jesus said, 'Empty thyself and I shall fill thee.' This corresponds to Patanjali's teaching, '*Yogaścitta vṛtti nirodhaḥ*' (Yoga is the restraint of all mental modifications). This emptying process, in which all the modifications are reduced to one, is a trying discipline. Continued intense practice, however, will bring success.

In addition to the practical suggestions outlined for concentration, there are a few other points for the serious Yoga aspirant to bear in mind. The first is the necessity of having a separate area for meditation. A small room kept under lock and key is best. If this is impossible, then the corner of a room can be set apart from the rest of the room with a curtain or screen. It is important that the meditation room be kept separate from other areas and not be used for any other purpose so that the mental vibrations in that place will continue to be pure. The room should be decorated with pictures of saints, sages, prophets and world teachers. Incense and candles should be burned in the morning and evening. Do not allow anybody else to enter the room and disturb its vibrations. It should be regarded as a temple of God, and should be entered with reverence. No worldly talk or thoughts should be indulged in. No word that is uttered, thought that is cherished, nor deed that is done is lost. They are reflected on the subtle layers of ether encircling the room, and invariably affect the mind.

Because of the many strains and pitfalls on the yogic path, a guru is essential. If an aspirant meditates upon his guru, even from far away, a connection is established between them. In response to his thoughts the guru radiates power, peace and joy to the student. The stream of spiritual magnetism flows steadily from the preceptor to his disciple, just as oil flows from one vessel to another. The student draws from the teacher in proportion to his degree of faith. When he sincerely meditates on the teacher, the latter actually feels the thought current touching his heart. He who possesses inner astral sight can clearly visualise a thin line of bright light between disciple and teacher which is caused by the movement of pure thought vibrations.

Advanced Meditation

While meditating, various experiences will manifest from time to time. An aspirant may notice a light appearing in the center of the forehead, or small fiery balls moving about before the mind's eye. Sometimes various *anahata* sounds may be heard more clearly. Occasionally beings or objects from the astral world manifest. There may even be brief sensations of bliss. These phenomena are covered in more detail in the chapter on spiritual experiences.

When these extraordinary experiences of meditation occur, one should not be frightened. Nor should the mistake be made that *samadhi* has been attained simply because some lights and a little rising above body consciousness have been experienced. Do not cling to these visions. Simply accept them for what they are—encouragements to keep the aspirant on the path and to convince him of the existence of super-physical realities.

During deep meditation, the aspirant forgets the external world first, and then the body. The idea of time disappears. He hears no sounds and is unaware of his surroundings. The feeling of rising up is a sign of going above body consciousness. In the beginning this feeling will last for only a minute. It is accompanied by a peculiar sensation of bliss. As the meditation deepens, body consciousness is lost. The loss of sensation usually occurs first in the legs, then the spinal column, back, trunk and hands. When this happens, the head feels suspended in air and mental consciousness reigns supreme.

Should there be a disinclination for work and a desire for meditation only, one should lead a life of complete seclusion, living on a diet of milk and fruits. There will be rapid spiritual progress. When the meditative mood vanishes, work should be taken up again. Thus by gradual practice, the mind will be molded.

In time the awareness of ego gradually vanishes, and reasoning and reflection cease. A higher type of indescribable peace descends. However, it takes a long time to transcend the body completely, to merge with the object of meditation, or to receive a true spiritual experience. *Samadhi*, the superconscious state, is the highest goal to be attained through meditation, and is not achieved merely through a little practice. To attain the ultimate state of merging with the Divine, one must also observe celibacy and strict dietary restrictions; have purity of heart and be completely devoted to God.

After prolonged and steady meditation, Cosmic Consciousness is first experienced as a glimpse, and then becomes natural and permanent in realised souls. Therefore, when there is a flash of illumination, do not be frightened. It will be a new experience of intense joy. Do not turn away or give up meditation. It is a glimpse of Truth, a new platform but not the whole experience. Do not stop. Keep ascending until the final goal is reached.

Similarly, different minds are comfortable with different kinds of meditation. As the various techniques and approaches work differently for each person, one should experiment with a variety of methods, and then stay with the one that seems most comfortable.

It cannot be stated too strongly that all of the systems arrive at the same destination, despite differences. Which method is easiest: Raja, Mantra, Kundalini, Jnana or Bhakti Yoga? Each has its own problems and temptations. In Raja Yoga there is the danger of identifying with one's purity, and building up egoism because of pride in one's mental control. In Hatha Yoga one may spend years awakening the kundalini. By the time it happens, a few spiritual powers will have manifested, and one may be sidetracked. Despite asserting their identify with Brahman, Jnana

Yogis tend to be attached to the intellectual sheath. When a Bhakta Yogi surrenders to the Lord, he will encounter severe tests to see if his surrender is complete. Whatever the means, terminology and techniques employed, the basic concepts are the same, and the methods often overlap. There are no sharp lines of definition or fundamentally distinct concepts. All Yogas culminate in the merging with the Absolute.

The state of Cosmic Consciousness is sublime beyond description. The mind is most inadequate to grasp and describe it. It inspires awe, joy, and freedom from pain, sorrow and fear. It bestows enlightenment, and places the experiences on a new plane of existence. One experiences a sense of universality, an awareness of eternal life. This is not merely conviction; it is an actual experience of knowledge. Although this knowledge is an inherent natural faculty, training and discipline are necessary to awaken it. Because of ignorance, it is non-functioning in the majority of people.

The Absolute can be experienced by all through regular practice of meditation with a pure heart. Abstract reasoning and study of books do not suffice. Direct experience is the source for this higher intuitional knowledge, or divine wisdom. The experience is superconscious and transcendental; senses, mind, emotions and intellect are at perfect rest. It is not the imaginary reverie of a visionary dreamer, nor is it a hypnotic trance. It is absolute Truth, cognized through the spiritual eye, the eye of intuition.

The little ego melts, and the differentiating mind vanishes. All barriers, sense of duality, differences, separateness and distinctions disappear. There is no time or space; there is only eternity. The experiencer has the feeling that he has obtained all his desires and that there is nothing more to be known. He feels perfect awareness of the superconscious plane of knowledge and intuition. He knows the whole secret of creation.

There is neither darkness nor void; all is light. Dualities vanish. There is neither subject nor object. There is neither meditation nor *samadhi.* There is neither meditator nor the meditated upon. There is neither pleasure nor pain. There is only perfect Peace and Absolute Bliss.

6

Japa Meditation: Theory

Mantra Yoga is an exact science. Mananat trayate iti Mantrah—*'By the constant thinking of Mantra, one is protected and released from the round of births and deaths.' A Mantra is so called because it is achieved by the mental process. The root* 'man' *in the word Mantra comes from the first syllable of that word meaning 'to think' and* 'tra' *from* 'trai' *meaning 'to protect or free' from the bondage of the phenomenal world. A Mantra generates the creative force and bestows eternal Bliss. A Mantra when constantly repeated awakens the consciousness.*

—Swami Sivananda
Japa Yoga

A Mantra is mystical energy encased in a sound structure. Every Mantra contains within its vibrations a certain power. Upon concentration and repetition of a given Mantra, its energy is elicited and takes form. Japa, or Mantra Yoga, is that practice by which the power contained within Mantras is applied for specific purposes.

Each Mantra is constructed from a combination of sounds derived from the fifty letters of the Sanskrit alphabet. Sanskrit is also known as *Devanagari*, or language of the gods. The ancient sages, who were attuned to higher levels of consciousness, were well aware of the inherent power contained in sound, and they utilised combinations of sounds to set up specific vibrations. These vibrations applied systematically could literally move mountains. In fact, one theory on the building of the pyramids suggests that it was the highly developed science of manipulating sound vibrations that enabled the early Egyptians to sculpt and move stones of such enormous proportions.

Whether such feats can be attributed to the control of sound is a question modern science has not yet covered. Yet there is no doubt that sound does have a definite and predictable effect on the human psyche and body. An obvious example is the difference between classical and rock music. The first tends to be relaxing while the other is inclined to excite the senses. On a more subtle level, various Mantras are applied for certain purposes. Most specifically, they turn the mind toward concentration on the Supreme and release spiritual energy in the *chakras* of the body.

There are different types of Mantras. Some, called *bija* or seed Mantras, are such that they have no exact meaning. They act directly on the *nadis*, or nerve tubes of the astral body. They vibrate in the *chakras* along the spine, acting as a subtle massage, releasing blockages and allowing the kundalini energy to flow more freely. In these the name and form of the sound are merged and cannot be separated. There are also Mantras that have meaning which can be translated. These *nirguna* or abstract Mantras also set up powerful vibrations in the body, but verbally assert union with unmanifest pure consciousness.

More common, however, is the Deity Mantra, in which a specific form with attributes is visualised along with the repetition of the sound. For example, a reclusive person bent on destroying his negative qualities would repeat a Siva Mantra. A family person, whose ideal was to be a loving and responsible husband or wife, might meditate on the name of Rama. An individual who sees God as infinite, all-loving, and even a little playful would build these qualities in himself by repeating a Krishna Mantra.

The Yoga of Physics

It is important to understand, however, that the visualisations of deities are only an aid to focussing the mind. Repeating Mantras which are the names of deities internalises the power of the vibrations that are contained in the name. When the name of Siva is repeated with concentration, the sound actually breaks down one's lower qualities. Long ago, Siva was explained in a mythological way; now scientists explain that when energy breaks down, it forms patterns, it dances. This is the same as the dance of Siva. Fritjof Capra, author of *The Tao of Physics*, notes the similarity between the Hindu Lord Siva, the Power of Destruction, and the Quantum Theory, which states that matter is never quiet but is always in a state of motion. In the following excerpt entitled 'The Yoga of Physics,' Dr. Capra explains this relationship. It is taken from his keynote address at the Los Angeles Symposium on Physics and Metaphysics, on 29 October 1977.

'What is the nature and origin of the universe? What is the nature of human existence? What is matter made of? What is the relation between spirit and matter? What is space? What is time? Throughout the ages men and women have been fascinated by these questions. Different approaches have been developed in different cultural contexts and at different times.

'Artists, scientists, shamans, mystics—all have their own way of describing, both verbally and non-verbally, the world. We shall focus mainly on two approaches. We shall look at modern Western science, on the one hand, and Eastern mysticism—particularly the tradition of Yoga—on the other. We shall see that they lead to very similar views of the world.

'My field is physics, a science which, in the 20th century, has led to a radical revision of many of our basic concepts of reality. For example, the concept of matter is very different in sub-atomic physics from the traditional idea of a material substance that was held in classical physics. The same is true of other concepts of reality such as space, time, objects or cause and effect. Out of these changes in our concepts of reality, a new world view is emerging. This view turns out to be closely related to the views of mystics of all ages and traditions, particularly the religious philosophies of the Far East–Hinduism, Buddhism, Taoism.

'In the Yoga tradition it is said that there are many paths, all leading to spiritual knowledge and Self-Realisation. I believe that modern physics, to some extent, can be such a path. Its view of the universe is in harmony with those of the great yogis and sages. In that sense, I'm going to talk of the Yoga of physics.

'Classical Western physics has its roots in the philosophy of the fifth century Greek Atomists, a philosophical school which saw matter as made up of basic building blocks called atoms. These were believed to be hard, solid, basically passive chunks of matter. This inert matter was said to be moved by external forces of a totally different nature and category, which was identified with the spiritual realm. In this way, a dichotomy was created which became characteristic of Western thinking in subsequent centuries. It gave rise to the dualism between spirit and matter, between the mind and the body.

'In contrast to the mechanistic view of classical Western science, the Eastern view could be called an organic, holistic, or ecological view. Things and phenomena are perceived as being different manifestations of the same reality. The division of the world into separate objects, though useful and practical on the everyday level, is seen as an illusion—*Maya*, as the Indians say. To Eastern mystics, objects have a fluid and ever-changing character. Change and transformation, flow and movement, play an essential role in their world view. The cosmos is seen as one inseparable reality, forever in motion. It is alive, organic, spiritual and material at the same time. A very similar view is now emerging from modern physics.

'In the 20th century Western scientists began probing the atom. They discovered that atoms were not hard and solid, but consisted mainly of empty space. Each atom had a tiny nucleus made up of particles around which whirled other particles. At first, scientists decided that these sub-atomic particles must be the essential building blocks of matter. But they found that this was again wrong. This was shown in the 1920s when Quantum Theory, the theoretical framework of atomic physics, was worked out.

'Quantum Theory showed that the sub-atomic particles have no meaning as isolated entities, but can only be understood as interconnections between various agencies of observation and measurement. Particles are not things but interconnections between things; and these things are interconnections between other things, and so on.

'Quantum Theory thus reveals a basic oneness of the universe. It shows that we cannot decompose the world into independently existing smallest units. As we penetrate into matter, Nature does not show us any isolated basic building blocks, but rather appears as a complicated web of relations between the various parts of a unified whole.

'This network of relations, furthermore, is intrinsically dynamic. According to Quantum Theory, matter is never quiescent, but always in a state of motion. Macroscopically, the materials around us may seem dead and inert. But if you magnify a piece of metal or stone, you realise that it is full of activity.

'Modern physics pictures matter, not as passive and inert, but as continuously dancing and vibrating. This is very much like the Eastern mystics' description of the world. Both emphasise that the universe has to be grasped dynamically. Its structures are not static, rigid ones, but should be seen in terms of dynamic equilibrium.

'Physicists speak of the continuous dance of sub-atomic matter which goes on all the time. They have actually used the words "dance of creation and destruction" or "energy dance." This naturally comes to mind when you see some of the pictures of particles taken by physicists in their bubble chambers.

'Of course, physicists are not the only ones talking about this cosmic dance. Perhaps the most beautiful example of this metaphor exists in Hinduism—the idea of the dancing Lord Siva. Siva is the personification of the cosmic dance. According to Indian tradition, all life is a rhythmic interplay of death and birth, of creation and destruction.

'Indian artists have created beautiful pictures and statues of dancing Lord Siva. These statues are visual images of the cosmic dance, and so are the bubble chamber tracks photographed by modern physicists. They are a modern version of the dance of Siva, obtained by using the most modern and advanced of our Western technological instruments. To me, the effect is as beautiful and as profound as the magnificent Hindu statues. In both cases, we are picturing an eternal dance of creation and destruction, which is the basis of all natural phenomena, the basis of all existence. Therefore, I have put the two together—here you have the "Dance of Siva" merging the 12th and 20th century versions. You can see that this image of the cosmic dance unifies, in a very beautiful way, ancient mythology, religious art, mystical insight and modern science.'

Sound: The Seed of All Matter

'In the beginning was the Word, the Word was God and the Word was with God.' The Word of the Bible is the *Sabdabrahman* of the Hindu *Tantra*. Word, sound and Mantra are integral parts of Indian cosmology, and cannot be separated from it. Taking cosmological principles out of the realm of theory, *japa*, or Mantra repetition, puts them to work in a pragmatic way. It is the path from microcosm to macrocosm; it is the vehicle that carries the individual back to the Source.

In the beginning, *Shakti*, the unmanifest Cosmos, floats like an egg in the silent, motionless Void. A mass of latent, undifferentiated energy, it contains the seed power of all the universes. It rests in the Void, alternately flowering as the manifest, evolved Cosmos, and then withdrawing itself in dissolution, *pralaya*. Throughout eternity, like day and night, the universe alternately expands into matter and recedes into primal energy.

During the period of dissolution, *Shakti*, also known as the Divine Power or Cosmic Energy, lies quiescent. Just as the tulip is latent within the bulb, so this universe of names and forms, as we know it, lies enfolded in *Shakti*. Within its heart rests the three qualities, *sattwa* (purity), *rajas* (activity), and *tamas* (inertia), whose kaleidoscopic shifting permeates all aspects of the universe. Cosmic evolution proceeds from the unconscious, unmoving, unknowable and unmanifest to the conscious, moving, knowable and manifest microcosm. On the other hand, human evolution is a return journey from the gross physical plane of the microcosm back to the Absolute. In one case the force is centrifugal, in the other, centripetal.

In the Tantric view, sound, as a vibration of undifferentiated Intelligence, is the catalyst that sets into motion the unfolding of the manifest cosmos. A primal shudder disturbs the slumbering equilibrium of *Shakti* and arouses *rajas*, the active principle, to carry out the creation of the manifold universes. The causal vibration, *Sabdabrahman*, is undifferentiated, soundless Sound. It is the wavelength experienced as God.

This great Cosmic Vibration splits *Shakti* into two fields of magnetic force, and projects it as two aspects, *Nada* and *Bindu*. As centrifugal, positive male force, *Bindu* is the ground from which *Nada* operates. As centripetal, negative female force, *Nada* unfolds the manifest universe. They are regarded as Father and Mother aspects of the Supreme Power. The bifurcation of *Shakti* is a duality in unity, not a separation. This duality of poles in the substratum of manifested *Shakti* actually provides the magnetic force holding together in a state of vibration of molecules of the physical world.

Through the medium of time-lapse photography, it is possible to watch a rosebud explode into full flower. Like a rosebud, the universe unfolds and expands. After the first differentiation containing the seed energies of the universe, the vibrating mass of energy continues differentiating and expanding as wavelengths. By the fifth differentiation, the energy is evolved on the gross plane, with the creation of fifty articulate sounds or *varnas*. *Varna* means colour, and all sounds have corresponding colour vibrations in the invisible world.

From the combinations and permutations of these root sounds, the universe of forms is created. Sounds, as physical vibrations, are able to produce predictable forms. Combinations of sounds produce complicated shapes. Experiments have demonstrated that notes produced by certain instruments can trace out on a bed of sand definite geometrical figures. In order to produce a particular form, a specific note at a particular pitch must be generated. Repetition of the exact note and pitch creates a duplication of the form.

Underlying all the forms of the physical world are the oscillating wavelengths of the fifty primeval sounds in varying combinations. Sound is thus potential form, and form is sound made manifest. Because of the oscillatory nature of matter and of mind as perceiver, the world of manifest forms can only be experienced in distortion as illusion.

Fragmented and fractured, the fifty basic sounds themselves have faded down the corridor of time, and are lost to human memory. The Sanskrit language, however, is directly derived from them, and of all languages it is the closest approximation. Mantras are sound powers evolved from the *varnas* and revealed in Sanskrit syllables to the ancient sages.

Sound as Energy

The sacred syllables used in meditation by spiritual aspirants are usually Sanskrit names of the Absolute. As divine power made manifest in sound, the Mantra itself is the subtle body of Deity. The theory of *japa* meditation, or Mantra repetition, holds that by repeating the syllables with accuracy and intense devotion, the form of the Mantra's presiding deity will be evoked. Meditation on *OM Namah Sivaya* produces the form of Siva, while *OM Namo Narayanaya* produces that of Vishnu. The vibrations produced by the tones of a Mantra are all important, and pronunciation cannot be a haphazard matter. Through attunement with the wavelength of the Mantra, one is led from the gross plane of articulate sound back through the obscuring veil of the material universe to personalised Deity, and ultimately to the primal undifferentiated energy of the Supreme Power.

At this point it is necessary to consider the microcosm, which is the macrocosm in miniature. It is the vehicle by means of which the return trip from articulate sound to the Causal Power is made. Like the cosmos, the individual continually undergoes the flowering and dissolving of countless lifetimes, the periods of activity and rest. Centrifugal and centripetal forces manifest in him as breath and in the beating of the heart. In the human body, *Nada*, the vital power of the universe, takes form as kundalini, the psychic force lying coiled in astral slumber at the base of the spine. This energy pulsates with the wavelengths of the fifty basic sounds, which eventually reach gross articulation through the vocal chords.

In yogic theory, thought, form and sound are all the same, just as steam, water and ice are all the same substance. They are different aspects of a particular wavelength, or the same vibrational energy as passed through different levels of consciousness. Form manifests in the mind the moment the name is heard by the ears and transmitted to the consciousness.

Thought and sound manifest in four fundamental states, with sound at one end of the spectrum and thought at the other. *Japa* meditation leads one from the lowest to the highest of these states. *Vaikhari*, the spoken word, is dense, audible sound at its maximum differentiation. It is thought translated into the coded state called language. As the spoken word, it is the most concrete state of thought. In this first stage, thought implies both name and form. The name is the same as the thought wave, and they cannot be separated. When the word 'cat' is pronounced, a form is visualised. The reverse is also true. However, the more abstract the word, such as 'God', the more difficult is the conceptualisation.

The use of language calls for differentiation of thought into word. This process occurs during the second stage, *madhyama*. Through a mental prism clouded by preconceptions, impressions, emotions and other limitations, the speaker or writer selects his words. They are translated back into thought by the listener or reader, whose mind in turn is clouded by his own ideas. The transmission of thought into language inevitably leads to confusion.

Suppose for a moment that a computer is given the job of translating from English to Russian the sentence, 'The spirit is willing, but the flesh is weak.' In translating a second time, from Russian back to English, the result could very well be, 'The ghost is wishing, but the meat is raw.' The mechanism of language is extremely crude and inadequate.

Pashyanti, the third stage, is visible sound. It is the telepathic state, in which one can literally feel the form of the thought. It is the universal level on which all thought takes place, whether a person is English or Chinese. There is no differentiation of thought, name and form. An Indian, Eskimo, German, and Bantu can all look at the same flower and experience the thought of it at the same time and the same non-verbal language.

Para, the fourth and highest state, is transcendental. Formed into no particular wavelength, it is above all names and forms. It is the unchanging, primal substratum of all language and is pure energy, or *Shakti*. As undifferentiated potential sound, it corresponds to *Sabdabrahman*, the Divine Vibration that unites all.

Thought cannot be held at the first level of vocal or visual experience. Its vibrations are too rapid, even on the lowest plane. In the telepathic state, it can travel anywhere instantly. In the transcendental state everything merges together. This state of thought or vibration, which can be reached in meditation, is commonly called God.

Using Sound Vibrations for Meditation

Japa meditation is a method of channeling one's consciousness from the lowest to the highest level of pure thought. Repeated verbally or mentally, a Mantra lifts one into the telepathic stage and beyond to the transcendental. 'Rama,' for instance, has a specific form that merges with the name in the telepathic state. On the fourth level, name, form, and one's own Self as witness are indistinguishable. They unite and a state of bliss prevails.

One does not enjoy bliss, but becomes Bliss itself. This is the true experience of meditation.

The power of sound is tremendous. In addition to image and form, it can generate ideas, emotions and experiences. By merely hearing words the mind can undergo pain or pleasure. If somebody shouts, 'Snake! Snake!' one immediately jumps with fright. Consciousness of the presence of something considered dangerous has been created. The mind reacts with terror, and the body jumps in fear. When such is the power of the name of an ordinary thing of this world, imagine what power resides in the name of the Lord.

Japa is one of the most direct ways of Self-Realisation, or Universal Consciousness. It removes the dirt of the mind, the anger, greed, lust and other impurities that hide the light within. Just as a dusty mirror acquires the power of reflection when cleaned, the mind from which impurities have been removed acquires the capacity to reflect higher spiritual truth. Even a little recitation with feeling and one-pointed concentration on the meaning destroys mental impurities. *Japa* meditation done with faith, devotion and purity augments the power of the aspirant, bestowing on him the virtues and powers of the Mantra's presiding deity. Revealing God to his consciousness, it confers illumination and eternal bliss.

The Supreme is not an individual entity. God is an experience realised on a particular wavelength. *Japa* produces in the mind the form of the deity connected with the Mantra. Through constant practice, this form becomes the center of one's consciousness and can be directly realised. The Mantra of the deity, therefore, is the same as the deity. Repetition with concentration on the meaning of the Mantra and on the attributes of the particular deity will bring God-Realisation quickly. However, through sheer vibratory power, *japa* with no knowledge of the meaning will also bring realisation, although it will take more time.

Initiation into a Mantra

If possible, before attempting *japa* seek out a guru and receive Mantra initiation. Mantra initiation is the spark that ignites the dormant spiritual energy residing in every human heart. Once lit, the fire is kept going by daily *japa* meditation.

Only those who are themselves pure can give initiation to others. Therefore it is important to find a qualified guru. For him to successfully implant the Mantra in the disciple's heart, he must have broken its power himself. Breaking the power of a Mantra means that one has meditated and obtained the mystic experience of God through it, making its power one's own. At the time of initiation, the guru arouses the Mantra's *Shakti*, or power, in his consciousness and transmits it, along with his own energy, to the disciple. If the disciple is receptive, he receives the radiant mass of energy in his own heart and is immeasurably reinforced and strengthened. Guru, Mantra and disciple are bound together in Divine Power made manifest in consciousness.

There must be psychic affinity between teacher and student; the spiritual path is a lifetime involvement. The guru continues to guide and purify the aspirant, to prepare and strengthen him for God-Realisation, whether it be through *japa* meditation or other means. There are no shortcuts to the goal. Needless to say, the commercial peddlers of instant-mix mumbo-jumbo, which is sold as Mantras, should be assiduously avoided. They are opportunists preying on the spiritual instincts of those who are sincerely looking for Truth.

If no guru can be found, select any Mantra that seems appropriate. It should be repeated mentally with faith and devotion every day. This in itself has a purificatory effect, and the realisation of God-consciousness will eventually be attained.

Everything in the universe vibrates on specific wavelengths. These wavelengths can be manipulated. For example, when its pitch is increased high enough, a violin note can shatter glass. The various Mantras, although equally efficient, vibrate on different wavelengths. At the time of initiation, a Mantra is selected, either by the guru or by the initiate himself, in accordance with the latter's mental type. The vibrations of the Mantra and those of the disciple's mind must be mutually compatible. The mind must also be receptive to the deity whose form it will eventually assume. The process of attuning body and mind to the Mantra through *japa* meditation is prolonged. When attunement finally is achieved, meditation takes place.

In the state of meditation the flow of inner thought waves, which has been channeled by repetition of the Mantra, is greatly intensified. The deeper the meditation, the more marked the effect. The mind's upward concentration sends a rush of force through the top of the head. Response comes in a fine rain of magnetism which bathes the body in a downward flow of soft electricity. Thus the power of *japa* meditation leads to the Divine Vibration. One experiences that eternal Silence which encompasses all sound.

7

Japa Meditation: Practice

The efficiency of the Japa is accentuated according to the degree of concentration. The mind should be fixed on the Source. Then only you will realise the maximum benefits of a Mantra. Every Mantra has got tremendous force. A Mantra is a mass of Tejas or radiant energy. It transforms the mental substance by producing a particular thought movement. The rhythmical vibrations produced by repeating the Mantra, regulate the unsteady vibrations of the five sheaths. It checks the natural tendencies of objective thoughts of the mind. It helps the spiritual power and reinforces it.

—Swami Sivananda
Practice of Yoga

Mantras are Sanskrit invocations of the Supreme Being. Reinforced and propelled by *japa* meditation, they pass from the verbal level through the mental and telepathic states, and on to pure thought energy. Of all languages, Sanskrit most closely approaches telepathic language because of its affinity to the fifty primeval sounds. It is the most direct way to approach the transcendental state.

Mantras cannot be concocted or tailor-made for the individual, despite some current claims. They have always existed in a latent state as sound energies. Just as gravity was discovered but not invented by Newton, Mantras were revealed to the ancient Masters. They have been codified in the scriptures and handed down from guru to disciple. Although it is customary for the guru when giving initiation to accept voluntary offerings of fruit, flowers or money, the selling of Mantras is strictly against all spiritual rules.

Neither Mantra, deity nor guru, once chosen, should be changed. There are many paths up the mountain. Perseverance on one alone will bring the aspirant to the top faster than if he were to spread his energies in exploring all the alternative paths.

Saguna Mantras

Mantras used by spiritual aspirants to achieve God-Realisation are called deity Mantras. They are *saguna*, with qualities or form-producing, and aid the conceptualisation process, just as do visual symbols. In time, recitation gives rise to the actual form of the particular deity.

As a specialised sound-body of consciousness, the Mantra is the deity itself. The form of the deity manifests as the visible portion of the sound. The Mantra, therefore, must be repeated in the proper way, with attention to the syllables and rhythm. If translated, it ceases to be a Mantra because sound vibrations newly created in translation are no longer the body of the deity, and therefore cannot evoke it. Only the rhythmical vibrations of the Sanskrit syllables properly recited can regulate the unsteady vibrations of the worshipper and permit the form of the deity to arise.

Westerners are prone to think that the various Mantras refer to different gods, and that there is a wide diversity in the culminating experience. It must never be forgotten that the deities are aspects of the one Divinity whose grandeur is too vast for the mind to comprehend at the beginning of spiritual practice. To use again the analogy of the hill, the many paths to the top can be viewed as the worship of the various aspects of God. The hill itself is one hill, and the summit is the same. After reaching the pinnacle, one will have the vision to encompass the totality.

Every true Mantra fulfils six conditions. 1) It was originally revealed to a sage, who achieved Self-Realisation through it and passed it down to others. 2) It has a presiding deity and 3) a specific meter. 4) It possesses a *bija*, or seed, investing it with a special power that is the essence of the Mantra. 5) It also has dynamic divine power, or *Shakti*. 6) Lastly, there is a plug that conceals the pure consciousness hidden in the Mantra. As soon as the plug is removed by constant prolonged repetition, pure consciousness is revealed, and the devotee receives the vision of his deity.

All devotees are really worshipping the same Supreme *Atman*. Differences are only the differences in worshippers. These differences arise from the need for multiplicity in approach to the Godhead. Various temperaments are attracted to particular manifestations of the Divine. Some people are drawn by silence, others by activity; some lose themselves in nature, others in intellectual abstractions. One can approach God more easily if there is a compatible relationship with the most suitable manifestation. Harmony between aspirant and chosen deity is essential. However, the goal will be reached only when one can see his chosen deity in all deities and in all beings.

At the time of initiation by a guru, one's deity, or *ishta devata*, is chosen. Every person has worshipped some deity in previous lives; the impressions of this worship are imprinted in the subconscious mind. These impressions have influenced the mental vibrations and have helped to form the particular mentality. Worship of Lord Siva in a previous birth would incline one to Siva worship in this life also; it would impart certain mental characteristics, such as stoicism and love of solitude. One who chooses Siva as his *ishta devata* would be most drawn to abstract forms of thought and meditation as his method of worship.

The householder to whom family, responsibility, order and ideals are important is drawn to Rama, the ideal son, husband and lawgiver. Krishna attracts most people, particularly devotional types and active, balanced extroverts who are concerned with the welfare of others. As the mischievous baby, a young man engaged in divine play in the fields and forests of Vrindavan, and inspired giver of the wisdom of the Bhagavad Gita, His range is all-inclusive. Those who feel reverence for the Mother aspect as divine universal energy might worship Durga. If one cannot discover his own natural inclination, the guru will choose the deity in accordance with his insight.

Once the deity and appropriate Mantra have been selected, and the aspirant has received initiation, he works with the Mantra until reaching enlightenment. The Mantra becomes his theme song, so to speak. He makes its vibrations his own, and to the extent that he can do this, he is drawn closer to God.

Other deity Mantras can also be used in a supplementary way, such as for acquiring particular attributes. Repetition of *OM Aim Saraswatyai Namah* bestows wisdom, intelligence and creative achievement. *OM Sri Maha Lakshmyai Namah* confers wealth and prosperity. The Ganesha Mantra removes obstacles in any undertaking.

The *Maha Mrityunjaya* Mantra prevents accidents, incurable diseases and calamities, and bestows longevity and immortality. It is also a *moksha* Mantra, bringing liberation. Those who do *japa* of it daily will enjoy health, long life and ultimate enlightenment. The translation of this most powerful Mantra is: 'We bow to that three-eyed Lord (Siva) who is full of sweet fragrance, who nourishes human beings. May he free me from the bondage of births and deaths, just as the ripe cucumber is separated from the vine, and may I be fixed in immortality.'

The *Gayatri Mantra* is the supreme Mantra of the Vedas. It is the one Mantra that can be commonly prescribed for all, for *Gayatri* is the Mother of the universe, *Shakti* herself, and there is nothing She cannot do. Her Mantra purifies the mind; destroys pain, sin and ignorance; brings liberation; and bestows health, beauty, strength, vitality, power, intelligence and magnetic aura.

Repetition of the *Gayatri Mantra, OM Namah Sivaya, OM Namo Narayanaya*, or *OM Namo Bhagavate Vasudevaya* 125,000 times, with feeling, faith, and devotion secures for the devotee the grace of the presiding deity. *OM Sri Ramaya Namah* and *OM Namo Bhagavate Vasudevaya* enable one to attain realisation of God with attributes first, and subsequently realisation without attributes.

Mantras for Japa

1. ॐ श्रीमहागणपतये नमः
OM Śri Mahā Gaṇapataye Namaḥ
Prostrations to the great Lord Ganesha
OM is the original, most powerful Mantra sound. It is a part of almost every other Mantra, and serves to invoke pure supreme vibrations. Sri is a title of reverent respect. Maha means great. Ganapati is another name for Ganesha who is symbolised as the elephant-headed god, representing strength and fortitude. He is the remover of obstacles and bestower of success.

2. ॐ नमः शिवाय
OM Namaḥ Śivāya
Prostrations to Lord Siva

Siva is the lord of ascetics and recluses. He is part of the Hindu Trinity. Brahma and Vishnu, the other two parts, are associated with creation and preservation, respectively. Siva, the Cosmic Dancer, presides over the destructive energies which break up the universe at the end of each age. This is the process of the old making way for the new. In a more personal sense, it is Siva's energy by which one's lower nature is destroyed, making way for positive growth.

3. ॐ नमो नारायणाय
OM Namo Nārāyaṇāya
Prostrations to Lord Vishnu
Narayana is a name of Vishnu, the Preserver of the world. After the Creation, it is the energy ofVishnu which maintains order to the universe. It is Vishnu who regularly takes on a human form and incarnates on earth to benefit mankind. People who are closely involved in the running of the world and maintaining the harmony of life are drawn to this aspect of God.

4. ॐ नमो भगवते वासुदेवाय
OM Namo Bhagavate Vāsudevāya
Prostrations to the Lord God, Vasudeva
Rhagavan means Lord, referring to Vishnu. Vasudeva, meaning 'He Who abides in all things and in Whom all things abide,' is a name of Krishna. Krishna is one of the most loved of all deities. He is considered to be a world teacher for he is the source of the Bhagavad Gita, one of the most popular of all Eastern religious texts. People are drawn to Krishna because of his playfulness and joyful nature.

5. हरि ॐ
Hari OM
OM Vishnu

Hari is another name for Vishnu. It is that aspect which forgives the past actions of those who take refuge in Him and destroys their negative deeds. Thus Hari is a redeemer and a guide to personal salvation as well as the World Preserver.

6. ॐ श्रीरामाय नमः
OM Śrī Rāmāya Namaḥ
Prostrations to Lord Rama
Rama, an incarnation of Vishnu, took life on earth for the purpose of upholding righteousness and rewarding virtue. His life is the subject of the Ramayana. Rama lived the life of perfection and responsibility. Rama and Sita epitomised the devotional relationship between husband and wife. They are the model for all householders and people with family duties.

7. ॐ श्रीदुर्गायै नमः
OM Śrī Durgāyai Namaḥ
Prostrations to Mother Durga
Supreme Divinity is without qualities or attributes, and as such It contains all qualities and attributes. The masculine principles are important, yet they must be balanced with the feminine principles. Masculine and feminine are but obverse and reverse of the same coin. Durga represents the motherhood aspect of God. She is the force, or *Shakti*, through which Divinity manifests. Durga is power. She is the protector and benefactor. According to Hindu mythology, the chaitanya, or pure consciousnesses, of Brahma, Vishnu and Siva were united to form the being of Mother Durga. She is commonly pictured riding a tiger and having eight arms with which she carries flowers and weapons of protection and gives the gesture of blessing.

8. ॐ श्रीमहालक्ष्म्यै नमः
OM Śrī Mahā Lakṣmyai Namaḥ
Prostrations to the great Mother Lakshmi

Lakshmi is the bountiful provider. As Vishnu's consort, She aids in the preservation of the three worlds by bestowing wealth and abundance of a material and spiritual nature. She is pictured as a beautiful woman standing on a lotus blossom with her arms open and giving.

9. ॐ ऐं सरस्वत्यै नमः
OM Aim Saraswatyai Namaḥ
Prostrations to Mother Saraswati
Aim is the *bija* of Saraswati, the source of all learning, and knowledge of the arts and music. She is Brahma's consort and is involved with the creation of new ideas and things. Responsible for bestowing wisdom and knowledge, She is often worshipped by people in the creative arts.

10. ॐ श्री महा कालिकायै नमः
OM Śrī Mahā Kālikāyai Namaḥ
Prostrations to Mother Kali
Kali is that divine aspect which is responsible for the destruction and eradication of negative qualities in this world. She is the transformative power of Divinity which dissolves the individual into cosmic union. Maha Kali is one of the most fearsome of all the expressions of Divinity. Because of the intensity of her purgative nature, very few people are initiated into this Mantra.

11. ॐ श्रीहनुमते नमः
OM Śrī Hanumate Namaḥ
Prostrations to Blessed Hanuman
Hanuman is the perfection of devotion. He is the greatest and the most selfless devotee of Lord Rama. In the Hindu tradition, he is considered to be a semi-deity, for he is the son of the wind god. He possesses great strength and courage.

12. हरे राम हरे राम राम राम हरे हरे
हरे कृष्ण हरे कृष्ण कृष्ण कृष्ण हरे हरे

Hare Rāma Hare Rāma, Rāma Rāma Hare Hare,
Hare Kṛṣṇa Hare Kṛṣṇa, Kṛṣṇa Kṛṣṇa Hare Hare
My Lord, Rama! My Lord, Krishna!
Hare is a glorified form of address for calling upon God. Rama and Krishna were two of the best known and most beloved incarnations of Vishnu. They took human birth on this earth to lead mankind to eternal salvation. This is the *Maha Mantra*, the easiest and surest way for attaining God-Realisation in this present age.

13. ॐ श्रीराम जय राम जय जय राम
OM Śrī Rāma Jaya Rāma Jaya Iaya Rāma
Victory to Rama
Jaya means 'victory' or 'hail.'

14. श्रीराम राम रामेति रमे रामे मनोरमे
सहस्रनाम तत्तुल्यं रामनाम वरानने ।।
Śrī Rāma Rāma Rāmeti, Rame Rāme Manorame;
Sahasranāma Tattulyaṃ, Rāma Nāma Varānane
All these sacred names Rama are equal to the highest name of God
This Mantra cures gossiping and backbiting, and makes up for time lost in idle chit-chat.

15. ॐ त्र्यम्बकं यजामहे सुगन्धिं पुष्टिवर्धनम् ।
उर्वारुकमिव बन्धनान्मृत्योर्मुक्षीय माऽमृतात् ।
OM Tryambakaṃ Yajāmahe Sugandhiṃ Puṣṭivardhanam
Urvārukamiva Bandhanān Mṛityor Mukṣiya Mā'mṛitat
We worship the three-eyed Lord (Siva) who is full of sweet fragrance and nourishes human beings. May he liberate me from bondage, even as the cucumber is severed from the vine.
This is the *Maha Mrityunjaya Mantra*. It removes diseases, prevents accidents and bestows liberation. It should be repeated daily.

16. ॐ नमोऽस्तु ते महायोगिन् प्रपन्नमनुशाधि माम् ।
यथा त्वच्चरणांभोजे रतिः स्यादनपायिनी ।।

OM Namo 'stute Mahāyogin Prapannamanuśādhi Mām
Yathā Twaccaraṇāṃ Bhoje Ratiḥ Syadanapāyinī
Salutation to thee, O great Yogi! Pray direct me that have fallen at Thy feet, so that I may find unfailing delight at Thy lotus feet.
This is the Mantra for self surrender. It should be repeated with a pure heart free of personal desires.

Gayatri Mantra

ॐ । भूर्भुवः स्वः । तत् सवितुर्वरेण्यम् ।
भर्गो देवस्य धीमहि । धियो यो नः प्रचोदयात् ।।
OM Bhūr Bhuvaḥ Swaḥ, Tat Savitur Vareṇyam
Bhargo Devasya Dhīmahi, Dhiyo Yo Naḥ Pracodayāt
We meditate on that Ishwara's glory, Who has created the universe, Who is fit to be worshipped, Who is the embodiment of Knowledge and Light, Who is the remover of all sins and ignorance. May He enlighten our intellects.

ॐ	*OM*	Symbol of the Para Brahman
भूः	*Bhūr*	Bhu-Loka (Physical plane)
भुवः	*Bhuvaḥ*	Antariksha-Loka (Astral plane)
स्वः	*Swaḥ*	Swarga-Loka (Celestial plane)
तत्	*Tat*	That; Transcendent Paramatman
सवितुः	*Savitur*	Ishwara or Creator
वरेण्यम्	*Vareṇyam*	Fit to be worshipped or adored
भर्गो	*Bhargo*	Remover of sins and ignorance; Glory Effulgence
देवस्य	*Devasya*	Resplendent; Shining
धीमहि	*Dhīmahi*	We meditate
धियः	*Dhiyo*	Buddhis; Intellects; Understandings
यः	*Yo*	Which; who
नः	*Naḥ*	Our
प्रचोदयात्	*Pracodayāt*	Enlighten; Guide; Impel

Gayatris of Different Deities

Gayatri is a verse of specific length and meter. Although the *Gayatri* described above is one of the most sacred of the Vedic Mantras, and is called 'Mother of the Vedas,' this verse form is also used to praise and invoke many of the deities.

1. ॐ एकदन्ताय विद्महे वक्रतुण्डाय धीमहि । तन्नो दन्ती प्रचोदयात् ॥
OM Ekadantāya Vidmahe Vakratuṇḍāya Dhīmahi, Tanno Dantī Pracodayāt
This is the *Gayatri* of Ganesha.

2. ॐ नारायणाय विद्महे वासुदेवाय धीमहि । तन्नो विष्णुः प्रचोदयात् ॥
OM Nārāyaṇāya Vidmahe Vāsudevāya Dhīmahi, Tanno Viṣṇuḥ Pracodayāt
This is the *Gayatri* of Vishnu.

3. ॐ तत्पुरुषाय विद्महे सहस्राक्षाय महादेवाय धीमहि । तन्नो रुद्रः प्रचोदयात् ॥
OM Tatpuruṣāya Vidmahe Sahasrākṣāya Mahādevāya Dhīmahi, Tanno Rudraḥ Pracodayāt
This is the *Gayatri* of Siva.

4. ॐ दाशरथये विद्महे सीतावल्लभया धीमहि । तन्नो रामः प्रचोदयात् ॥
OM Dāśarathaye Vidmahe Sītāvallabhayā Dhīmahi, Tanno Rāmaḥ Pracodayāt
This is the *Gayatri* of Rama.

5. ॐ देवकीनन्दनाय विद्महे वासुदेवाय धीमहि । तन्नः कृष्णः प्रचोदयात् ॥
Om Devakīnandanāya Vidmahe Vāsudevāya Dhīmahi, Tannaḥ Kṛṣṇaḥ Pracodayāt
This is the *Gayatri* of Krishna.

6. ॐ कात्यायन्यै विद्महे कन्याकुमार्यै धीमहि । तन्नो दुर्गा प्रचोदयात् ॥
OM Kātyāyanyai Vidmahe Kanyākumāryai Dhīmahi, Tanno Durgā Pracodayāt
This is the *Gayatri* of Durga.

7. ॐ महादेव्यैच विद्महे विष्णुपत्न्यै च धीमहि । तन्नो लक्ष्मीः प्रचोदयात् ॥
OM Mahādevyai Ca Vidmahe Viṣṇupatnyai Ca Dhīmahi, Tanno Lakṣmīḥ Pracodayāt
This is the *Gayatri* of Lakshmi.

8. ॐ वाग्देव्यै च विद्महे कामराजाय धीमहि । तन्नो देवी प्रचोदयात् ॥
OM Vāgdevyai Ca Vidmahe Kāmarājāya Dhīmahi, Tanno Devī Pracodayāt
This is the *Gayatri* of Saraswati.

9. ॐ सर्वसंमोहिन्यै विद्महे विश्वजनन्यै धीमहि । तन्नः शक्तिः प्रचोदयात् ॥
OM Sarvasaṁmohinyai Vidmahe Viśvajananyai Dhīmahi, Tannaḥ śaktiḥ Pracodayāt
This is the *Gayatri* of *Shakti*, Cosmic Power.

10. ॐ गुरुदेवाय विद्महे परब्रह्मणे धीमहि । तन्नो गुरुः प्रचोदयात् ॥
OM Gurudevāya Vidmahe Parabrahmaṇe Dhīmahi, Tanno Guruḥ Pracodayāt
This is the *Gayatri* of the guru.

11. ॐ भास्कराय विद्महे महाद्युतिकराय धीमहि । तन्न आदित्यः प्रचोदयात् ॥
OM Bhāskarāya Vidmahe Mahādyutikarāya Dhīmahi, Tanna Ādityaḥ Pracodayāt
This is the *Gayatri* of Surya, the Sun.

Nirguna Mantras

As *saguna* Mantras have form, *nirguna* Mantras are without form. There are no deities or personalised aspects of God to be invoked. Rather, one uses the abstract Mantras and Vedantic formulas to assert identification with all of Creation. Because people are of many different temperaments, not all spiritual aspirants are drawn to a personal deity. Many perceive the universe as diverse energy patterns, all connected and interrelated, and stemming from one Source or Primal Cause.

For this type of temperament, the abstract Mantra creates a vibration in which the meditator identifies with the whole of the Cosmos. With the repetition of one of these Mantras, the meditator loses his individual identity and merges with Nature. He avows that he is identical with that homogeneous substratum, that energy or power of existence, which underlies and permeates all that exists.

All Mantras are hidden in OM, which is the abstract, highest Mantra of the cosmos. OM is the manifest symbol of the *Sabdabrahman* vibration, or God; but, it must not be equated with the Divine. The universe has come from OM, rests in OM and dissolves in it. AUM, as it is sometimes written, covers the threefold experience of man; A represents the physical plane, U represents the mental and astral plane, and M represents the deep-sleep state and everything beyond reach of the intellect. The transcendental sound of OM is heard only by yogis, not by the ordinary ear.

Letters of the alphabet are emanations from OM, which is the root of all sounds and letters. A is the first sound the vocal apparatus can utter, and M is the last. In between is the middle range of U. The three sounds comprising OM encompass all sound. There is no language, music or poetry outside its range. Not only do all language and thought arise from this word, but also the energy vibrations of the universe itself.

Because of its universality, OM can be used as a Mantra by all who are unable to find a guru. However, its very universality and lack of particular form make it very difficult for a beginner to grasp. The mind must be very strong to be able to concentrate on formless and abstract Mantras such as OM.

Japa meditation on OM has a tremendous influence on the mind. Vibrations set up by this word are extremely powerful. By holding the hands over the ears and intoning it, one can experience its vibrations on a rudimentary physical level. No other sound similarly intoned will have the same vibrational power within the head.

Correctly pronounced, the sound proceeds from the navel, with a deep and harmonious vibration, and gradually manifests itself at the upper part of the nostrils. The larynx and palate are the sounding boards; no part of the tongue or palate is touched. As the U is pronounced, the sound rolls from the root of the tongue to the end of the sounding board of the mouth. M is the last sound, and is produced by closing the lips. Pronounced merely as spelled, OM will have a certain effect upon the nervous system, and will benefit the psyche. Pronounced correctly, it arouses and transforms every atom in the physical body, setting up new vibrations and awakening dormant physical and mental powers.

Just as the various deities are aspects of the One Supreme, so the various *bija*, or seed Mantras are aspects of the supreme Mantra, OM. *Bija* Mantras are seed letters directly derived from the fifty primeval sounds, and are very powerful. Generally a *bija* Mantra consists of a single letter, although some, such as HRĪM, are compounded. Each has a significant inner mystic meaning, although on the surface the sound itself appears to have no meaning at all. Each element of the universe has its corresponding *bija*. The sounds for ether, air, fire, water and earth are, respectively, HAM, YAM, RAM, VAM and LAM. Every deity also has its own seed syllable. Because of their innate force, *bija* Mantras generally are not given for initiation. *Japa* on them may be practiced by those who are in a pure state, and their use is preceded by intricate rituals.

Abstract Mantras

1. सोऽहम्
So'ham
I am That I am

The meditator is existence itself. He is without form, without quality, without past, present or future. No bonds or limitations restrict the aspirant who has *So'ham* firmly fixed in his mind.

2. अहं ब्रह्मास्मि
Ahaṃ Brahma Asmi
I am Brahman
Aham Brahma Asmi is a great Vedantic formula. The meditator asserts himself to be One with the ever-present Brahman. In doing so, he denies confinement to the body and mind, and affirms unity with the Absolute.

3. तत्त्वमसि
Tat Twam Asi
That Thou Art
'That' is the eternal Brahman, and 'thou' is the meditator. *Tat Twam Asi*, one of the greatest of the Vedantic statements, identifies the individual as one and the same with Brahman, the Absolute Substratum of Creation.

4. ॐ
OM
There is no translation of OM. It consists of three letters: *A*, *U*, and *M*. It signifies the three periods of time, the three states of consciousness and all of existence. *A* is the waking state, *U* is the dreaming state, and *M* is the deep-sleep state. OM contains *nada* and *bindu*. *Nada* is the prolonged vowel sound and *bindu* is the humming sound, made with closed lips, with which the Mantra ends.

Bija Mantras, Mystic Seed Letters

1. (हौं) HAUM
In this Mantra, *Ha* is Siva and *au* is Sadasiva. The *nada* and *bindu* mean that which dispels sorrow. With this Mantra, Lord Siva should be worshipped.

2. (डुं) DUM
Here *Da* means Durga, and *u* means to protect. *Nada* means Mother of the universe, and *bindu* signifies action (worship or prayer). This is the bija Mantra of Durga.

3. (क्रीं) KRĪM
With this Mantra Kalika should be worshipped. *Ka* is Kali, *ra* is Brahman, and *ī* is Mahamaya. *Nada* is the Mother of the universe, and *bindu* is the dispeller of sorrow.

4. (ह्रीं) HRĪM
This is the Mantra of Mahamaya or Bhuvaneshwari. *Ha* means Siva, *ra* is prakriti, *ī* means Mahamaya. *Nada* is the Mother of the universe, and *bindu* is the dispeller of sorrow.

5. (श्रीं) ŚRĪM
This is the Mantra of Maha Lakshmi. *Sha* is Maha Lakshmi. *Ra* means wealth. *Ī* is satisfaction or contentment. *Nada* is the manifested Brahman, and *bindu* means the dispeller of sorrow.

6. (ऐं) AIM
This is the *bija* Mantra of Saraswati. *Ai* stands for Saraswati, and *bindu* is the dispeller of sorrow.

7. (क्लीं) KLĪM
This is the *Kamabija. Ka* means Kamadeva, the lord of desire; it also means Lord Krishna. *La* means Indra, the ruler of Heaven, also lord of the senses. *Ī* means contentment or satisfaction. *Nada* and *bindu* mean those that bring happiness and sorrow.

8. (हूँ) HŪM
In this Mantra *Ha* is Siva, and *ū* is Bhairava. *Nada* is the Supreme, and *bindu* means dispeller of sorrow.

9. (गं) GAM
This is the Ganesha *bija. Ga* means Ganesha, and *bindu* is the dispeller of sorrow.

10. (ग्लौं) GLAUM
This is also a Mantra of Ganesha. *Ga* means Ganesha, *la* means that which pervades, *au* means luster or brilliance, and *bindu* is the dispeller of sorrow.

11. (क्ष्रौं) KṢRAUM
This is the *bija* of Narasimha, a very fierce half-man half-lion incarnation of Lord Vishnu. *Ksha* is Narasimha, *ra* is Brahma, *au* means with teeth pointing upwards, and *bindu* means dispeller of sorrow.

The science of Mantra is very complex. There are even Mantras for such specific purposes as curing snake bite and chronic diseases, but these are of a lower order. In the modern world, the power of gross sound vibration is just beginning to be utilised in physical therapy, and its potential is being tapped in other fields. The ancient Indian sages had this sophistication thousands of years ago. They have used sound in its gross and subtle states to penetrate the planes of human consciousness and to reach the divine vibration that is the experience of God. Beginning in OM and dissolving in OM, the Mantra comes full cycle.

Meditation with the Mantra

There are various practical aids to progress in *japa* meditation that have been tested for thousands of years and are based on sound psychological and natural principles.

The telling of rosary beads is the form of *japa* most familiar to Western experience. A *japa mala*, similar to a rosary, is often used in Mantra repetition. It helps to foster alertness, acts as a focus for the physical energy and is an aid to rhythmic, continuous recitation. It consists of 108 beads. An additional bead, the *meru*, is slightly larger than the others. It is the signal indicating that with one Mantra recited for each bead, *japa* has been done 108

times, or one *mala*. The fingers should not cross the *meru*. When it is reached, the beads are reversed in the hand; one continues reciting the Mantra, moving the *mala* in the opposite direction. The thumb and third finger roll the beads; the index finger, which is psychically negative, is never used. The rosary must not be allowed to hang below the navel, and should be wrapped in a clean cloth when not in use.

An appropriate prayer before beginning induces purity of feeling. With eyes closed and concentration focussed either between the eyebrows on the *ajna chakra* or on the *anahata chakra* of the heart, one should invoke the aid of his chosen deity and guru. The Mantra must be pronounced distinctly and without mistakes, for it and the deity itself are one and the same thing. Repetition must be neither too fast nor too slow, and thought must be given to its meaning. Speed should be increased only when the mind begins to wander. Because the mind will naturally try to drift away after a time, it is necessary to keep alert throughout the practice.

Variety in *japa* is necessary to sustain interest, avoid fatigue and counteract the monotony that can arise from constant repetition of the same syllables. This can be provided by modifying the volume. The Mantra can be repeated loud for a while, then whispered, and then recited mentally. The mind needs variety or it becomes tired. However, even mechanical repetition that is devoid of feeling has a great purifying effect. Feeling will come later, as the process of purification continues.

Audible repetition is called *vaikhari japa*, while that done by whispering or humming is termed *upamsu japa*. Mental repetition, *manasika japa*, is the most powerful; it requires keener concentration, for the mind tends to shut off after a period of time. The advantage of loud *japa*, which should be used with discretion, is that it shuts out all worldly sound and distractions. One should alternate when necessary, particularly when drowsiness sets in.

Unaccustomed to this kind of activity, the beginner at first may find himself giving up too soon, after five or ten minutes of repeating the Mantra. The syllables in this case may sound meaningless—mere syllables and nothing more. But by persevering for at least half an hour without interruption, he will give the Mantra time to work itself into his consciousness, and benefits will be felt in a few days.

Meditation on the image of the chosen deity while the Mantra is being repeated adds tremendously to the efficacy of *japa*. Sound and form correspond and reinforce each other. Sound vibrations alone, if made with care and devotion, are capable of producing the form in the consciousness of the aspirant. The process can be greatly facilitated by visualising the deity in the heart area or the space between the eyebrows. With the visualisation, there should be awareness of the various attributes of the deity. Feel that the Lord is seated within, emanating purity to the heart and mind, and manifesting his presence by the power of the Mantra.

Thus, in meditating on Siva, the physical energy is focussed on rolling the *mala* beads. The image of the deity, with the third eye and the symbolic crescent moon, serpents, trident, drum, etc., occupies the mind on one level. The Mantra *OM Namah Sivaya* is simultaneously being repeated, and on another level is being embedded in the consciousness. Repetition of the Mantra has a cumulative effect, and with continued practice it gains in power. It should be evident that *japa* meditation is far more than a verbal exercise. It is a state of complete absorption.

Concluding prayer and rest are important. When *japa* practice is finished, it is advisable not to plunge immediately into worldly activity. Sitting quietly for about ten minutes, one should reflect on the Lord and feel His presence. As routine duties are commenced, the spiritual vibrations will remain intact. This current should be maintained at all times, no matter what one is engaged in. When doing manual work, give the hands to work but give the mind to God. Like a woman who continues knitting while talking to her friends, one can sustain mental *japa*. With practice, the manual work will become automatic. When the Mantra can be repeated throughout the day, God-consciousness will permeate one's life.

Mantra writing, *likhita japa*, is another, supplementary form of *japa*. The Mantra should be written daily with a special pen and notebook which have been set aside for this purpose. It should be done for half an hour, during which time complete silence and concentration are observed. While writing, simultaneously repeat the Mantra mentally so that the impression made in the consciousness will be intensified. *Likhita japa* may be done in any language or script. It greatly helps the aspirant to concentrate and leads to meditation. This practice helps to set up a continuous vibration of divine energy that guides and protects, regardless of what one is doing.

Advanced meditation should not be attempted without the guidance of guru. *Bija* Mantras and certain mystic Mantras, such as the *Sri Vidya*, should not be repeated by those who are not well acquainted with them and with the Sanskrit language. When improperly repeated, they can actually bring harm to the psychic system. Those who are not qualified, and who do not have access to a guru who has broken the power of these advanced Mantras, should concentrate on their own Mantras.

Deity Mantras are used for *purascharana*, which is concentrated *japa* meditation extended over a long period of time. When performing a *purascharana*, the aspirant sets aside a certain number of hours each day for *japa*. The Mantra is repeated 100,000 times for each syllable of the Mantra. The Mantra is repeated with feeling, and in a particular manner with the right observance, until the fixed number of Mantras have been recited. Slow repetition of the Maha Mantra may take as long as three years to finish. The practitioner must observe certain rules and regulations laid down in the scriptures in regard to *purascharana*, and must observe perfect dietary discipline in accordance with those injunctions.

Anushthana is the practice of religious austerity for the sake of obtaining some object or goal, the highest being spiritual. For success, the desire should be spiritual, and it should be kept in view throughout the practice. The rigor of the austerity, which may be of various kinds, depends on the constitution and health of the aspirant.

For *japa anushthana*, a deity Mantra should be selected in accordance with the desired goal. Although his personal deity might be Krishna, if one wanted to compose sublime music, he would repeat the Mantra for Saraswati; if he wished his spiritual obstacles to be removed, he would select a Ganesha Mantra. *Japa* meditation is then performed for a protracted period, with intense concentration of mind and no thought of the external world. This leads to achievement of the desired goal.

There may be other types of *japa* meditation, but the broad theory and techniques do not greatly vary. Approached with faith and devotion, and carried out with perseverance, *japa* is the most direct path to God-Realisation.

Mantras	Speed Per Min			No. Japa Done in One Hour				Time Required, at 6 Hrs Daily, For 1 Purascharana				
	Low	Med.	High	Low	Med.	High		Yrs	Mo.	Day	Hrs	Mins
OM	140	250	400	8400	15000	24000	Low	–	–	–	11	54
							Med.	–	–	–	6	40
							High	–	–	–	4	10
Hari Om or Sri Rama	120	200	300	7200	12000	18000	Low	–	–	1	3	47
							Med.	–	–	–	16	40
							High	–	–	–	11	7
Om Namah Sivaya	80	120	150	4800	7200	9000	Low	–	–	17	2	10
							Med.	–	–	11	3	30
							High	–	–	9	1	35
Om Namo Narayanaya	60	80	120	3600	4800	7200	Low	–	1	7	0	15
							Med.	–	–	27	4	45
							High	–	–	18	3	15
Om Namo Bhagavate Vasudevaya	40	60	90	2400	3600	5400	Low	–	2	23	2	0
							Med.	–	1	25	3	30
							High	–	1	7	0	15

(*contd . . .*)

Mantras	Speed Per Min			No. Japa Done in One Hour				Time Required, at 6 Hrs Daily, For 1 Purascharana				
	Low	Med.	High	Low	Med.	High		Yrs	Mo.	Day	Hrs	Mins
Gayatri Mantra	6	8	10	360	480	600	Low	3	0	16	0	45
							Med.	2	5	8	5	30
							High	1	7	15	3	35
Maha Mantra or Hare Rama Mantra	8	10	15	480	600	900	Low	3	0	16	0	45
							Med.	2	5	8	5	30
							High	1	7	17	3	35

8

Hatha Yoga Meditation: Kundalini

Kundalini is the cosmic power in individual bodies. It is not a material force, like electricity or magnetism. It is a spiritual potential, Shakti or cosmic power. In reality it has no form. It is the coiled-up, sleeping Divine Shakti that lies dormant in all beings. This mysterious Kundalini lies face downwards at the mouth of Sushumna Nadi. When it is awakened, it makes a hissing sound like a serpent, hence it is also called serpent power. Kundalini is the goddess of speech and is praised by all. She Herself, when awakened by the Yogin, achieves for him the illumination. It is She who gives liberation and knowledge for She is Herself that. She is also called Saraswati for She is the source of all knowledge and bliss. She is pure consciousness itself. She is Brahman. She is Prana Shakti, the Supreme Force. It is by this Shakti that the world exists. Creation, preservation and dissolution are in her.

—Swami Sivananda
Kundalini Yoga

Kundalini Yoga, or Laya Yoga as it is sometimes called, is the culminating meditative experience of Hatha Yoga. It is for the advanced student who is practicing under a guru. It requires thorough knowledge of the psychic body and its structure, as well as great purification of the physical and psychic bodies. Kundalini *Shakti* is primordial, cosmic power, and cannot be trifled with. Premature attempts to arouse it without proper preparation can cause great damage to the aspirant's mental, physical and psychic balance. The guidance and grace of a guru are absolutely necessary.

In kundalini meditation, the divine power that lies dormant in every human being is aroused and pulled upward through the *chakras*, the psychic centers of the body. At the top of the head, the seat of the highest consciousness, the union of the individual and Absolute Consciousness takes place. This is expressed symbolically as the union of *Shakti*, or kundalini, with Lord Siva.

Kundalini Shakti

The equilibrium of the universe is maintained by a polarity of positive and negative, male and female, the static and the dynamic. Whatever exists in the universe, the macrocosm, exists also in Man, the microcosm. The masculine passive ground force, Siva, resides in the *sahasrara*, the seventh *chakra*, located in the crown of the head. *Shakti*, the feminine active power, lies coiled at the base of the spine. It is the manifestation of cosmic power in the body and is in a dormant, potential state. Not a material force, it is the pristine psychic and spiritual power that underlies all organic and inorganic matter. Because of its spiral-like upward motion when awakened, it is referred to as serpent power, and is depicted iconographically as a serpent coiled at the base of the spine. The arousal of kundalini leads to union with Lord Siva. It is the state of supreme consciousness and spiritual enlightenment

Hatha Yoga awakens the kundalini by disciplining the body; purifying the *nadis*, the astral channels 'through which flows the *prana*; and controlling *prana*. Through the physical postures of Hatha Yoga the nervous system is toned, enabling it to withstand the experience of the rising energy. It regulates the flow of *prana* by means of body locks and seals, known as *mudras* and *bandhas*. *Kriyas*, special cleansing techniques, purify the inner organs of the physical body, and breath control steadies the mind. Vigorous *pranayama*, asanas, and meditation are not enough, however. Mental purification requires selfless service, for seeing and serving the Supreme in all beings is essential for any spiritual progress.

Kundalini and its channel for movement are not to be found in the physical body. Every portion of the physical body has its counterpart in the astral body, and both bodies are interdependent on the material plane. The seven psychic centers, or *chakras*, and *sushumna nadi*, the passage through which the kundalini rises, are in the astral body and correspond to the nerve plexuses and the spinal cord.

According to yogic theory, there are approximately 72,000 *nadis*, astral nerve tubes, the most important of which is the *sushumna*, the astral body's counterpart to the spinal cord. On either side of it are two *nadis* known as *ida* and *pingala*, which correspond to the left and right sympathetic cords in the physical body. *Prana*, vital energy, flows through them. As long as it does so, man is engaged in worldly activities, and is bound by time, space and causation. However, when the *sushumna* operates, he is beyond such limitation.

While Western anatomy recognises only the gross form and functions, Kundalini Yoga acts on the subtle level. The aspirant, therefore, must have a thorough knowledge of the major *nadis*. The *sushumna nadi* extends from the *muladhara chakra*, the second vertebra of the coccygeal region, to the *Brahmarandhra*, in the crown of the head. The physical spinal cord is made up of gray and white brain matter, and is suspended within the spinal column. Within this cord is a central canal, called in anatomy the

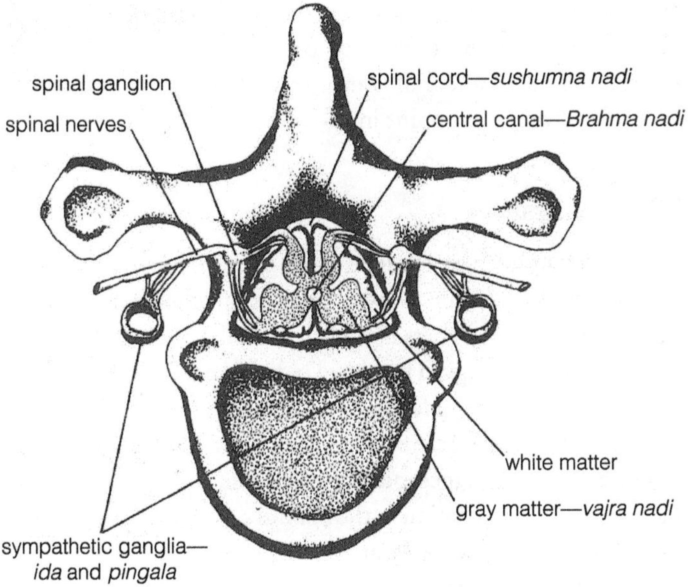

The Spinal Cord and the Nadis Cross Section of a Vertebra

The nadis, *indicated in italics, exist in the astral body. They are shown here in relation to their counterparts in the physical body.*

canalis centralis. The *sushumna*, located within this spinal canal, has several subdivisions.

Within the fiery red *sushumna* is another *nadi*, *vajra*, lustrous as the sun, which in turn contains another, the *chitra*, which is pale in colour. Inside the *chitra* is a very fine, minute canal known as *Brahma nadi*. When the kundalini is awakened, it passes through this canal from the *muladhara chakra* to the *sahasrara*. In this canal exist all of the main *chakras*, each representing a different state of consciousness.

The *chitra nadi* is the most vital part of the body, and is sometimes referred to as the 'heavenly way.' Within it, at the lower extremity, is the beginning of the *sushumna*, which is called the *Brahma Granthi* or 'knot of Brahma.' This obstruction is penetrated as the kundalini is aroused and passes upward toward the *nadi's* termination point in the cerebellum.

The Chakras

The six *chakras* are way stations along the *sushumna*, to the final destination, the *sahasrara chakra*. They are of consciousness, with specific tones of awareness and bliss, as well as storage places for the subtle, vital energy. They have corresponding centers in the spinal cord and nerve plexuses of the gross physical body, with which they are closely related. Vibrations produced in the physical centers by prescribed methods create specific desired effects in the subtle centers. The location of the *chakras* and their corresponding centers in the physical body are:

1. *Muladhara*: at the lower end of the spinal column, corresponding to the sacral plexus.
2. *Swadhishthana*: in the region of the genital organs, corresponding to the prostatic plexus.
3. *Manipura*: at the navel, corresponding to the solar plexus.
4. *Anahata*: at the heart, corresponding to the cardiac plexus.
5. *Vishuddha*: in the throat region, corresponding to the laryngeal plexus.
6. *Ajna*: between the eyebrows, trikuta; corresponding to the cavernous plexus.
7. *Sahasrara*: at the crown of the head, corresponding to the pineal gland.

During meditation, each *chakra* is visualised as a lotus with a certain number of petals. The *muladhara*, *swadhishthana*, *manipura*, *anahata*, *vishuddha* and *ajna chakras* have four, six, ten, twelve, sixteen and two petals respectively, while the *sahasrara* has one thousand. The number of petals is determined by the number and position of the *nadis* that emanate from the *chakra* and give it the appearance of a lotus. Hanging downward when the kundalini is dormant, the *nadis* turn upward with its ascendency.

Associated with each petal is one of the fifty Sanskrit letters, representing the vibration produced on it by the kundalini as it passes through the *chakra*. These sounds exist in latent form and, when manifested as vibrations of the *nadis*, can be felt during concentration. Besides petals and sound vibration, each *chakra* has its own geometric form representing a specific power, as well as its own color, function, element, presiding deity and *bija*, or mystic vibration.

There are various methods of locating the *chakras*, all of which may be approached from the front as well as the back. It may help initially to think of the *muladhara*, *manipura*, *anahata*, and *ajna* as localities rather than concentrated points. When attempting to locate the *chakras* from the back, one moves one's concentration directly upward along the spinal cord, from *chakra* to *chakra*. If approaching from the front, one moves from the base of the spine up to the navel, the heart, the throat, etc. At all times the consciousness is kept internalised and receptive to experiencing—the inner vibrations indicating an energy center. In all exercises, a comfortable meditative posture should be assumed; a straight spine is essential.

The *chakras* may be focussed upon by chanting OM, the all-inclusive universal sound vibration, in different pitches. Fixing the concentration on the *muladhara chakra*, OM is chanted at the lowest pitch. Then moving up the spinal cord to the area of each successive center, the pitch is raised higher each time. The OM sound gradually becomes imperceptible. Another method utilises the Indian musical scale to locate the psychic centers. There is a definite relationship between the scale and the principal *chakras*. Sa corresponds to the *muladhara*, re to the *swadhishthana*, ga to the *manipura*, ma to the *anahata*, pa to the *vishuddha*, dha to the *ajna* and ni to the *sahasrara*.

When the kundalini is awakened, it does not proceed directly to the *sahasrara* unless one is an exceptionally pure yogi. It must be moved up from one *chakra* to another, and a great deal of concentration and patience is required. It may drop back and have to be raised again with great effort. Even when the kundalini is raised to the *ajna chakra*, it is difficult to keep it there. Only great yogis such as Sri Ramakrishna, Sri Aurobindo and Swami Sivananda were able to keep it there for any length of time. When the kundalini finally rises from the *ajna* to the *sahasrara*, union takes place. But even here it does not remain long. Only after lengthy and continuous practice does the evolved and purified adept experience permanent union and final liberation.

The speed at which the kundalini is aroused depends upon the aspirant's purity, stage of evolution, dispassion, purification of the psychic nerves and vital sheath, and yearning for liberation. In due time, Nature awakens the power and gives the student knowledge as he is ready. Until he is able to absorb it totally, nothing of deep importance is revealed to him.

There are numerous other exercises, both physical and breathing, to facilitate *chakra* meditation. It cannot be stressed too strongly that this kind of meditation must be done under the guidance of a guru, and then only after many months of purification and preparation. No teacher, however, can give the student the power or the necessary self-discipline.

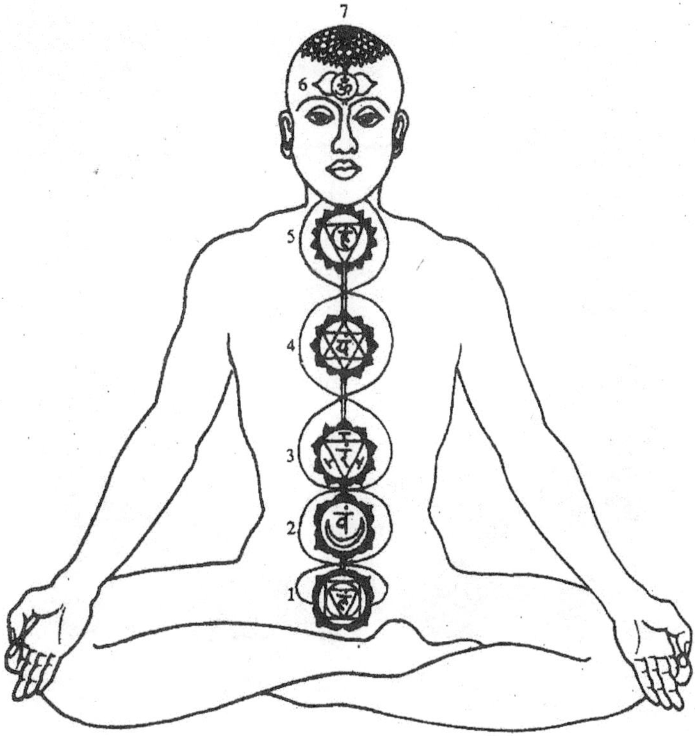

The Chakras and the Ida, Pingala and Sushumna Nadis

1. *Muladhara*, 2. *Swadhishthana*, 3. *Manipura*, 4. *Anahata*, 5. *Vishuddha*, 6. *Ajna*, 7. *Sahasrara* (Thousand-petalled Lotus)

Muladhara Chakra

The *muladhara chakra* is located at the base of the spinal column. It has a square mandala representing the earth principle which is yellow in colour, and has the *bija* Mantra of *laṃ*. The four petals which are crimson-coloured are associated with the sound vibrations of *vaṃ*, *śaṃ*, *ṣaṃ*, and *saṃ*. These *bijas* begin on the upper right-hand petal and are read in a clockwise direction. Brahma is the presiding deity. Within this *chakra*, kundalini lies dormant. Here also is the *Brahma Granthi*, or knot of Brahma, which must be forced open through rigorous ***sadhana*** and intense purification for the kundalini to rise.

Meditation on the *muladhara* confers knowledge of the kundalini, as well as the means of awakening it. It bestows breath and mind control, and knowledge of the past, present and future.

Swadhishthana Chakra

The *swadhishthana chakra*, situated in the *sushumna* at the genital area, controls the lower abdomen, kidneys, etc., in the physical body. Its element, water, is associated with the white crescent moon, and the *bija* is *vaṃ*. The six vermillion petals are represented by *baṃ*, *bhaṃ*, *maṃ*, *yaṃ*, *raṃ* and *laṃ*. Vishnu is the presiding deity.

Meditation is fixed on the crescent moon in the *chakra*. It gives control over the water element and confers psychic powers, intuitional knowledge and knowledge of astral entities. Many impure qualities are annihilated.

Manipura Chakra

The *manipura chakra* is located in the *sushumna nadi*, at the navel, and corresponds to the solar plexus. The red triangular mandala in its center contains its element, fire. The *bija* Mantra is *raṃ*. The ten petals which are dark purple, like heavy rain clouds, are represented by *ḍaṃ*, *ḍhaṃ*, *ṇaṃ*, *taṃ*, *thaṃ*, *daṃ*, *dhaṃ*, *naṃ*, *paṃ* and *phaṃ*. The presiding deity is Rudra.

He who concentrates successfully on this chakra has no fear of fire and is free from disease.

Anahata Chakra

The *anahata chakra* is located in the *sushumna* in the region of the heart. Its element air is located in the smoke-coloured mandala, shaped like the Star of David, in its center. Its *bija* is *yaṃ*. The twelve deep red petals are represented by *kaṃ*, *khaṃ*, *gaṃ*, *ghaṃ*, *ṅaṃ*, *caṃ*, *chaṃ*, *jaṃ*, *jhaṃ*, *ñaṃ*, *ṭaṃ* and *ṭhaṃ*. Isha is the presiding deity.

The *anahata* sound, the primal sound of *Sabdabrahman*, is heard at this center. Meditation on the *anahata chakra* bestows pure qualities, cosmic love and various psychic powers.

Vishuddha Chakra

The *vishuddha chakra* is situated in the *sushumna nadi* at the base of the throat, and corresponds to the laryngeal plexus in the physical body. It also corresponds to the fifth cosmic plane. Within a pure blue circle is its element, ether. The seed *bija* is *haṃ*. The sixteen smokey purple petals contain the Sanskrit vowels: *aṃ, āṃ, iṃ, īṃ, uṃ, ūṃ, ṛṃ, ṛṃ, ḷṃ, ḷṃ, eṃ, aiṃ, oṃ, auṃ, aṃ, aḥṃ*. The presiding deity is Sadasiva.

He who concentrates and ultimately achieves meditation on this *chakra* attains high success. He enjoys complete knowledge of the four Vedas and knows the past, present and future.

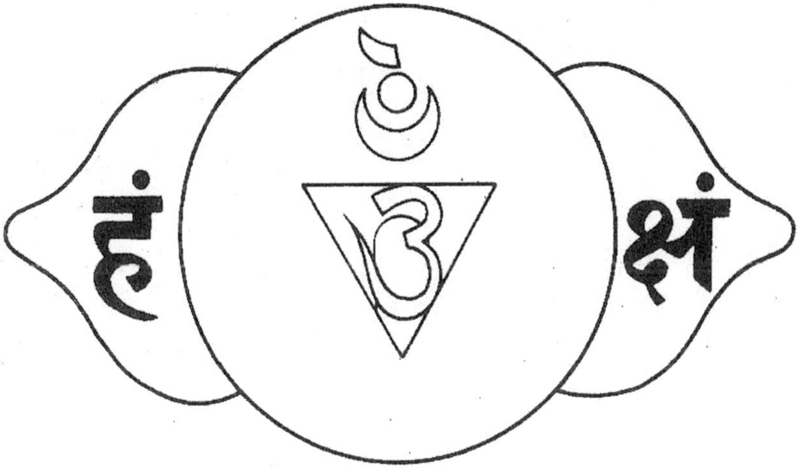

Ajna Chakra

The *ajna chakra*, in the *sushumna*, corresponds to the space between the eyebrows, the *trikuta*. OM is the seed letter for this *chakra* which is the seat of the mind, and is found in the pure white circle within it. On each side are two petals, also pure white, their vibrations represented by the Sanskrit letters haṃ and kṣaṃ. The element is *avyakta*, the primordial cloud of undifferentiated energy and matter. Paramasiva is the presiding deity.

He who meditates successfully on this center destroys the Karma of all past lives, and becomes a liberated soul. Intuitional knowledge is obtained through this *chakra*, the seat of primordial power and soul. It is here that yogis consciously put their *prana* at the time of death. All yogis, particularly *jnanis*, concentrate on this center and OM.

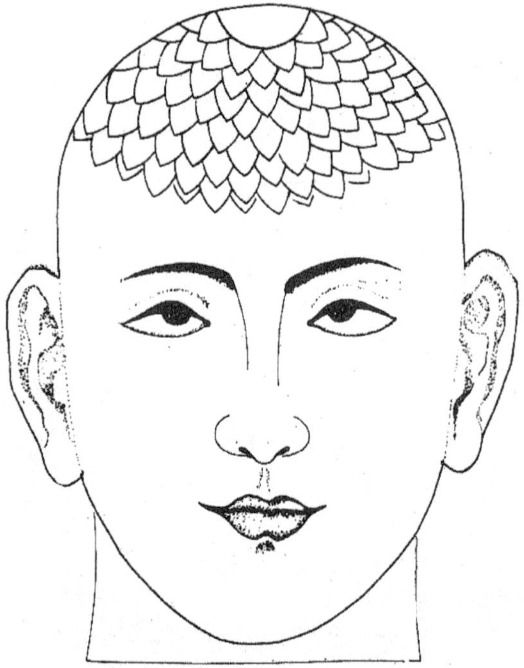

Sahasrara Chakra

The *sahasrara* is a subtle center, above and beyond the other six centers. All others are intimately connected with it. Situated at the crown of the head, it corresponds to the pineal gland of the physical body. It has a thousand petals, on which are repeated the fifty letters of the Sanskrit alphabet. It is the abode of Siva.

The area in the crown of the head, known as the anterior fontanelle in a newborn child, is called *Brahmarandhra*, the 'hole of Brahma.' At the time of death, when the advanced yogi separates himself from the physical body, it bursts open and the *prana* escapes through it.

When Kundalini *Shakti* is united with Siva at the *sahasrara*, the yogi experiences extreme bliss. He attains the superconscious state and the highest knowledge. He becomes a fully developed *jnani*.

9

Jnana Yoga Meditation: Vedantic Theory

A Jnana Yogi sees Atman everywhere through his eye of wisdom. There is absolutely no personal element in him. There is no thought of the self. He has not a bit of selfish interest. The lower self is completely annihilated. He lives for serving all. He feels the world as his own self. He actually feels that all is himself only. There is not a single thought or feeling for a personal little self. He has cosmic vision and cosmic feeling. Just as the river has joined the ocean, he has joined the ocean of bliss, knowledge and consciousness. He thinks and feels and works for others.

—Swami Sivananda
Vedanta in Daily Life

Jnana Yoga is one of the four main paths of Yoga. *Jnana* means wisdom; Jnana Yoga is the intellectual approach to spiritual evolution or realisation. Through inquiry and analysis, the mind is used to examine its own nature. Jnana Yoga is said to be the most difficult path, not because it is superior to any other path, but because one must be firmly grounded in the other yogic disciplines before attempting Jnana Yoga. There must be a strong base of selfless service—serving humanity without thought of personal gain—and love of God, or deep yearning to merge with the Absolute. One must have a strong, healthy body, control of the vital energies and of the mind before it is possible to use the mind as a vehicle to transcend this world of ignorance. Without these preliminary disciplines, there will not be the strength or discernment to stay on this path. It is easy to be confused, tempted, and led astray by the illusion of the world and the workings of the mind: It is the synthesis of all Yogas that rounds out the imbalances of life. Without this integration, there is the risk of becoming a dry intellectual from too much book learning.

Jnana Yoga is a path of evolution toward spiritual realisation. It employs and incorporates different methods to achieve this end, but its main tool is Vedanta philosophy. Vedanta is a body of knowledge based on ancient Indian texts. The practice of Jnana Yoga involves inquiry into the nature of the world by putting to use the teachings of Vedanta.

Vedanta

Vedanta literally means 'end of the Vedas;' Vedanta is based on the teachings of the Upanishads, which form the concluding section of the Vedas. The Vedas are the most ancient scriptural texts of India. Their origin is unknown, but it is said that they were given through inspiration to the holy men who sat meditating upon God. There are four Vedas: Rig, Yajur, Sama, and Atharva.

The Rig Veda deals with questions and commentaries on the world and the nature of reality. The Yajur Veda lays down all the rituals and sacrifices and the rules for performing them. It is also a discourse on all the Mantras. The Sama Veda gives all knowledge on the theory and practice of music and singing. The Atharva Veda deals with magic and the black arts. Each of these Vedas is divided into four sections: the *Mantra Samhitas*, which are hymns in praise of God; the *Brahmanas*, or guides for performing sacrifices and pronouncing the Mantras; *Aranyakas*, which are the mystical books that give the philosophical interpretation to the rituals; and the Upanishads, which contain the essence or knowledge portion of each of the Vedas.

The philosophy of Vedanta is composed of the teachings of all the various Upanishads which are still known to man. It is also one of the six major systems of Indian philosophy. Indian philosophy can be divided into six categories, or schools, each of which was developed by a particular sage, or wise man. He promulgated it to his disciples who then passed it on. These six systems are:

1. *Purva Mimamsa*, founded by Jaimini, prescribes rituals to invoke and placate the gods, and to attain Heaven: *Dharma* and *adharma*, righteous and unrighteous actions, create the world which is based on reward and punishment.
2. *Uttara Mimamsa*, founded by Maharishi Vyasa, is pure, non-dualistic *Advaita Vedanta*. It states that all is Brahman, or unmanifested God, and everything else which appears to exist is only a projection of that Absolute Brahman. It is also the basis of Jnana Yoga.
3. *Sankhya*, by Kapila Rishi, differs from Vedanta in that it is dualistic. That is, it sees a separation between matter, called *Prakriti*, and spirit, called *Purusha*. The material world, *Prakriti*, is seen as the creation and interaction of the three gunas, or qualities: *sattwa*, *rajas* and *tamas* (purity, activity and inertia).
4. *Yoga*, of Pantanjali; is a practical system of concentration and control of the mind, for it is the mind which creates all illusions. It is similar to Vedanta, but suggests that *Purusha* (Brahman), which is untouched by Karma or time, is the cause of creation. Pantajali's *Yoga Sutras*, (see chapters on Raja Yoga)

are the essence of Raja Yoga, although *Yoga*, meaning union, actually applies to a broader range of disciplines.

5. *Vaisheshika*, of Kanada Rishi, presents a material or scientific view of the universe. That is, all things are made of basic units called atoms. This has proven to be unsatisfactory because scientists now know that the atom can be broken down indefinitely and the ultimate essence of matter cannot be determined.
6. *Nyaya*, founded by Gautama Rishi, argues that God, or *Ishwara*, is responsible for the creation of the world.

The Vedantic thought of *Uttara Mimamsa* challenges all other systems. It maintains that liberation cannot be attained by ritual, action, duty or charity. Change is the law of this manifest universe. Because of this impermanence, it cannot be real. Brahman alone is real; the world of illusion is unreal, and the individual soul is nothing but Brahman Itself. This Ultimate Reality is beyond the reach of the limited intellect and the knowable world. Renunciation alone, the abandonment of all worldly attachments, can lead to knowledge of the Absolute. This is achieved through a process of negation of all worldly desires, identifications, qualifications and extensions. That which is left after complete abandonment is God.

Vedanta philosophy has a triple basis—in scripture, reason and experience. Although the basic authority is scriptural, this does not mean that Vedanta is a matter of blind, unthinking acceptance. Reasoning is necessary for intellectual understanding of the scriptures. The Vedantin uses logic to distinguish between the real and the unreal and then discards that which is unreal. Intellect can explain only the finite. After exhausting itself through the process of discrimination and negation of all that is unreal, it too must be discarded when it reaches the point where all that is left is the real.

While the path of the Self lies through exhaustive intellectual inquiry and analogy, language is of service only in indicating the nature of the Real. The final Court of Appeal is intuitional experience. Western philosophy tends to ignore direct intuition. It brings the intellect to the brink and abandons it there. Vedanta approaches Self-Realisation with the intellect and then pushes on to the final leap, through intuition, to direct experience.

Some religions hold that the universe was created out of nothing, by a fiat of God, and will lapse again into nothingness. It is not possible for something to come out of nothing. A tree, for example, is preceded by invisible energy in the form of a seed. God did not create the universe from nothing. What would be the purpose? Nor did he do so out of love for humanity, for there were no human beings at the time of the Creation. The Law of the Conservation of Matter and the Law of the Conservation of Energy say that neither matter nor energy can be created or destroyed; only its form can be changed.

For all practical purposes, it does not matter whether the world as we know it is real or unreal. If a starving man sees a fruit tree, does he first analyze the tree and count its leaves before plucking the fruit? If a man catches his clothing on fire, will he ask himself, 'Hmm, I wonder where this fire came from?' or will he immediately try to extinguish the flames? Time and energy are wasted in useless intellectual speculation and discussion. Concepts lead to no final answer. One's notions of God do not arise from reason. They are preconceptions, mere projections of somebody else's ideas. One group's ideas differ from those of another group, just as individual ideas vary. Vedanta does not try to convert to 'isms.' It offers a technique for one to experience Ultimate Reality by approaching first through intellectual inquiry and then through direct realisation.

Although the questions one runs into during the quest for spiritual fulfillment cannot be appropriately answered through the intellect, nonetheless inquiry, as opposed to discussion or debate, is necessary to lead the true spiritual seeker along the path. If the mind is open and free from prejudice and preconceived ideas, inquiry will eventually lead to direct knowledge.

The Veils of Illusion

Brahman, Absolute Consciousness, has neither name nor form. It is infinite, unqualified and undifferentiated. In Raja Yoga, it is called *Purusha*. Just as moonlight is actually reflected sunlight, so also this manifest world, *Maya*, is a reflection of Brahman. Reflected through *Maya*, or *Prakriti* in Raja Yoga, Brahman takes on qualities and is called *Ishwara*, or God.

Maya is the veiling power of Brahman. It creates the idea of limitation, an illusion that the world is different from Brahman. An empty glass creates the idea of space within defined boundaries, but when it breaks, the illusion disappears. With Self-Realisation, the world-illusion disappears and all is experienced directly as the unchanging, unlimited Brahman.

The difference between the individual soul and Brahman is only apparent. The individual soul is Brahman veiled by the illusions of body and mind. As long as man accepts only the manifest world of *Maya*, he is caught in its meshes and bound in Karma. Yet, it is only an apparent binding, for the Self cannot be bound by anything. Like the sky, it is eternally free. It is, however, overlaid with various phenomena, just as the motion picture screen is overlaid with the lights and shadows that play over its surface. Floods, fires, murders, love and death all take place in the shadow play, but they in no way affect the underlying screen.

Like the screen, the 'I' is subject to manifold illusions—I am a painter, I am an actor, I am a Catholic, I am a Protestant, etc.

These names and forms are only illusions superimposed on the Self and change from lifetime to lifetime and sometimes within a lifetime. They disappear in the light of Self-Realisation, just as the shadows vanish from the screen the moment the light is switched on.

Until realisation takes place, man is wrapped in *avidya*, which is ignorance or nescience. *Avidya* is the multilayered veil that lies over knowledge of the Self, which is the only true knowledge. Ignorance is erroneous identification with limiting adjuncts. Unlike the concept of sin, ignorance does not imply guilt, but rather a condition in which knowledge is yet to be acquired. The *Panchadasi*, an ancient Indian text, asserts, 'Man's present miseries and sufferings, his pains and limited pleasures, births and deaths, are all due to his erroneous identification with the five sheaths and three bodies.' The three bodies are the physical body, the astral body and the causal body, while the five sheaths are the food sheath, the vital sheath, the mental sheath, the intellectual sheath and the bliss sheath. They are described in detail in *The Complete Illustrated Book of Yoga*.

When someone says, 'I am Mr. California Muscle Beach; look at my body,' he is identifying with the physical food sheath. Its qualities are existence, birth, growth, decay and death. He identifies with the vital sheath when he is concerned with hunger, thirst, heat, cold and other such sensations. The mental sheath deals with thinking, emotions, doubt, exhilaration, depression, etc. When one boasts of intellectual achievements, it is identification with the intellectual sheath. Such associations constitute true ignorance. When one identifies with the blissful sheath there is an attachment to striving for realisation of the Self. Even this must ultimately be transcended. Attachment to the food sheath will bring only pain; muscular accomplishments will wane. So it is with them all. Only by throwing off bondage to these shadows can one be free. Vedanta is an intellectual method of disassociating from all the sheaths.

A person may identify with one of these limiting sheaths more than another. For instance, if the intellectual sheath predominates, one might assume the role of philosopher. Identifying with that role, a momentum would be created that translates everything into intellectual terms of experience, thus setting up obstacles to balanced integration as a human being and to finding true identity with the Divine. Thus in addition to being misplaced attachment, *avidya* is also causal ignorance, that which creates binding karmic actions. It is the root of all actions and reactions.

Attachment to the various sheaths also affects relationships with others. Someone who dwells predominantly on the emotional plane may have difficulty communicating with another who associates with the intellectual sheath. Depending on which sheath prevails, people are attracted to various gurus. A true guru, however, is unattached to any body or sheath. His only identification is with I AM.

In essence all is Brahman. Nature, as the reflection of Brahman, manifests in the individual soul as *avidya* or a veil of ignorance. As it is only a reflection, the material world, emotions and intellect, are all illusion. This illusion is called *Maya*. To be more exact then, *avidya* is the state of being trapped in *Maya*. This ignorance is present until Unity is realised. As long as one experiences diversity, there will also be the experience of fear. In regarding others as different from himself and from Brahman, man becomes prey to various fears of what might happen to him in his separateness.

Avidya, manifesting through illusion or *Maya*, has neither beginning nor cause. As the projection of Branman, *Maya*, which is the manifest world, cannot exist independently. It is both real and unreal—real to mankind, unreal in the light of Brahman.

The magician who pulls a rabbit out of a hat or saws a woman in half creates an illusion. He does not really cause a rabbit to materialise inside an empty hat, nor does he bisect a woman and then put her together, yet the illusion exists while the audience sits and watches. Thus the trick is both real and unreal. This universe is real because man participates in the *illusion*, but when he reaches Self-Realisation, its reality dissolves. In the same way, a dream is real at the time that it occurs but is recognised as unreal upon awakening. Its unreality lies in its impermanence.

The beginning of a dream cannot be fathomed. Its subtle roots lie in the unknown reaches of the past. Even the beginning of the actual experience of dreaming is unknown to the dreamer. Suppose you go to sleep at 11:00, begin dreaming of a Hawaiian vacation at 11:30, and wake up at midnight, thus ending the dream. While asleep, can you know what time your dream begins? It has an infinite past, just as it has an infinite future while it is being dreamed. After awakening, however, you know that it must have taken place between 11:00 and 12:00. In the waking state, the dreamer knows that the dream had not an infinite past, infinite future, nor reality.

The dream of *Maya* does not begin with one's birth. It weaves through many lifetimes and has an infinite past. Although archaeologists and anthropologists keep pushing back their theories on the dates of man's origin, his past is infinite. In the highest state of consciousness on the path of man's spiritual evolution, there is neither past nor future; time and space are transcended. Such concepts are recognised to be illusory. There is only one eternal now.

There is no real difference between the dream of sleep and the dream of *Maya*. When we identify with the body and mind, they seem real enough; but on reaching the fourth, or highest state of evolution, *turiya*, we realise that they are not real. Just as darkness disappears in the light of the sun, the illusion of space and time vanish in the light of realisation. As long as *Maya* exists as the projection of Brahman, man will be subject to its illusion. While the dream action is taking place, it is impossible to remove the illusion by any action within the dream. One must step outside the dream to see clearly. Likewise, man must learn to step outside of *Maya*. All of man's sufferings stem from identification with the shadow of *Maya*.

It takes light only an instant to remove darkness. Darkness, however, can never remove light. Though ignorance enshrouds man, it can never bring darkness to the Self which remains untouched. Man is eternally the pure Self. Space is always space whether occupied by air, water, earth or any other form of dense matter. It can never be removed, negated or destroyed. So, too, the Self remains the same in all conditions.

True knowledge refers only to the Immortal Self, untouched by causal ignorance. Vedanta uses the analytical method to break the attachment to the five sheaths. By following this method, a highly advanced student will eventually experience the feeling of separation from the sheaths. When the veil of ignorance is thus lifted, he will realise his true identity.

Throughout life, one is conditioned to think of oneself in terms of qualifications. The question 'Who are you?' may elicit such response as, 'I am Fred,' 'I am the sales manager,' or 'I am a black man.' There is a lifelong process of brainwashing going on in which people think of themselves as rich or poor, tall or short, Prime Minister or bricklayer. They go on endlessly with this charade, becoming more and more limited in their ideas of themselves.

How does one realise identity with the Immortal Self which existed before one was born and will exist after the death of the body? The authority for such knowledge is the scriptures as revealed through the sages and passed on through the instrumentality of a teacher. The classic Vedantic analogy for enlightenment of the deluded human condition is that of 'The Snake and the Rope.'

A man is walking along a poorly lit path at dusk when he sees what appears to be a snake and he becomes frightened. When a light is produced, he sees with relief that it is only a rope. The illusion of a snake has disappeared and no further convincing is needed. The moment the Self is realised, ignorance, ego and limiting adjuncts disappear. You know who you are. Illusion disappears in the light of Reality. Nothing can stop anyone from eventually reaching this goal. It is your very birthright.

Who Is This 'I'?

In all of Vedanta nowhere is it stated that the Self is an object which is to be obtained. One can obtain an external object, but the Self is not an external object. More to the point, how can one obtain what he already has? One Vedantic path to Self-Realisation is that of negation, 'Neti, Neti,' meaning 'not this, not this.' Everything that can be known is experienced through the senses and the mind, and therefore cannot be the attributeless Brahman. After negation of the sheaths, what is left IS. Just as the idea of a snake is negated from the coiled rope when the light is brought, the non-Self also is negated from the Self which is eternally existing.

That which one must strive hardest to control is the *ahamkara*, or ego. The ego is that quality of the mind which considers itself to be separate from others. It is the ego that creates the illusion that people are entities separate from the rest of reality. The illusion separates one from the Self. Because of its proximity to the Self, the ego appears to be conscious. Hence, the two ideas 'I' and 'mine' are fabricated causing a false perception of the Self. Identification with the false self causes the ego to emerge. The world when seen as separate from the individual becomes an adversary and an object of exploitation, rather than a harmonious whole. Then various objects are needed to satisfy the ego's voracious appetite.

The Self is the Indweller; body and mind are its reflection, like the sun reflected in a mirror. A mirror has no inherent light. Reflected light, however, has certain qualities. It can illumine a dark object, blind the eyes and be mistaken for the real sun.

The ego experience is the reflected experience of the Self. If it reflects through the blissful sheath, one is a holy man. If it reflects through the intellectual sheath, one is an Einstein. Reflected in all five sheaths, the ego will manifest strongest in the higher ones. With meditation, these higher sheaths become more developed and tranquility and joy are experienced.

The reflection of a face in a mirror is different from the face itself. It imitates the real face and partakes of the mirror's qualities. It depends on the mirror for its very existence. The real face is not subject to this dependency and therefore differs from the reflection. Similarly, the reflection of the Self in the ego is different from the real Self. The individual ego depends on limiting qualities, *upadhis*, but the real Self depends on nothing.

In the case of the reflected face, it is not real, for it is not always there in the mirror. At the same time, it is not totally unreal, as it can sometimes be seen. It is also used at times, such as when combing the hair. By extension, the existence of the ego cannot be denied. Yet by analysis, we know that reflected things are only temporary.

The mirror has an existence independent of the face. The intellect, however, which is the reflecting medium of the pure Self, does not exist independently of and apart from the Self. Therefore, the distinction between pure Self and its reflection is only apparent.

The reflection of the Self in the ego is the individual soul experiencing and acting in this universe. It is sometimes said that the individual soul is a real entity with its own properties, like the shadow of a tree that refreshes those who come into it on a hot day. However, the shadow does not have an existence of its own, for it is merely the result of the leaves blocking the sun's light and heat. Therefore, it is said that the shadow is only the ever-changing result of the sun and the tree's leaves. Pure Self remains unacting, untouched and unchanging. It does not participate in the experiences of existence, birth, death and non-discrimination. A Self-Realised person knows that death and birth are false experiences.

Knowledge of the appearance and disappearance of the mental modifications or changes of the mind rests on the existence of the Self as witness, and that it alone exists after the negation of everything else. If one accepts the idea that the Self is reflected in the individual soul, then it is possible for the intellect to know itself to be Brahman. The intellect, like the body and senses, is not conscious. The knowledge I AM BRAHMAN can be possible only through the agency of reflection.

Ignorance leads us to regard ourselves as individuals suffering transmigratory existence; we are born again and again, and we will die again and again. This idea results from identification with the body, and is only a reflection. Transmigratory existence cannot be predicated of the Self, which is actionless, nor can it be predicated of the ego, which has no real existence. Those who maintain that the Self is the experiencer of transmigratory existence, and is therefore subject to change, mistake the ego to be the Self.

We have all looked into the distorting mirrors of a carnival. Each mirror reflects differently, although we ourselves remain the same. Wars occur because people look into the mirror and cannot agree upon the image. The Self is neither good nor bad, but the *upadhis*, or limiting adjuncts, create the problems of pain, suffering, birth and death. The wheel of birth and death reflects in different egos, and the continuously differing reflections create endless problems.

Adhyaropa

In reality, the world as we know it was never created. This world is superimposed on Brahman. Understanding of Vedanta is impossible without understanding the principle of superimposition, *adhyaropa*. *Adhyaropa* means superimposing the idea of the world with all its qualities and pairs of opposites upon the one attributeless Cosmic Existence.

The classic example of superimposition, 'The Snake and the Rope,' has already been cited. As another example, suppose someone were to visit a friend and discover that he is out but will be returning in half an hour. The person waits outside the house for about half an hour, when he sees someone approaching. Although it is actually a stranger whom he has never met, he mistakes him for his friend. This is called positive superimposition. On the other hand, assume that the person approaching really is the friend but he is thought to be somebody else. This is called negative superimposition. In both cases, a certain false attribute is superimposed upon the original friend.

Adhyaropa is illusion resulting from ignorance of the real object. It vanishes with the realisation that the apparent snake was, in fact, a rope. The snake was not there in the past, is not there in the present, and will not be there in the future. The snake exists only in the imagination. Once enlightenment takes place, the same mistake will not be made again. In the same way, all that one sees as diverse objects and conditions in this world is really Brahman. It was Brahman, alone, in the past, and will remain so in the future.

Dream is a vivid example of superimposition on reality. Mind and the manifest world have power, however, to create illusions far more pervasive and lasting than dreams that occur in sleep. Everyday life is full of illusory transactions. For instance, in getting a bank loan to pay off a mortgage, all sorts of papers are signed by various people. The bank manager lends money that does not exchange hands and is not even seen. It is only a record on a piece of paper somewhere in the bank. The entire transaction is pieces of paper: a paper dream. But at the same time, it seems very real.

One is continually getting into this type of situation. The ordinary man gets completely caught up in it. The Vedantin, or *jnani*, on the other hand, keeps his awareness of the world as illusion and remains unattached as he performs his duties. Jnana Yoga teaches that even though one is dreaming, one can intellectually dissociate from the 'world dream' and associate with the Self.

Vedanta leads to the detachment necessary for successful meditation. When there is no detachment, worldly objects and thoughts—the play of *Maya*—intrude in meditation and the aspirant identifies with them rather than with the Self or God. Accepting the world of appearance, he hungers for diverse objects, feels pleasure and pain, undergoes sufferings and tribulations, and is subject to likes and dislikes. But to a *jnani* there is no world at all; he resides in the Self.

Awareness of unity and identity with Brahman may seem hopelessly unattainable, for we are conditioned to think of ourselves as unique individuals. No man stands alone. We are all the body of Brahman. One part of the body is not regarded as different, or better, or more useful than another part. The brain cells are not treated better than the bladder cells. There are trillions of cells in the body, but they are not differentiated. Even though they are actually independent and can function independently in the laboratory test tube, we regard the body as one. In the light of the Supreme Brahman, the whole universe is one body. Individuals are like cells. We think that we are different from the body of Brahman, however, and we cling to the idea of our little independent identities.

The organs of knowledge and action enable man to discern the diverse objects of the world. But when reality is cognized, the world no longer appears real. Brahman, the Self, alone is everywhere. You may dislike your body or anything outside of yourself, but it is impossible to dislike the Self. When everything is seen as the Self, who can be hated? One becomes the embodiment of pure cosmic Love.

Man has been made in the image of God. This does not mean that God has eyes, nose, liver, freckles, pain, death and ignorance. This is man's image, not God's. God is what remains after all such qualifications have been negated. There is a natural limit to the play of loving the body and enjoying the physical world. Real love begins when people are seen, not as individuals, but as the beholder's own Self.

Nyayas

Because its abstract truths cannot be easily understood by the finite intellect, the philosophy of Vedanta is best taught through practical illustrations. Its main purport is that Brahman alone is real, the whole world of appearance is unreal, and the individual soul is nothing but Brahman Itself. This truth is taught by the following classical analogies, or *nyayas*.

Rajjusarpa Nyaya (Snake and Rope): At night, a man treads upon a rope and mistakes it for a snake. When a light is brought, he sees his error and his fears vanish. This illustrates how qualities of the world are superimposed on Brahman until Realisation is reached.

Mrigatrishna Nyaya (Mirage in the Desert): A mirage gives the appearance of water and lures the wanderer to his destruction.

Just so, the pleasures of this world appear to be real and lure the *jiva*, the individual soul, away from the spiritual path. Ultimately, however, the attachment to pleasure brings pain.

Shuktirajata Nyaya (Man and the Post): At dusk, a post is seen in the distance and it is imagined to be a man. Like the 'Snake' illustration, this is another example of superimposition. The unreal is superimposed upon the real.

Kanakakundala Nyaya (Gold and Ornament): Although ornaments are of diverse forms, they are gold in essence. Likewise, there are various kinds of pots—big, small, round, narrow—but basically, all of them are only clay. This *nyaya* illustrates that the names and forms of the world are in essence Brahman alone; Brahman appears in all shapes and forms.

Samudrataranga Nyaya (Ocean and Waves): There are countless waves in the ocean, and each can be perceived separately. But all are water, inseparable from the ocean. In reality, they are identical with it. Brahman and the individual souls are the same body.

Sphatikavarna Nyaya (Crystal and Color): Crystal is pure and colorless. Yet, when it is placed near a colored object, it will reflect that color. Brahman is attributeless, but the limiting adjuncts and the reflection of the three qualities of nature, or *gunas*, make it appear to have qualities.

Padmapatra Nyaya (Lotus Leaf): When it rains on the lotus, the drops will gently roll off the leaves and fall from them without wetting the leaf. So also, Brahman is the untainted substratum of the world. It is like the movie screen—unaffected by the play of light and shadow upon it.

Vatagandha Nyaya (Wind and Odor): Wind carries whatever scent is exposed to it, whether good or bad, but itself is unaffected by it. Although Brahman puts on various names and forms, it is unattached.

Oornanabhi Nyaya (Spider and Thread): The spider brings forth its web from its own body, and later reabsorbs it (it is said). The thread is nothing but the body of the spider and is one with it. Even so, this world is projected from Brahman, withdrawn into Brahman, and is always one with Brahman.

Surya Bimba Nyaya (Reflection of the Sun): The sun may be reflected in ponds, rivers and puddles, yet there is only one sun. Despite the many reflections of Brahman, there is but one Reality. It appears as many in the form of *Maya*.

Ghatasasha Nyaya (Pot and Space): Space, ether, is unaffected by the walls of a pot which appear to separate the space into 'inside' and 'outside.' But when the pot is broken, what was 'inside' and what was 'outside' are seen to be the same and have undergone no change at all. The *Atman* may seem limited by the mind and body, but it is one with the Supreme.

Dagdhapata Nyaya (Burned Cloth): If a cloth is burned, its form will remain intact until touched, when it will crumble to ashes. In the same way, the *jnani's* ego is burned in the fire of wisdom; only his body remains.

Arundhati Nyaya (Star): If it is difficult to find a certain star in the heavens, the teacher may point to stars which are brighter and easier to locate. From these, one is guided to look at the star he seeks. Thus the aspirant is first shown Karma Yoga, Bhakti Yoga, Hatha Yoga, etc. These lead him to Self-Realisation.

Bija Vriksa Nyaya (Seed and Tree): The seed is the cause of the tree, yet the tree is the cause of the seed. It cannot be said which came first. This illustrates that each statement has a counter-statement, and the world is bound up in relativity.

Markata Kishora Nyaya (Monkey and Baby): A baby monkey will cling to its mother, by its own strength, while she travels about the trees. Even so, an aspirant of Jnana Yoga struggles for himself to attain wisdom. In contrast, the Bhakti Yogi is helpless in his surrender to the Lord, like a kitten dependent upon its mother to pick it up.

Ashma Loshtra Nyaya (Stone and Mud): Mud is hard compared to cotton, but soft compared to stone. There is no quality in things by themselves. Qualities exist by virtue of their relativity.

Kakadanta Nyaya (Crow and Teeth): Looking for happiness in this world is like looking for the teeth of a crow, or the son of a barren woman. It is meaningless to question the contradictions and mysteries of existence, for in reality, there is no creation at all.

Dandapoopa Nyaya (Stick and Cakes): In India, cakes, that is, pastry-like breads, are often tied to a stick and carried to the marketplace. It is said that when many cakes are tied to a stick and the stick disappears, the cakes are missing also. That is to say, that all the doubts and delusions of this world disappear when the world disappears and Self-Realisation occurs.

Kshaurikaputra Nyaya (Barber and Son): When asked by the king to find the most beautiful boy in the kingdom, the barber searched in vain until he thought of his own son, who, in reality, was the embodiment of ugliness. This illustrates the blinding quality of attachment. Everyone is shut up within his own limited experience.

Visha Krimi Nyaya (Poison and Worms): Worms thrive in poison that would kill a man. One man's cake is another man's poison. This illustrates that good and bad are relative. Sensual pleasures are poison for evolved beings.

Kakataliya Nyaya (Crow and Palm Tree): A crow sat on a palm tree and was killed by a falling coconut. Is the death of the crow attributed to the coconut, or to his being in that place at that time? We each experience the world independently. Experience of this world that is common to all is accidental and has no meaning. Reality is the experience of the undifferentiated Self.

A child might see the sun reflected in a dozen pots of water, and think that he sees a dozen different suns. The reflected suns will have certain qualities, but they are not comparable to the real sun which is many times brighter and more powerful. When the water in the pots dries up, the illusions are gone but the sun still remains.

The Self, like the sun, is reflected in all. The quality of the reflection depends on the purity of the reflecting surface. It is only limited by ignorance, *avidya* of the mind. A person whose reflection is obscured by ignorance might be called a sinner, and one whose reflection is bright could be called a saint. But a Jnana Yogi never forgets that there is no difference between a saint and a sinner, for both are the same unlimited Self.

10

Jnana Yoga Meditation: Vedantic Practice

Vedanta must enter your bones, nerves, cells and interior chambers of your heart. I do not believe in lip Vedanta. This is pure hypocrisy. Even a little of real practical Vedanta will elevate a man quickly and make him immortal and fearless. I believe in practical Vedanta. I believe in solid spiritual practice. I believe in thorough overhauling of worldly nature and worldliness of all sorts. We should become absolutely fearless. That is the sign of life in Atma. No more words. No more talk. No more arguments, heated debates or discussions. No more study. No more wandering. Live in OM. Live in truth. Enter the silence. There is peace. Peace is silence.

—Swami Sivananda
Sadhana

There are various Vedantic methods for realising the Self. All are based on the removal of limiting ideas, or *upadhis*, in regard to oneself and the universe. Just as a container creates the illusion that the space inside it is separate and smaller, so the mind creates its own walls, and hence, the illusion of separation from the Self. Removal of the limiting adjuncts is the very core of

Vedantic meditation regardless of the mode used. In the practice of Jnana Yoga, one does not merely sit for meditation at a specific time, but one also applies the meditative process throughout the day. In this way, even though participating in the world, the Jnana Yogi is untouched by it.

Neti Neti: Not This, Not This

Neti Neti, meaning 'Not this, not this,' is the method of Vedantic analysis by negation. It is the keynote of Vedantic inquiry. It is a means of approach. By finding out what a particular subject is not like, one can move toward an understanding of what it is like. Through this process of negation, one can approach an understanding of real happiness by realising that it does not lie in wealth, power, fame or any other object of worldly pursuit. Through negation of everything that can be known via the senses, one exhausts the mental modifications and finds the answer within. Ultimately, direct experience is necessary, for it is not a matter of intellectual understanding. When the intellectual resources have been completely drained, the goal is 99.99% reached. The 100% mark is direct intuitive realisation.

A man is not his house nor is he his job, for these are subject to change but the man remains the same. It is useless to identify with clothing or hairstyle, yet all are subject to this form of illusion from time to time. The Self, which is one's essential nature, is neither body nor senses; the body and senses are mere external qualities of the Self. The *jnani* negates identification with all things of this world which are not *Atman*. He negates the mind by saying, 'I am not these desires,' 'I am not these fears,' 'I am not this personality,' until eventually, all things within worldly experience are negated. Finally, worldly experiences are transcended for all has been negated and nothing remains but the Self.

In this kind of meditation, union with the Absolute is achieved by denial of body, mind, name, form, intellect, senses and all limiting adjuncts. The true 'I' remains, which is *Sat-Chit-Ananda*, or Absolute Existence-Knowledge-Bliss. Meditate with full concentration, bringing the mind back when it wanders to externals. They are not the *Atman* or Self. Eventually the mind will become steady and will rest in thoughtless, motionless state of pure Bliss.

Sakshi Bhav: Witness State

The *Sakshi Bhav* method is the witnessing approach. One observes the play of life as though one were watching a movie but, again, does not identify with it. Whatever situations the aspirant experiences, his reaction is, 'I am not involved in this; I am only watching it happen.' It entails introspection and close awareness of the mental waves. The mind does not want to be watched and will soon slow down its activities, but it does not give up without struggle. In many ways it will deceive and persuade one to stop watching it. It is such a powerful force that it is capable of dragging the attention wherever it goes, unless extreme vigilance is practiced. Many, many times it will divert the attention from its focus. One must observe this with patience, then firmly return to the witness state, taking care not to fight the mind but only to gently guide it. With the repetition of OM *sakshi aham* (I am witness of all my actions), and continual disassociation from those actions, the individual ego eventually vanishes.

Abheda Bodha Vakya: Eliminating Name and Form

This method recognises that every sentient being and insentient object in the universe has five components—name, form, existence, knowledge and bliss. All things, whether animal, vegetable, or mineral, have these attributes, but it is the names and forms that seem to differentiate them and set one thing apart from another. Name and form are impermanent and illusory, while existence, knowledge and bliss are permanent. Matter is the visible manifestation of spirit, and inseparable from it, but through the meditative technique of *Abheda Bodha Vakya*, name and form are discarded. Only man has the vehicle to realise that what remains is Existence-Knowledge-Bliss, or *Sat-Chit-Ananda*, the eternal 'I' which continues through many changes of name and form.

When parts of the body are damaged, such as eyes, heart, kidneys, liver and blood, they may be replaced with spare parts from other beings. What then becomes of the body's identity? What becomes of the individual's identity? The consciousness of 'I' remains constant and cannot be taken from anything animate or inanimate. A tree may be destroyed to become a plank, or gold may become a ring, but only the name and form have changed. By identifying with the underlying, attributeless essence of all objects of the universe, the final stage of meditation is reached.

Laya Chintana: Absorption

The *Laya Chintana* method is one of involution or absorption. In this system, effect is absorbed into cause. Each cause is the effect of its preceding cause, so this process continues progressively. There are three avenues of this approach. First, one concentrates on merging into the understanding, *buddhi*, which is then merged into the unmanifest universe, *avyaktam*, that state where the three qualities of nature (*sattwa, rajas, tamas*) are in equilibrium. Finally *avyaktam* is merged into the Supreme Imperishable Brahman. In the second approach, the elements of the world merge with each other, starting with the grossest and proceeding to the subtlest.

This is the reverse of the process by which the earth was formed, where a mass of swirling gasses gradually cooled and condensed to a solid planet. The focus is on manifestation of the five traditional elements: earth, water, fire, air and ether. Earth is merged into its cause, water; water is merged into its cause, fire; air, which is the cause of fire, absorbs the fire and, in turn, is absorbed into ether. The ether is absorbed into the unmanifest, *avyaktam*, and that finally merges with Brahman. In the third path, the microcosm merges with the macrocosm. The individual merges with the universe; in other words, the *jiva*, soul, merges with Brahman. Thus all external attributes are gradually merged into their Source.

There are no qualities in the universe that are not in the human body. An atom is a complete replica of the solar system, with electrons encircling a nucleus just as planets revolve around the sun. The atom is a microcosm and everything that is happening in the microcosm of the human body is also occurring in the earth and in the universe. Individual cosmic creation and destruction are taking place all the time. Instead of identifying with the individual self, which is only a tiny fraction of the universal scheme, one can find his larger identity by merging with the Cosmos itself. It is matter in its most subtle state. Before the sun and earth came into existence, they were gas molecules, and before evolving into the molecular state, they existed in the etheric or energy state.

The water molecule is composed of the atoms of hydrogen and oxygen. When atoms were smashed in the cyclotron, it was discovered that this was not the end of matter. No matter how much scientists subdivide atoms, they continue to find smaller and smaller particles. If the earth and sun were suddenly blown to pieces, the matter would revert to ether. Ultimately it would return to the Supreme Mind, compared to which ether itself is gross. Mind is the last reduction of matter to its original source, Brahman. As such, it is the source of ether, which evolves into air or gas, and then condenses into fire, water and earth. It can evolve no further than that. Gross matter is thus the last stage of Cosmic Mind's evolution. On this gross level, mind becomes physical nature.

In its most dense manifestation as gross matter, mind exhibits the least amount of consciousness. It is too far away from its Source to express itself. Take for instance a rock. It contains the potential for infinite energy and power, but unless put to intelligent use, it remains inanimate. The further matter moves from its Source toward gross evolution, the more limited is its effect.

A close look at these elements which we take for granted leaves one in awe of the guiding Cosmic Intelligence. Water, for instance, is made up of two hydrogen atoms and one oxygen atom. When hydrogen by itself comes into contact with fire, it reacts with an explosion. Oxygen reacts with fire to make it burn more fiercely. Yet in combination, as water, they will quench fire and cool the body. What is the source of this intricate engineering? Only an intelligent power is capable of such creation.

All life is interconnected. Animals inhale oxygen, the by-product of plants, and exhale carbon dioxide. In their bodies the oxygen combines with glucose to produce energy for the various bodily functions. Plants take in carbon dioxide and release oxygen into the air which is then used by animals. They take nutrients from the soil and use the sunlight for photosynthesis. Man eats the plants for nourishment and when he dies, his body is returned to earth where it becomes food for the plants. This is but one small example of the complicated and interdependent relationships that exist among all things. It hardly seems possible that such a world could have been created by an accident of nature.

Relationships like this exist throughout the cosmos. Consider the size of the universe. It is impossible that these miracles occur only on earth. How many suns with planets can there be in our galaxy, and how many galaxies can there be? How large is this universe? Its size cannot be imagined, nor can the number of planets capable of supporting life be counted.

There are physical laws which cause the planets to rotate and to revolve around the sun in certain, precise ways. These same laws cause whole solar systems, indeed even galaxies, to hurtle through space at tremendous speeds—all in perfect coordination. These laws could not have come about accidentally without an originating cause. Only a guiding intelligence could be responsible.

Panchikarana: Doctrine of Quintuplication

Allied to *Laya Chintana*, which is meditation by thinking rather than stilling the thought waves, is the Doctrine of Quintuplication. It further develops the concept of absorption of the gross into the more etheric by breaking down the components of the body and its functions into the five basic elements called *tanmatras*. When it is seen that these are not Brahman, they may be either absorbed into each other as in *Laya Chintana* or discarded by negation as in *Neti Neti*. In either case, one arrives at the Self, which is beyond them all. To this end, the Doctrine of Quintuplication is applied.

According to this ancient theory, owing to ignorance one identifies with the physical body which is made up of five basic, pure elements: *akasha*, ether; *vayu*, air; *agni*, fire; *apas*, water; and *prithivi*, earth. These undergo permutation, and combine with each other in definite proportions. This is called quintuplication. Thus it is said that wherever there is hardness in the body, it is due to the portion of earth; wherever there is fluidity, it is due to the portion of water. Body warmth is due to the portion of fire, and movement, to air. The quality of space found in the body is attributed to the ether. These differentiations are also the basis of *ayurvedic* medicine.

The three most gross elements, earth, water and fire, can be easily experienced by the five senses. Although air cannot be seen, it can be sensed indirectly through smell and hearing, and directly through touch. Ether has two meanings, one of which denotes the sky. When used as an element, however, it signifies primordial energy, or the primordial cloud.

In the process of Creation, primordial energy came first, then matter on a subtle level, and then the world as we know it now. Behind it all is *Shakti*, the cosmic energy. It is also known as *Maya*, that power which is both veiling and projecting, for it veils the knowledge of Brahman and projects the illusion of this universe. Drawing energy from the Source, *Shakti* forms the various elements, resting only after reaching the grossest form.

In their subtle or pure form, the five basic elements combine in definite proportions to form gross elements. It is these gross elements upon which the existence of the earth depends. While this traditional Vedantic view may not seem to correspond exactly with modern science, by following the essence of the thought behind it, one gains insight into the intricate relationship between matter and spirit. According to the Doctrine of Quintuplication, each gross element is made up of one half of its corresponding pure element and one-eighth of each of the four other subtle elements. An example of this can be seen clearly in the chart for gross earth

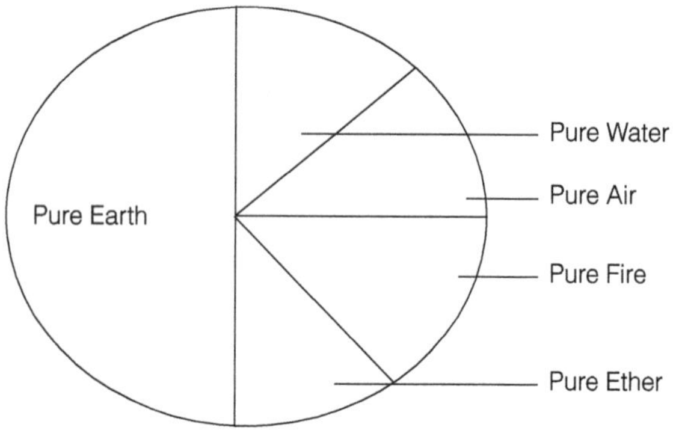

Gross Earth

in which the earth is composed of one half subtle earth and one-eighth each of subtle ether, subtle air, subtle water and subtle fire.

It can be seen that each element, when quintuplicated, is not pure, but contains a portion of each of the other elements. Each quintuplicated element produces a special effect according to its predominance. Each contains qualities of the others, and has a particular function in nature and in man.

Further, each of these elements has five properties. These properties are based upon the interaction of the subtle elements within the gross elements, and total twenty-five in number.

Quintuplicated Elements

Gross Elements	Subtle Elements				
	1/8 Ether	1/8 Air	1/8 Fire	1/8 Water	1/8 Earth
Ether	Grief	Desire	Anger	Delusion	Fear
Air	Running	Bending	Walking	Expansion	Contraction
Fire	Hunger	Thirst	Laziness	Sleep	Luster
Water	Semen	Blood	Saliva	Urine	Sweat
Earth	Bone	Flesh	Skin	Arteries	Hair

In order to better understand this portion of the theory, let us examine the properties associated with quintuplicated ether. The five properties of ether are grief, desire, anger, delusion and fear, which are all generated in the ether which belongs to the space of the heart. Grief is the chief part of ether for with grieving the body feels empty like space. Desire is fleeting like the wind, therefore it belongs to that part of air found in ether. When anger arises, the body becomes hot. Anger belongs to that part of fire found in quintuplicated ether. Delusion is as pervasive as water and belongs to that portion of water found in ether. Finally, when we are frozen with fear, the body becomes inanimate and statue-like; thus, fear belongs to the earth principle. The remaining twenty properties can be understood in a similar manner.

Although the emotions are actually attributes of the astral body, they are treated as if they belonged to the physical body for this is where their influences are directly perceptible. Because the emotions belong to the ether portion of the quintuplicated elements, they cannot be the Self. They are negated and identification with them is not possible. 'I am not these emotions. I am not this body. I am not these actions. I am the Self.' The Jnana Yogi abandons the idea of I-ness and my-ness and identifies with the imperishable *Atman*, which is entirely different from the five elements. He is the knower, seer and witness of all these products.

The physical body is reduced to nothing as it is analyzed and all temporary qualities are removed. It is merely a product of the five elements and their twenty-five combinations. Modern scientists and doctors understand only the gross attributes of the body. The five elements and twenty-five properties are mere limiting adjuncts. When the body is stripped of them, that which remains is the Self.

Jnana Yoga teaches the aspirant not to identify with these quintuplicated elements that make up the five sheaths. The body is a fictitious play of illusion and ignorance (*Maya* and *avidya*). Attachment to it is bondage. By negating the ideas of possessiveness and attachments to its illusory qualities, one can achieve emancipation.

Mahavakyas or the Great Proclamations

Where there is true knowledge, knowledge of the immortal Self, there is no trace of causal ignorance. The scriptures, the Vedas and the Upanishads exist to impart knowledge to humanity. Scriptural declarations can be grouped under three heads: injunctions, prohibitions, and proclamations of the highest truth.

The first two, injunctions and prohibitions, give the aspirant a glimpse of the Truth and raise him to the proper level of understanding and receptivity. They are similar to the *yamas* and *niyamas* of Raja Yoga or the Ten Commandments in that they give basic spiritual instruction. The third, the proclamations, is a set of four Upanishadic statements which express the highest truth of the identity between the individual soul and the supreme Soul. They are only for those who have purified their minds and are capable of sublime understanding. They are known as the *Mahavakyas*. Understanding them enables the individual soul to identify with the Supreme Soul. There are four *Mahavakyas*, one contained in each of the four Vedas. They are:

1. *PRAJNANAM BRAHMA* (Consciousness in Brahman)—The nature of Brahman is existence, or absolute knowledge, or cosmic consciousness.
2. *AHAM BRAHMA ASMI* (I am Brahman)—This is the idea on which the aspirant fixes his mind during meditation, Identification is with the Supreme, not with limiting adjuncts.
3. *TAT TWAM ASI* (That Thou Art)—*Tat* represents Brahman, *Twam* is the individual, and *Asi* is union. This is the *Mahavakya* through which the teacher instructs the spiritual aspirant.
4. *AYAM ATMA BRAHMAN* (This Self is Brahman)—This expresses the inner intuitive experience of the meditator.

Of these four declarations, *TAT TWAM ASI* is the most important. The guru initiates the disciple into the knowledge of Brahman through this declaration, for it is the one that gives rise to the other three. The disciple reflects and meditates on it, and eventually experiences *samadhi*, or superconscious state. He is then able to give expression to the other three statements.

The words *Tat Twam Asi* must be dissected carefully, for they are pregnant with meaning. They can be repeated to different people and interpreted in different ways depending on the person's evolution. When right understanding is reached, the aspirant is better able to disown all actions, reactions and attributes. He can lead a worry-free life.

To begin with, one must have a basic understanding of the relationships of the Absolute, the world and the individual. Brahman, the unmanifest Absolute, projects itself as *Prakriti*, the world as we know it. *Prakriti* is made up of the three qualities of nature: purity, activity, and inertia (*sattwa*, *rajas* and *tamas*). In turn, it manifests into two aspects as *Maya*, the phenomenal world, and *avidya*, identification with the individual self.

In the phenomenal world, Brahman reflects through *sattwa*, purity, as *Maya*, and it is called *Ishwara*. *Ishwara* is a name meaning God with qualities, God with attributes. *Ishwara* has full control over the world, and can appear as Jesus, Rama, Siva, and the Holy Mother. *Ishwara* appears as any aspect of divinity to which one relates in a personal sense. In its other projection, *Prakriti's* natural purity is adulterated and overbalanced by the qualities of action and inertia (*rajas* and *tamas*). These produce the impure state of ignorance, *avidya*. Brahman reflecting through it results in individual souls who are colored by the same ignorance.

As both are reflections of the same unqualified Brahman, there is no basic difference between *Ishwara* and the individual soul, or *jiva*. However, the clarity of the reflection differs. When a clean mirror and a dirty mirror are placed in the sun, more light reflects from the clean mirror. The amount of Divine Reflection that a being projects depends upon his degree of purity.

The only real distinction is that *Ishwara* has full control over *Maya*, while the individual is caught in the web of *Maya*. Just as a spider weaves a web for itself, Brahman has projected the world. The spider can move anywhere within the web and is not affected by the threads of its own creation. When a fly gets caught in it however, it becomes entangled. We are like flies caught in the web of *Maya*.

Like the spider, *Ishwara* can move in his own creation on any level and in any manifestation. He can be incarnated on any plane and can withdraw the incarnation. As Vishnu, Rama and other avatars, *Ishwara's* manifestations remain unaffected by *Maya*. In such stories as the *Ramayana* in which Rama is shown as experiencing emotions, God has had human traits and responses superimposed upon Him. He is not really subject to human emotions, however. Just as the spider must follow its own threads, Rama cannot interfere with the karmic laws of his own creation. The game must be played out. To sum up, when Brahman reflects through *Maya* the reflected consciousness is called *Ishwara* and it controls the universe. Reflected through *avidya* the consciousness is the individual soul. No matter what the name, Brahman is One, just as milk is milk whether produced by a French, German or Indian cow. The brand name and the container are irrelevant. *Maya* is the container inside of which is only one *Ishwara*. The reason one is unable to feel THOU ART THAT is because his reflection is tarnished by the veil of ignorance.

When Christ said, 'I and my father are One,' He was in effect saying, 'Aham Brahma Asmi,' 'I am Brahman.' Moses had the same revelation with the burning bush: '*Jahweh*—I am that I am.' 'I and my Father are One' could be added to the *Mahavakyas*. Jesus was a highly developed Jnana Yogi, but he was crucified because his contemporaries could not understand his statements. If He were to appear today, He would still be crucified. People look for a Messiah who fits their own preconceptions. They are not interested in proclamations of truth.

Avidya, ignorance, is the cause of conflict. Why do Protestants and Catholics fight in Ireland? They are not fighting for God, because God already exists. Why do Hindus and Muslims fight? Ignorance is responsible for all misunderstanding and dissention. Only true spiritual aspirants can transcend it by long, hard discipline and practice.

Because of ignorance, the common man could not understand when Christ said, 'The Truth shall make you free.' Although Jesus was a highly advanced *Advaita Vedantin*, He used Bhakti Yoga (i.e. the Path of Devotion) to encourage worship of the Father, and a little Raja Yoga in the form of *yamas* and *niyamas*. He could not take them beyond that even though He had the highest knowledge. Vedanta was never meant for the masses. When Jesus said, 'I and my Father are One,' He meant *Aham Brahma Asmi*—I am Brahman—eliminating body, name and external qualifications. The disciples assumed that these words applied only to Christ and not to themselves. Jesus did not find a single person who actually understood his meaning.

Bhagatyaga Lakshana

The *Bhagatyaga Lakshana* method of Jnana Yoga explains the proclamation *TAT TWAM ASI*, That Thou Art. In Vedanta, the word *Tat* represents unqualified Brahman and *Twam*, the individual soul; *Asi* represents union. Meditation on these words is a process of de-hypnotisation. One negates all the qualifications and attributes that limit the individual soul which is then realised as Brahman.

To explain in more detail, the meaning of a word or phrase can be approached in three ways:

1. *Vachyartha*—Primary meaning, conveyed directly by the word
2. *Lakshyartha*—Implied meaning
3. *Vyangartha*—suggested meaning, hinted at by the words associations.

A word and its meaning are linked by a *vritti*, mind wave. When the word 'fire' is pronounced the corresponding mind wave is energised and there is visualisation of the concept. The reverse also takes place. When one sees a fire, the mental image gives rise to the corresponding verbal utterance, 'Fire.' This relationship between word and meaning can be simple or complex. It is simple when it generates the word's primary meaning. 'The sun is hot,' is an example of *Vachyartha*, for 'hot' is directly related to 'sun.' If a child is asked to draw a leaf, he copies it from nature, but an artist will draw it indirectly. Similarly, *Lakshyartha* is based on an indirect relationship between word and meaning. In the statement, 'It is hot today,' the implied meaning is that the sun is hot. Indirect relationships between word and meaning fall into three categories: *Jahallakshana*, *Ajahallakshana* and *Jahadajahallakshana*.

When the direct meaning of a word is dispensed with and only the implied meaning is taken into account, it is called *Jahallakshana*. The statement, 'The house is on the river' does not mean that there is a house on the surface of the river, but on the bank of the river. The direct meaning of a flowing river is discarded and the implied meaning 'on the bank' is substituted. Although the river and its bank are quite different things, one being water and the other earth, there is a spatial proximity which creates a relationship. The implied meaning is based on the direct meaning, which is then discarded.

In the *Ajahallakshana* category, both the direct and implied meanings are operative. Imagine a man is at a horse show and asks, 'Which horse is jumping?' He might receive the reply, 'The white is jumping.' A color cannot jump, but in this case, the direct meaning 'white' refers to the implied meaning 'horse,' both of which are relevant to the sentence. The whole is understood to mean, 'The white horse is jumping.'

Jahadajahallakshana, the third category, is also known as *Bhagatyaga Lakshana*. Here a portion of the direct meaning is retained and a portion is discarded. Assume that ten years ago a certain Dr. Smith lived in New York City and was last seen by a friend at the opera. Now imagine that this same friend sees him, ten years later, as a derelict on Skid Row in San Francisco. He exclaims, 'This is that same Dr. Smith.' There is a certain discrepancy in this statement because the word 'this' refers to the Dr. Smith that is seen here and now, associated with the idea of a derelict in rags is San Francisco. But the word 'that' refers to the Dr. Smith known before. It is associated with the idea of a successful professional man, dressed in a tuxedo and separated in time and space by ten years and three thousand miles.

Certain elements are contradictory and must be eliminated. A successful doctor is not an unemployed derelict. San Francisco is not New York and Skid Row is not the Metropolitan Opera House. Also, the period of ten years cannot be equated with the time at which the statement was made.

In the statement, 'This is that same Dr. Smith,' only a portion of the direct meaning of 'this' and 'that' is retained. The contradictory factors of time, space and external appearances are eliminated while Dr. Smith himself, the person, remains. It is only the idea of a Dr. Smith free of impermanent qualities which is non-contradictory. Only after the mind has gone through this complicated process—which it does in a flash—can 'this Dr. Smith' be identIfied with 'that Dr. Smith.' After the opposing associations of name and form have been set aside THIS IS THAT remains. Dr. Smith, the person common to both, stands as the implied meaning.

Tat Twam Asi can be understood only in light of this kind of reasoning. 'That Thou Art' does not refer to the direct meaning of the body. It asserts that each individual soul is in reality the Supreme Absolute. Such impermanent qualities as body, color, sex and religion are eliminated. Although we may now be in the garb of human beings, before being incarnated here on earth, each existed in the Brahmic state. *Tat*, That, refers to pure consciousness or Brahman; *Twam*, Thou, refers to reflected consciousness in ignorance, or the individual soul; *Asi*, Art, proclaims their unity, which alone exists, for all are projections of Brahman.

Thus, *avidya* leads the individual soul, *jiva*, to identify with his intellect, emotions and physical body, creating activity, suffering and pain. The *upadhis* give the appearance of individualisation and separation, although there is only one Brahman. In identifying with the various sheaths of the individual being, we fail to realise our true nature. An Olympic champion identifies with the physical sheath; a politician with the vital sheath; someone in love, with the emotional sheath; a college professor, with the intellectual sheath. One who is happy and pure all the time identifies with the bliss sheath. Who is closest to Self-Realisation? None of them for they are all prisoners; they are all at a distance. Even goodness is binding, for the bliss sheath is an *upadhi* as are all the others. Chains may be made of gold or of iron, nonetheless they are chains.

Once Indra, king of the Gods, and Virochana, king of the demons, approached Prajapati, the Creator, to learn knowledge of the Self. After thirty-two years of rigorous discipleship, they were told to look at themselves in a looking glass and report what they saw. After doing so, they replied, 'We see ourselves as we are.' Prajapati then asked them to put on their best clothes and to look again. On hearing the same reply, he told them, 'That is the immortal Self.'

Virochana, satisfied, preached to his followers that the body alone is to be worshipped. Indra, however, was unconvinced that the body is the Self. After a second period of thirty-two years' discipleship he decided that the dreaming self is the true Self. Still dissatisfied however, he underwent an austerity program of one hundred and one years, and learned that the real Self is above all individualistic implications.

Like Virochana, most people misunderstand the body to be the Self. They cannot understand TAT TWAM ASI, because they lack the patience to consider deeply the significance of the words. Words are double-edged weapons. If misunderstood, they will be detrimental to one's progress; properly understood, they can carry one across the abyss of ignorance. The significance of TAT TWAM ASI can be grasped only after long, detailed and careful consideration. Then it will be apparent that if man was made in God's image, it does not mean that God resembles a human being. Rather, one must look into man and realise the God nature enshrined therein.

11

Bhakti Yoga Meditation

True religion does not consist in ritualistic observances, baths and pilgrimages, but in loving all. Cosmic love is all-embracing and all-inclusive. In the presence of pure love all distinctions and differences as well as all hatred, jealousy and egoism are dispelled just as darkness is dispelled by the penetrating rays of the morning sun. There is no religion higher than love. There is no knowledge higher than love. There is no treasure higher than love because love is truth, love is God.

—Swami Sivananda
Practical Lessons In Yoga

Bhakti Yoga is the path of devotion. While Jnana Yoga appeals to the intellectual, and Raja Yoga to the rational and scientific mind, Bhakti Yoga comes naturally to those who are predominantly emotional in temperament. Stemming from the innate and unselfish drive toward Unity, it is the most direct way to God-Realisation. It is the approach of pure love, which is poured upon the chosen deity, or aspect of God. The path of Bhakti Yoga is essentially the same as that of the Christian tradition. Through placing all his concentration on God, the devotee endeavors to increase his remembrance of and communion with the Lord. With faith, prayer and self-surrender he attains direct perception of his Ideal. When merging takes place and Oneness alone remains, the goal is reached.

Converting the Emotions

Emotions have no place in other paths of Yoga, and, because they are bound up with attachment, they are rigorously uprooted. However, the *bhakta* converts the emotions into unconditional love for God, which is neither binding nor selfish. The emotions, when channeled properly, can be used to attain liberation.

The practice of Bhakti Yoga transmutes the lower emotions into devotion. Emotion is weakness, and must not be equated with divine love, which manifests as peace and joy. The lower emotions are not suppressed, however, but are utilised and sublimated. Without emotion there is no love, and without love one cannot approach the infinite Love that is God. Through the higher emotions the devotee reaches out to the Divine. His practice is carried out by both formal worship and by seeing the Lord in all names and forms at all times. With purification the receptive heart receives the continual flow of divine love.

The barrier between the individual soul and the Supreme Soul is the ego, the ever-present enemy. It manifests as a feeling of separateness. Bhakti does away with this feeling of separation, for in the ecstasy of pure love and devotion, the consciousness of the individual self is lost. With the surrender of the ego, the individual becomes an instrument in the hands of God. This state is beautifully symbolised by the image of Krishna playing the flute. Just as the flute is a hollow instrument through which the breath of God moves, so the individual must empty himself of all egoism, to enable the Lord to act fully through him. He takes neither credit nor blame for his actions, for God does the action. The devotee thinks of nothing but God. The Lord is his constant thought wave, and fills every mental space. He is the consummation of everything; hence everything is to be worshipped.

God is experienced by each individual in his own way. This idea is strikingly illustrated in the *Srimad Bhagavatam*, in which Krishna assumes as many forms of himself as there are cowherd women, his disciples, and manifests to shower love on each individually. Their yearning for him lies in their knowledge that he is the Lord, and their fulfillment is the fulfillment of divine love. While immersed in the bliss of dancing with him, they experience *samprajnata samadhi*, in which there is still awareness of duality. This gives way to *asamprajnata samadhi*, the highest superconscious state, when they become one with him. However, Krishna separated himself from them when their egoism made them feel that they had ensnared and could control him. A true spiritual master treats his devotees in the same way, relating to each individually, but withdrawing temporarily when pride and egoism infect the disciple.

Control of the mind and annihilation of the ego are the essence of all yogic disciplines, including Bhakti Yoga. Even on this essentially emotional path, the intellect must not be neglected. If it is disregarded, Bhakti Yoga can degenerate into fanaticism. If, on the other hand, it is transcended, the devotees experiences *para-bhakti*, the highest state of supreme devotional ecstasy.

Ashrams and solitude are not necessary for the Bhakti Yogi. The mental attitude alone is important. This attitude of devotion is also necessary for progress on the paths of Yoga. Even the intellectual approach of Jnana Yoga needs the element of *bhakti* for success in attaining God's grace.

Those who turn to Bhakti Yoga are moved by one of four general motivations. Distress can be a powerful factor. When all else has failed, there is no recourse left but to turn to God. How many soldiers in battle and people burdened by extreme sorrow have found God as their final refuge! Curiosity is another impetus. Looking beyond the external trappings of worship, the mind seeks to understand what lies behind the symbolism, words and rituals, and pushes on to the other shore. A third motive is desire for gain, whether it be of love, knowledge or wealth, etc. God is petitioned as the benevolent father who will grant favors if approached with faith and devotion. The highest *bhakti* is selfless. The motivation is the simple desire to love and serve God. Only with this attitude will the ego disappear. One cannot attain liberation until all desires, including spiritual desire itself, have been burned.

The Bhakti Yogi makes use of gross forms and rituals as aids to self-surrender. Altars, statues, pictures, etc., are not in themselves objects of worship. Like the Christian Cross, which stands for Jesus, they are all symbols. The omnipresent Lord is as present in the image as anywhere else. The image is merely used as a focal point for worship of God.

Forms of Devotion

Indian tradition recognises nine forms of worship in the practice of Bhakti Yoga. From the simple to the more difficult, they are:

1. *Sravanam*—Listening to stories of the Lord's *lila*, or play. Book knowledge is not sufficient. The stories must be imparted by inspired teachers and wise men.
2. *Kirtanam*—Singing of God's glories. Christian hymns also fall into this category.
3. *Smaranam*—Remembrance of His name and presence, in mental attitude and unceasing prayer.
4. *Padasevanam*—Service at the Lord's feet. The world is seen as God's feet, and in serving humanity one mentally is offering worship to His feet.

5. *Archanam*—Worship of God through such rituals as puja. One offers himself to the Lord, thus breaking the ego.
6. *Vandanam*—Prostration to the Lord with full awareness of His presence in all names and forms. This develops humility.
7. *Dasyam*—Cultivation of the feeling of being a servant of God.
8. *Sakhyam*—Cultivation of feeling friendship toward the Lord, thus establishing a personal relationship.
9. *Atmanivedanam*—Complete surrender of self. This is the equivalent of *asamprajnata samadhi*, the seedless state in which there is complete acceptance and surrender, and no duality.

Practice of the lower stages, such as listening to stories, is relatively easy. It keeps the mind centered on the Almighty, creating positive thought waves and a receptive mind. Even those who are intellectually oriented derive benefit from the stories and chanting if they will open their hearts as well as their minds. When the devotee has been prepared by the earlier stages of worship, he can attempt the more difficult higher stages.

In any case, the *bhava*, or devotional feeling, of the devotee is of extreme importance. Accommodating the various temperaments of people, there are five different ways of relating to God:

1. *Shanta*—This pure feeling of peace is devoid of desire, ignorance and emotion. Its presence is not externally apparent. This is the devotional attitude of the Jnana Yogi.
2. *Dasya*—The devotee regards himself as the servant of God, whom he sees in everything but himself. He sees himself as inferior to the rest of humanity. Humbly placing himself in God's hands, he takes delight in service to all. Hanuman, the monkey chieftain of the *Ramayana*, who dedicated his life to the service of Rama, exemplifies this relationship.
3. *Sakhya*—God is regarded as a spiritual friend, to whom one can turn for advice, comfort and companionship. One becomes

unable to live without His company. Arjuna's relationship with Krishna, as set forth in the *Bhagavad Gita*, is of this nature.

4. *Vatsalya*—The relationship is that of parent and child, with God being viewed as a Divine Child. It is exemplified by Yashoda's relationship with the baby Krishna.
5. *Madhurya*—This is the feeling of the lover toward the beloved. It is pure love, untinged by lust, and is difficult to develop. Encompassing a pure desire to touch and embrace His physical and astral form, this method is encountered frequently in the poetry and writings of the Sufi and Christian mystics. In Yoga it is symbolised by the union of Siva and Shakti in the *sahasrara chakra* at the crown of the head. This is the highest type of devotional feeling.

There is one more *bhava*, which remains outside the pale of normal relationships. It is not deliberately cultivated as a path to God, nor is it easy to maintain. This is the feeling of extreme hatred toward God. When one is in constant remembrance of Him, even with hatred, the mind becomes one-pointed and fixed. Through this concentration one is redeemed, for evil always falls before goodness. Various demons of Hindu mythology such as Kamsa and Ravana, achieved salvation in this manner.

According to classical tradition, the human being experiences fourteen different states of consciousness: physical, astral, mental, supramental, superconscious, unconscious, subconscious, dream, supracosmic, dual, multiple, *virat* (God as Cosmos), divine and absolute. The practice of Bhakti Yoga can lead the aspirant through any or all of them. The devotee is particularly subject to visions, lights in the forehead and other manifestations of psychic phenomena. These experiences can be frightening, particularly the loss of physical consciousness, which may feel like dying. However, the aspirant must not be faint-hearted, nor should he cling to these experiences which will appear and reappear for brief periods at the beginning of serious spiritual progress. With persistent and regular practice, one goes beyond these phenomena to meditation, peace and bliss. One must struggle to reach meditation, and struggle even harder to reach *samadhi*, the superconscious state.

In all religions Truth becomes diluted by and for the masses. It becomes an external object to be sought after, rather than an inner state of Consciousness, which is its true nature. The essential attitude to be taken in any religion is one of taking refuge, of confession, prayer, and ultimate surrender to a higher power. It is this inner state of consciousness that Bhakti Yoga nurtures. Without its presence, all other paths of Yoga and any true spiritual progress will fall short of the mark.

12

Raja Yoga Sutras: Theory

There is something beyond the mind. That is the Self, Consciousness. Psychoanalysis should be combined with Raja Yoga. We must not only have a thorough knowledge of the Western science of psychology, but combine it with Raja Yoga and spirituality also. Psychologists should have a perfect knowledge of Patanjali's Raja Yoga. They will be better able to understand the workings of the mind. Then, they will be able to do more service to the world.

—Swami Sivananda
Conquest of the Mind

Raja Yoga, the royal path of mind control, is the most comprehensive and scientific approach to God-Realisation. The precepts and doctrines of this ancient science were first compiled and explained by Patanjali Maharishi, the greatest psychologist of all time. Never has man's mind been so completely analyzed. Never has a process for eliminating human woes and frailties been so succinctly presented. The methods of Raja Yoga are profoundly timeless. Though of ancient origin, they are still the most useful technique available to modern man beset by the tremendous stresses and strains of competitive society. The eight limbs of Raja Yoga have been described in the chapter 'Concentration: Practice.' They may be practiced by anyone regardless of religious or philosophical persuasion.

Raja Yoga, as a system for probing the mind, is not one to be practiced by one person on another. It is a method of self-inquiry that takes the individual through personal changes, step by step. Its essence was written down by Patanjali about 2000 years ago. He wrote in a simple an lyrical style, so that the *sutras*, or aphorisms, could be easily understood and committed to memory. The philosophy is contained in the next four chapters. The first chapter deals with the general theory of Yoga, how the mind functions, and the various levels of *samadhi*, the superconscious state.

समाधिपादः Samādhi-Pādaḥ

Chapter One: The Road to Samadhi

1. अथ योगानुशासनम् ।
Atha yogānuśāsanam
Now Yoga is explained.
The word *Yoga* means union. It refers to the process of uniting the individual with the Universal Soul. It brings about that state of mind which is unruffled and calm in all situations.

2. योगश्चित्तवृत्तिनिरोधः ।
Yogaścitta-vṛtti-nirodhaḥ
Yoga is restraining the activities of the mind.
The mind is neither visible nor tangible. It exists not in the physical body, as does the brain, but in the astral body. Its magnitude cannot be measured, for it carries all feelings, ideas and impressions from this life and all previous lives, as well as intuitive knowledge of what is to come. It is the mind, and nothing else,

that must be corralled and controlled in order to achieve the true peace of Union.

The Sanskrit word *citta* translates as mind stuff, or mental substance. It is, in a sense, the ground floor of the mind. In Vedanta philosophy, it is referred to as *antahkarana*, which means inner instrument. The *antahkarana* contains four main elements. The *manas*, mind, engages in thinking, doubting and willing. The *buddhi* is the intellect, and it performs the functions of discriminating and making decisions. That portion of the mind which is self-arrogating and sees itself as separate from the Source is the *ahamkara*, ego. Finally, there is the subconscious, which serves as a storehouse of past experiences and memory; this is also called the *citta*.

As can be seen, the word *citta* has several meanings. While in Vedanta philosophy it refers specifically to the subconscious, Patanjali uses *citta* in a broader sense, as that underlying substratum, the very foundation that makes up one's mental apparatus. The *citta* may manifest in one of five forms at any given time. They are: 1) *kshipta*, scattering; 2) *mudha*, darkening, dullness; 3) *vikshipta*, gathering, centering; 4) *ekagrata*, one-pointed, concentrated; 5) *niruddha*, absolute suspension of activity.

The *kshipta*, scattering, form is activity, and tends to be experienced as pleasure or pain. The mind acts to justify its desires, and does not care about consequences. It thinks of a frankfurter, and must have one. When warned of the poisons it contains, the reaction is to cover the frankfurter with more mustard and eat it anyway. In the *mudha* state of mind, the tendency is to see and cause suffering, and to negate happiness. The *vikshipta* form functions when the mind struggles to draw itself to its center. The rays of the mind are normally scattered, going in every direction. Here there is the conscious effort to gather and focus them. When the mind is in *ekagrata* state, it is one-pointed, which finally leads to the ultimate state, *niruddha*, where there is suspension of activity, and *samadhi*, the experience of supreme bliss.

The *citta* is thus the backgound of the mind. It is like a lake on which rise and fall waves, which are comparable to the thoughts. These thought waves are called *vrittis*. A *vritti* is a 'mental whirlpool,' or mental modification; it is the difference between action and the absence of action in the mind. In the average person there are thousands of *vrittis* arising each minute in the mind. It is impossible for the conscious mind to keep track of the minute and intricate changes through which the mind is traveling every second. It is no surprise, therefore, that it takes many years of observation of one's own mind to understand its workings.

The Self is the witness of all that is perceived, but it neither acts nor reacts, for all action and reaction take place in the mind, appearing as *vrittis*. Thought, the most powerful force in the universe, initiates all action. Activity carried out on the physical plane is only a mirror of the inner workings of the mind. That which is assumed to be reality, the physical environment in which each person lives, is only a projection of the mind. In truth, when the many mental modifications, *vrittis*, are restrained, one is no longer affected by the comings and goings of the world, and the Self shines forth in undisturbed purity.

3. तदा द्रष्टुः स्वरूपेऽवस्थानम् ।
tadā draṣṭūḥ svarūpe 'vasthānam
At that time (when the thought waves are stilled), the perceiver rests in his own true nature.

That state of pure consciousness is achieved when the mind is no longer modified by the activities of thought waves. When the waves of a lake are stilled, one can see the bottom clearly. Likewise, when the *vrittis* of the mind subside, one's essential nature becomes evident. When the mind's agitation stops, the world no longer exists for the meditator, for he is in union with the Self.

4. वृत्तिसारूप्यमितरत्र ।
vṛttisārūpyam-itaratra
When the mind is not concentrated, the perceiver identifies with its modifications.
When thought waves arise, there is the immediate tendency to identify with them. One thought wave spawns a host of others. If one's neighbor has a swimming pool that is two inches larger, the *vritti* arises that 'I must have a larger pool.' If not caught in its formation, this thought repeats itself, followed by others of a related nature. One follows in the wake of the previous, each giving more and more power to the overall attitude. If, out of covetousness, one buys his neighbor's pool and house, there will be more taxes to pay in addition to two swimming pools and two houses to be cleaned. This may entail hiring help, which further entails supervision. If the second house is rented out, perhaps the tenant will damage either it or the pool. To get away from the headache of it all, one goes for a vacation. The swimming pool is exchanged for one in Hawaii, and the bed and television, for those in the hotel room. One sits in the hotel lobby instead of his own living room, worrying about whether or not the neighbor is remembering to let the dog out each day, and how things at the office are going.

What is the real difference between the hotel lobby and one's own living room? There is none, for the mind is a slave to its preoccupations, identifying with the same problems wherever it is. One *vritti* gives rise to countless others, all in search of happiness. But in fact, it is only foolishness, for the very rising of the thoughts themselves destroys the peace that the mind craves. It is only when these thoughts are stilled in concentration that identification with agitation and desire are eliminated.

5. वृत्तयः पञ्चतय्यः क्लिष्टाक्लिष्टाः ।
vṛttayaḥ pañcatayyaḥ kliṣṭākliṣṭāḥ

There are five types of thought waves, some of which are painful and some of which are not.

Learning may be both enjoyable and painful for the student. He wants knowledge, and yet he wants to escape. The mind plays a tug of war. The painful thoughts are eliminated when the internal conflict ceases through concentration of the mind. Meditation is predicated on a gathered state of mind. If this could be maintained at all times, one would be continually resting in happiness.

6. प्रमाणविपर्ययविकल्पनिद्रास्मृतयः ।

pramāṇa-viparyaya-vikalpa-nidrā-smṛtayaḥ

The five kinds of thought waves are correct knowledge, erroneous understanding, verbal delusion, sleep and memory.

Correct knowledge brings painless experience. It is the only kind of mental modification that is beneficial.

7. प्रत्यक्षानुमानागमाः प्रमाणानि ।

pratyakṣānumānāgamāḥ pramāṇāni

Direct perception, inference and competent testimony are proofs of correct knowledge.

Correct knowledge, knowledge based on fact, can be proved in any of three ways, but none of the proofs may contradict any other. The first is direct perception, in which the knowledge is experienced directly through the senses. This is acceptable only if the senses are pure and not deluded, and if one perception of the experience does not differ from another. The second proof, inference, is based on reasoning. There may be no physical perception of the truth, but it is arrived at through logic and past experience.

The third proof, competent testimony, is knowledge given by a person of unimpeachable character. He has had direct experience himself; his words do not contradict the scriptures; his motives are pure and the knowledge he gives is of benefit to mankind; and his experience must be such that it agrees with men of wisdom.

The Truth is One. All proofs of correct knowledge arrive at the same conclusions.

8. विपर्ययो मिथ्याज्ञानमतद्रूपप्रतिष्ठम् ।
viparyayo mithyājñānam atadrūpa-pratiṣṭham
Erroneous understanding is a false conception of an idea or object whose real nature does not conform to that concept.
The second type of *vritti*, erroneous understanding, may also be based on a perception of an external object, but in this case the mental image does not correspond to the reality of that object. This may be caused by faulty perceptions, incorrect analysis of perceptions, or distortion of perceptions by the ego. It is like the mirage in the desert but is very common in daily life. Very often judgement is passed on a person or situation when there is no relationship between reality and the mental impression.

9. शब्दज्ञानानुपाती वस्तुशून्यो विकल्पः ।
śabdajñānānupātī-vastuśūnyo vikalpaḥ
Verbal delusion is caused by the identification with words that have no basis in reality.
Verbal delusion is the mental impression created by reactions to words that are not founded on fact. If one man calls another a fool, it is only a verbalisation, a vibration in the air. But what a thundering thought wave it creates. One simple, unreal word wreaks havoc, throwing the physical and emotional bodies into chaos, destroying all happiness and peace.

One is not a fool because he is called a fool. If a person were called a donkey, he would not grow long ears and a tail. Yet, it is not unusual for people to react in anger to such statements and, in the process, actually give validity to them. The mind attributes meaning and nuances to words, giving them a false reality. Such reactions to meaningless vibrations is the cause of countless human troubles.

Overreaction to words and jumping to conclusions are weakness of the mind. The *vrittis*, thought waves, must be restrained not only during meditation but at all times. One must be particularly wary of praise, for this too is verbal delusion, and the ego is ever ready to pounce on any opportunity to see itself as better or different from others. Not everyone is going to feel the same way as one who bestows a compliment. Inevitably the pendulum swings in the other direction, and criticism will be heard sooner or later. But happiness should not rest on praise or abuse, for in all conditions, the only reality is the Self which is beyond qualities and beyond change.

The Catholics and Protestants quarrel in Ireland; Jews and Arabs fight in the Middle East. In all parts of the world there are those who see themselves as different from others, rather than as one. Unable to control their thought waves, they are swayed by words that instigate action, which invariably leads to reaction. A strong mind will not be affected in this way. The weaker a person is, the less restraint he has over verbal delusion. Examine yourself the next time you are angry or miserable. Reason it out, and note the modifications of the mind. Gaining freedom from verbal delusion is essential for progress in meditation as well as for strengthening the mind.

A great Hindu holy man was once insulted in front of his disciples by a non-believer who spat upon his face several times. Not one muscle twitched, nor did his calm facial expression change, because he did not identify with his physical sheath. His mind was centered in God. Can you imagine the strength of that mind? Swami Sivananda prostrated before that man who tried to kill him, and Jesus forgave those who crucified him. No matter what was done to them, they responded with one thought, that of pure love. A true master will not react in anger, for to him insult and praise are the same.

Restraint of thought waves does not mean suppression. Suppression dams up violent emotions. For various reasons, people suffer abuse, suppressing anger or pain by smiling and carrying a stiff upper lip. The restrained thought waves must be given an outlet. They must be sublimated and channeled into such uplifting activities as Mantra repetition, exercise, singing and meditation on opposite, positive thoughts. Exchange love for anger and joy for sorrow.

10. अभावप्रत्ययालम्बना वृत्तिर्निद्रा ।
abhāva-pratyayālambanā vṛttirnidrā
That mental modification which encompasses an absence of any content in the mind is called sleep.
During the deep-sleep state the mind is blank, there is an experience of voidness in which the mind is attending to no thoughts. Some people may even experience this void state of mind with eyes open. But this *vritti* must not be mistaken for the superconscious state in which there is full concentration, awareness and realisation of the Self.

11. अनुभूतविषयासंप्रमोषः स्मृतिः ।
anubhūta-viṣayāsaṃpramoṣaḥ smṛtiḥ
Memory is the retention of past experiences.
Memory, or *smriti*, exists when the impressions received by the mind do not slip away permanently and can be recalled to consciousness. If one knowingly performs an action, it will be recorded in the mind. If there is no awareness of an action or event, it cannot be retained. Memory can arise out of the three previous *vrittis*—erroneous understanding, verbal delusion and sleep. Past impressions exist in the mind from thousands of years of life, but these are latent and are only considered memory when they surface to the conscious awareness.

12. अभ्यासवैराग्याभ्यां तन्निरोधः ।
abhyāsa-vairāgyābhyāṃ tan-nirodhaḥ
Their control (of chitta vrittis*) is brought about by practice and non-attachment.*

The different forms of mental modifications which bring about pain can be controlled in two ways. The first is *abhyasa*, which is practice or repetition. A change in character occurs only through formation of new habits. The second way is through non-attachment, or elimination of emotional reactions to situations and individuals. Non-attachment does not mean there should not be love or compassion, but rather that emotional thought waves are ignored. The *vrittis* may arise, but they are observed in a disinterested fashion, then put aside.

13. तत्र स्थितौ यत्नोऽभ्यासः ।
tatra sthitau yatno 'bhyāsaḥ
Abhyasa *is the continuous effort toward firmly establishing restraint of thought waves.*
In order to free the mind from the various thought forms, it is necessary to practice with regularity over an extended period of time. There are a great many means by which this practice is carried out. While the eight limbs of Raja Yoga are given here, there are many other forms of practice that lead to the same goal of Supreme Bliss, including other forms of Yoga explained in this book.

14. स तु दीर्घकालनैरन्तर्यसत्कारासेवितो दृढभूमिः ।
sa tu dīrgha-kāla-nairantarya-satkārāsevito dṛḍha-bhūmiḥ
Practice becomes firmly grounded on being continued over a long period of time without interruption and with sincere devotion.
If there are interruptions in the practice of stilling the mind, or if the effort is not continued over many many years, the results will only be temporary, and all progress will fade. Practice must be constant. It must also be done with an attitude of earnestness. Only when there is true desire to reach the Goal is success assured.

15. दृष्टानुश्रविकविषयवितृष्णस्य वशीकारसंज्ञा वैराग्यम् ।
dṛṣṭānuśravika-viṣaya-vitṛṣṇasya vaśīkāra-saṃjñā vairāgyam

Vairagya, *or non-attachment, is that state of consciousness in which the cravings for objects both seen and unseen are controlled through mastery of the will.*

Non-attachment is a state of mind. It is indifference to objects of the world. It involves being unaffected by the pull of likes and dislikes. Whenever the mind acquires a taste for a particular sensation of pleasure, it becomes attached to it. The mind recalls the experience and desires repetition of it. It is this craving that creates pain. The state of *vairagya* does not necessarily mean the cessation of life in society; it involves separating oneself from the binding emotions of that life.

Renunciation is a great aid to the attainment of *vairagya*. By giving up objects of the senses, the mind is quickly stilled. But it is best to remember that non-attachment is not synonymous with not having. One can own nothing and yet be full of desires. If a person is fond of cherry ice cream, binding his hands and taping his mouth will not keep his mind from dwelling on this treat.

The basis of *vairagya* is the internal realisation of the worthlessness of the external world. Objects and desires then automatically fall away. But renunciation does not mean running away from society, duties, and responsibilities, as is sometimes assumed. It means carrying on with one's duties in a dispassionate, unattached way.

16. तत्परं पुरुषख्यातेर्गुणवैतृष्ण्यम् ।

tatparaṃ puruṣa-khyāter-guṇavaitṛṣṇyam

The highest state of non-attachment stems from awareness of Purusha*; it renounces even the three qualities of Nature.*

True *vairagya* is identification with *Purusha* alone. *Purusha* is the Self, also referred to as Brahman in Jnana Yoga. It is unmanifest and without qualities. It is that all-pervading Supreme Being that exists in the soul of every person. It is to be distinguished from *Prakriti*, which is causal matter, the Lord manifested, appearing as the various aspects of the World. *Prakriti* has *gunas*, qualities, and these are *tamas*, inertia or lethargy; *rajas*, or passion and activity; and *sattwa*, purity.

In extreme non-attachment, there is no identification with the limiting adjuncts, which define the individual. Even these three qualities are renounced when the source of all knowledge is understood to be the Self. One who claims to be a saint is himself a sinner, he is identifying with the quality of spiritual lethargy that causes bad action. On the spiritual path, *tamas* is gradually replaced by *rajas*; that is, good actions replace inactivity. One is further balanced by taking on *sattvic*, or pure qualities. Then purity itself is ultimately transcended when one rests in the Self, for *Purusha* is limitless and thus beyond even the three qualities of *Prakriti*.

17. वितर्कविचारानन्दास्मितानुगमात् संप्रज्ञातः ।
vitarka-vicārānandāsmitānugamāt samprajñātaḥ
Samprajnata samadhi *(*samadhi *with conciousness) is accompanied by reasoning, discrimination, bliss, and an awareness of individuality.*
Samadhi, the superconscious state, is of two types. The first, *samprajnata*, means 'with seed,' and is the state where there is full concentration and experience of bliss, but duality still exists. Here there remains awareness of the object of meditation as separate from the individual who is meditating. The second type, *asamprajnata samadhi*, is said to be 'seedless.' It is the highest state of consciousness, in which there is no duality and the meditator is completely merged with *Purusha*.

Through *samprajnata samadhi* come all the powers of controlling the elements and, hence, nature. Knowledge alone is power, and when one has knowledge of something, he gains power over it. For example, one who meditates on the stars may lose track of all else, but as long as *vrittis* remain, there is still duality. In this concentrated state, even though there is no merging, knowledge of the stars is gained, and hence the powers of an astrologer. To control any element or its modification, one must concentrate on it, and with mediation comes power.

Those beings called angels or *devas* are entities who, through their good actions and meditations, have attained a place, or plane, where they can enjoy and use their powers. Many think this is the ultimate goal, but it is not. There is still duality, a sense of individuality. No matter how pure the ego is, as long as it exists, it must be transcended for the knower, knowledge and known to become One. *Samprajnata samadhi* is not an end in itself but is a state attained along the path. There are four kinds:

1. *Savitarka*: Meditation on elements in time and space.
2. *Nirvitarka*: Meditation on elements outside of time and space.
3. *Sananda*: Meditation on the mind, accompanied by bliss.
4. *Sasmita*: Identification with the unqualified ego.

When the mind fixes on a gross external element or object and meditates on it, it is called *savitarka* meditation. *Vitarka* means question; *savitarka*, with question. Because it has no reality, all matter is questionable and open to examination, and the faculty of reason is applied. This mode of meditation scrutinises the elements and the universe that they may yield up their secrets and powers to the meditator.

In their search to find out about matter, scientists employ this method. They concentrate on an element and experiment to discover its nature. Thus they have learned how to split the atom and utilise its energy for constructive or destructive purposes; modern man can now push a button and explode a hydrogen bomb.

Knowledge of something not only gives control over it, but over those who have no knowledge of it. One buys a certain brand of toothpaste in preference to another out of ignorance; the advertisers know human weaknesses. They claim that one brand has more sex appeal than another, and thus play on the weaknesses of the mind. Everybody manipulates power in this way. Politicians concentrate their energies on outwitting each other and the public. They come up with such Mantras as 'Law and order' and 'Peace with honor,' and bombard the public with their energy in order to control the mass mind. Even some yogis and swamis use such simple, silly tricks and devices as tiger skins, turbans and beards to capture one's imagination and hence the mind. If the mind can be tricked, it can be controlled.

Gaining power over an element is not a miracle; it is only knowing its secret. Laboratory experimentation is, in effect, scientific meditation. When the scientist discovers what has caused a certain mysterious disease, he will then have a basis for cure. He is trying to discover the secrets of nature in order to manipulate and control its energy. A sage knows directly how to tap this energy. By concentrating on one element and excluding all others, he gains direct knowledge. This is *savitarka* meditation. Its goal is the acquisition of powers, but one can never go beyond that.

When meditation is on the same gross elements, but they are isolated from time and physical space, and considered as being in the original state, it is called *nirvitarka*, without question. This is the mode of approach practiced in Kundalini Yoga. It is the type of *samadhi* that is reached through meditation on more subtle energy forces, *chakras*, visualisation, and symbols. In meditating on the *chakras*, or psychic centers, and their corresponding elements, no questions are being asked. The centers and elements involved in this subtle state are directly visualised. As they do not exist in the material world, they are outside of time and space. The object of mediation is thus a part of the meditative process itself. Questioning and experimentation are not involved, nor are meaning and powers being sought. Only discrimination is applied in order to remain focussed on the chosen image or sound.

Control over the elements and the attainment of power come as fringe benefits. They are not the goal.

Samanu pranayama, the process by which the astral tubes are cleansed, is another example of *nirvitarka* meditation. It is a breathing exercise accompanied by simultaneous concentration on the psychic centers, their corresponding elements, and repetition of the element's primal sound energy. One takes the elements out of time and space and directly uses their vibrational energy to purify the subtle astral channels. In repeating the seed sound RAM, one is not dealing with actual burning fire but with its subtle energy.

By controlling the subtle elements one can perform miracles in the eyes of ordinary people, but one is not necessarily progressing on the spiritual path. The mind, though concentrated, is fixed on unreal and limited objects, not on the Self. Meditation on the elements can only bring powers. It cannot bring liberation. Like a batter running down or a diminishing bank account, the powers run out, and their exhibition is limited. The higher the powers, the more voltage is used up. When they disappear, one must start at the bottom of the spiritual ladder again in the next lifetime.

There is no liberation in the acquisition of powers. They lead only to enjoyment of this life and to the reinforcement of the need for that enjoyment. In the end they bring intensified suffering. Even if one gained sufficient powers to become king of heaven, he could not stay there indefinitely. Power, like beauty, cannot be held forever.

The third kind of *samprajnata samadhi* is *sananda*. The elements, whether in or out of time and space, have all been progressively merged in the mind. As its own object of meditation, the mind rests in a state of bliss. One may not want to proceed further, for the ecstasy is supreme. But this is only a taste of the ultimate bliss, for there is still identification with the fruits of meditation. A duality exists in the very enjoyment of the blissful state.

When one offers flowers to the statue of the guru, the devotee is offering one gross element to another. There is awareness of both as concrete physical entities, but neither is important. What matters is the concentration of the mind, which is fixed on an external object. This is *savitarka*. Whether one worships a living guru or a statue makes no difference. Both are external and secondary to the devotional state of mind, which remains the same.

Meditation on the guru internally, seeing him not in time and space but in oneself, takes more concentration. If one puts him in the heart and mentally offers a flower, it is *nirvitarka*. Neither the body nor an outside object is brought into play. The mind alone acts in devotion with the mental offering of a flower.

In *sananda* the flower is forgotten, and association is with the guru as God. He is not seen as separate from the meditator; the previous apparent separation is now recognised as being a product of the mind. When the idea of separation is withdrawn and the thought wave stilled, the mental and emotional sheath is being transcended. The meditator experiences the supremely blissful awareness that the divinity worshipped is no different from himself.

In the last stage, *sasmita*, the mind itself is still the object of mediation, which deepens until only the awareness of the individual in his most purified form, the unqualified ego, remains. Unqualified egoism is identification with a limiting adjunct or false quality. The latter gives rise to such statements as 'I am a liberated woman' or 'I am a lawyer.' If really liberated, the only thing left is I AM. In *sasmita samadhi* the food, vital, and mental sheaths have faded out. The intellectual sheath, the purest ego state, remains predominant. Conscious only of his own pure ego and God, the aspirant still experiences duality.

Although it is possible at this point to merge in nature, the final goal is not yet reached. One still feels distinct from the Self. If he should die while in this stage of consciousness, there is no merging with the Absolute. He becomes a highly evolved angel, still subject to Karma and subtle ego. Like Swami Sivananda, he will be reborn as a sage, and will need only a word to speed him to God-Realisation.

The aforementioned stages are all phases of *samprajnata*, *samadhi* with seed. Their differences are those of degree, in progression of concentration and in disassociation from the gross ego. As the gross falls away, the psychic centers and elements dominate the consciousness. The elements, from dense to subtle, are then merged into the mind, which becomes its own object of meditation. On reaching the pure state of ego, one is unaware of physical, astral or blissful experience. Consciousness resides in the individual in his purest form, which remains separate from the object of meditation, just as the sun's reflection is separate from the sun.

This is a very difficult time for the spiritual seeker. He has reached a stage of development in which spiritual powers are thrown in his lap. Nature will hold him back as long as there is even a little ego. One is tested by the acquisition of powers, supramental experiences, obstacles and pressures. Do not be beguiled by external powers. Whether they are desired or not, they come naturally as the yogi advances along the path. Then people inevitably come to seek advice and counsel. This is a testing period for the ego. Credit should not be expected for the evolution of several lifetimes. It is necessary to push on to the unqualified experience of the *asamprajnata* state, in which there is no dualism.

18. विरामप्रत्ययाभ्यासपूर्वः संस्कारशेषोऽन्यः ।
virāma-pratyayābhyāsa-pūrvaḥ saṃskāraśeṣo 'nyah

Asamprajnata samadhi *(seedless state) is reached when all mental activity ceases and only unmanifested impressions remain in the mind.* *Asamprajnata* or seedless *samadhi*, is most clearly grasped if there is an understanding of the seven *bhumikas*, the stages of consciousness which lead to Self-Realisation. These are:

1. *Subhecha*, longing for truth. One realises his state of ignorance, and sincerely wishes to acquire spiritual knowledge.
2. *Vicharana*, right inquiry. One is convinced of the worthlessness of the world, and searches sincerely and deeply for the Truth.
3. *Tanumanasa*, fading of the mind. The mind loses its taste for objects of the world and becomes intensely immersed in knowledge of the Soul. This corresponds to the latter states of *savitarka* and *nirvitarka*.
4. *Sattwapatti*, purity of the mind. All mental modifications are reduced to identification with the Self. This corresponds to *sananda* and *sasmita*.
5. *Asamsakti*, detached state. The meditator is unaffected by anything in the world, due to his knowledge of the Self.
6. *Padarthabhavana*, knowledge of the truth. Karma is almost completed and external things do not appear to exist.
7. *Turiya*, the state of liberation. The yogi sees God everywhere. He does not perform action, for this state is of short duration while the body and sheaths are completely burned.

Asamprajnata samadhi begins with the fifth state of consciousness, and is characterised by an absence of thought waves. When the thought waves are active, they manifest as *samskaras*, or impressions in the mind. They can also exist in a passive state. When one meditates in *samprajnata*, which corresponds to the third and fourth stages of consciousness, the waves are stilled but not absent. Lurking deep in the subconscious, they will eventually emerge as desires. They are like seeds placed in a jar. Although temporarily dormant, they retain the potential for future germination.

For this reason a person in the fourth stage will never achieve liberation while in that stage. He is also in danger of toppling from whatever heights he has reached. No matter how high one goes, the possibility of slipping always lies in wait. The fourth stage is like a spiritual mountain peak, and one cannot perch eternally on top of it. Until nature and conscious concentration are transcended, and seedless *asamprajnata samadhi* is reached, there is the danger of falling.

It takes great strength and control to achieve the superconscious state. Without adequate preparation it is easy to be overpowered by lethargy. One can be deceived into thinking that it is *samadhi*, just as a little backache is sometimes mistaken for the awakening of the kundalini. A person in sleep and one who is experiencing superconsciousness appear to be in the same state, for energy at its lowest level resembles energy at its highest. When the blades of an electric fan are revolving with great velocity, they appear not to be moving at all.

Extremes are very much alike. Darkness cannot be seen, and neither can extreme light. In extreme lethargy there are no activities or desires. A person who is sleeping does not want to eat, make money or go to parties. Desires are absent. It is the same with *asamprajnata samadhi*, although this state is the height of awareness. One wants neither sensual nor sexual experience. The only difference is that in deep sleep there are still seeds in the jar, and the next morning they will sprout as desires.

When the mind is empty and the thought waves and impressions are completely gone, it is the seedless *asamprajnata* state. No seeds are left to manifest in the form of desires or tendencies.

Tendencies have the power to create. Who made one person male and another female? One's own thought impressions are responsible. This should be neither male nor female. When the mind begins acting and wants to behave like a woman, it creates a suitable body for those tendencies. As long as there are thought impressions and tendencies, there will be more reincarnation. The tendency of the ego itself must be broken down, for it, too, is illusion. *Maya* projects qualities onto the individual, and he thinks that he is tall, fat, man, woman, talented or dull. When all such ideas, good as well as evil, have been overcome, the soul stands alone.

Asamprajnata samadhi is that state of merging with the Absolute, which is beyond knowledge. Any objective experience is knowledge. If one sees Krishna, it is objective knowledge. However, if one knows that he is Krishna, that is beyond knowledge. Then there is no more seed, and nothing can touch him.

19. भवप्रत्ययो विदेहप्रकृतिलयानाम् ।
bhava-pratyayo videha-prakṛti-layānām
(Asamprajnata samadhi *may be attained) by birth (in those who have previously achieved) bodilessness or a merging with Prakriti.*
The highest state of *samadhi* is not achieved in one lifetime. It takes many incarnations to make the innumerable fine adjustments necessary for God-Realisation. Many who do reach *asamprajnata samadhi* have done the major part of their work in previous lives and return only to attain the final goal. Some have already reached the level of a *deva*, an advanced spriritual being not living with *Prakriti*, when meditation on the elements of nature has been perfected. In either case, merging with the Self is all that remains to be achieved.

20. श्रद्धावीर्यस्मृतिसमाधिप्रज्ञापूर्वक इतरेषाम् ।
śraddhā-vīrya-smṛti-samādhi-prajñapūrvaka itareṣām
For others, asamprajnata samadhi *is attained through faith, energy, recollection and keen awareness.*
For others, the highest state is reached through sincere lifelong application, as well as through past life efforts. Faith is the

firm conviction that the truth exists and that it can and will be attained. With this basic positive attitude, failure is impossible. Energy, or will, is the drive that carries one along the path, bouncing back after failures and maintaining courage through difficult times. Recollection is past spiritual *samskaras* rising to the surface of the mind and reinforcing the seeker's journey to his Goal. Keen awareness is focussed application of the mind, the intense intellectual input that is necessary for merging with the Supreme.

21. तीव्रसंवेगानामासन्नः ।
tīvra-saṃvegānām-āsannaḥ
Liberation comes quickly when the desire for it is intense.
The stronger the desire for liberation from the bondage of this world, the sooner will that goal be reached.

22. मृदुमध्याधिमात्रत्वात् ततोऽपि विशेषः ।
mṛdu-madhyādhimātratvāt tato 'pi viśeṣaḥ
Desire for liberation can be mild, moderate or intense.
The intensity of desire for liberation will reflect the effort that is put into achieving it, as well as the fruit—the success of one's endeavors toward God-Realisation.

23. ईश्वरप्रणिधानाद्वा ।
īśvara-praṇidhānād vā
(Success is swift for those who are) devoted to Ishwara *(God).*
While *Purusha* (Brahman or the Self) is the abstract view of the Lord in his purest absolute form, *Ishwara* is God as seen with attributes such as love, kindness, mercy, omniscience and so forth. Because the human mind is too limited to focus on abstractions, most people focus on his manifested form, *Ishwara*. In Western tradition, He is usually referred to as God, or Jehovah. In the Indian tradition, He is related to in various forms, such

as Vishnu, the Preserver; Rama, the Righteous; and Durga, the Divine Mother. These various deities are not different gods, but *Ishwara*, the one God, who is so omnipotent that he is able to manifest in as many forms as are needed by individuals of different temperament to help each focus on the Supreme.

Thus *samadhi* comes most quickly to those who place themselves in consciousness of God, however they may see him. That is, they have devotion, dedication and self-surrender to his will.

24. क्लेशकर्मविपाकाशयैरपरामृष्टः पुरुषविशेष ईश्वरः ।
kleśa-karma-vipākāśayair aparāmṛṣṭaḥ puruṣa-viśeṣa īśvaraḥ
Ishwara *is that particular center of Divine Counsiousness that is untouched by misery, Karma, or desires.*
Ishwara is the immortal Self, or *Purusha*, with form. He is perceived as a being, and yet He is totally untouched by the ignorance of unhappiness, the law of cause and effect, and cravings. For Him, the opposites of the phenomenal world, such as pleasure and pain, do not exist.

25. तत्र निरतिशयं सर्वज्ञबीजम् ।
tatra niratiśayaṃ sarvajña-bījam
In Him lies the seed of omniscience.
God, or *Ishwara,* is not just all-knowing, but is knowledge itself. In uniting with Him, the highest knowledge is obtained. This does not refer to intellectual knowledge only, but also knowledge of the entire universe through the eye of wisdom and intuition.

26. स पूर्वेषामपि गुरुः कालेनानवच्छेदात् ।
sa pūrveṣām api guruḥ kālenānavacchedāt
Unlimited by time, He is the Teacher of all other teachers, from the most ancient of times.

The highest teacher is the Self, *Purusha.* All ancient sages, such as Jesus and Buddha, realised the Self. While they may have had earthly teachers, the Source of their vast knowledge was not of this plane. Living in a superconscious state, they had direct access of the Truth, that knowledge which is absolute.

27. तस्य वाचकः प्रणवः ।
tasya vācakaḥ praṇavaḥ
He manifests in the word OM.
OM (AUM), the sacred word of the Hindus, is one of the oldest known words. Over 5000 years ago, and probably much earlier in ancient Sumer, OM was known and used as a secret word by Sumerian mystics and priests.

When the Indo-Aryan tribes wandered east from Sumer to northern India, they carried the precious and sacred word OM with them. In the oldest known Indian scriptures, OM has always had a place of prominence. Nearly all Mantras and hymns begin and end with OM. OM is also used alone as a Mantra and is considered to be the most powerful one.

There are countless stories still circulating in India telling that if a person can pronounce the word OM with the right vibration and proper concentration, he can attain all *siddhis,* that is power to perform all kinds of miracles, such as healing people, producing rain, or walking over water.

Some contemporary Indian authorities on the subject have also a rational explanation for the miraculous power of OM. For instance Swami Sivananda, who was a practicing medical doctor before he became a yogi, explains that the vibrations produced in nasal cavities by the continuous chanting of OM stimulate the activity of the hypophysis and gladula pinealis by a direct massage-like action. Since those organs have great importance in the psychological and physiological functions of man, it may explain part of the mystery behind OM.

It is impossible to describe the absolute meaning of OM, as it is said that only the enlightened can understand it completely. Its vibration is synonymous with union with the Divine. Its meaning is Supreme Reality itself. It is the same as *Sat-Chit-Ananda*, or Existence-Knowledge-Bliss Absolute.

All vibration, and hence all language, falls within the range of OM. Word and thought, name and form, cannot be separated, for word is thought manifested through the vocal cords. Every thought has its corresponding word of some kind, as well as weight, power, form and energy. OM contains within itself all language, all thought. It is the Primal Vibration and Divine Power.

28. तज्जपस्तदर्थभावनम् ।
tajjapastad-artha-bhāvanam
Constant repetition of OM and meditation on its meaning (leads to samadhi*).*
Focussing on the abstract is more difficult than focussing on concrete images of the Lord. However, because repetition of OM produces thought waves which correspond to those of the Supreme, it is a direct path to *samadhi*.

Swami Sivananda would always emphasise the power and glory of OM. In *Bliss Divine*, his greatest compilation of spiritual essays, he writes, 'Live in OM. Meditate on OM. Inhale and exhale OM. Rest peacefully in OM. Take shelter in OM.'

29. ततः प्रत्यक्चेतनाधिगमोऽप्यन्तरायाभावश्च ।
tataḥ pratyak-cetanādhigamo 'pyantarāyā-bhāvaś ca
From (the repetition of OM) is gained enlightening introspection and elimination of all obstacles.
Through meditation on OM, the highest of Mantras, Self-Realisation is possible. This is because the vibration of OM removes hindrances on the path and leads to realisation of the Self which exists within every individual.

30. व्याधिस्त्यानसंशयप्रमादालस्याविरतिभ्रान्तिदर्शनालब्धभूमि-कत्वानवस्थितत्वानि चित्तविक्षेपास्तेऽन्तरायाः ।
vyādhi-styāna-saṃśaya-pramādālasyāvirati-bhrānti-darśanālabdhabhūmi-katvānavasthitatvāni citta-vikṣepās te 'ntarāyāḥ
The obstacles to Realisation are disease, mental torpor, doubt, indifference, laziness, craving for pleasure, delusion, inability to practice and maintain concentration, and restlessness of mind due to distractions.

If the body is not healthy, cosmic consciousness cannot be reached. The practice of asanas and *pranayama* wards off disease and helps to maintain alertness. Doubt and the various mental obstacles can be dispelled by the spiritual experiences that come through meditation. Especially when progress seems to be at a standstill, it is essential to plod on doggedly with the practice. Yoga, like any other kind of learning, is never a straight ascent; there are ups and downs and plateaus. Bear this in mind, do not become discouraged, and be aware that all seekers encounter these same obstacles. They should be regarded as challenges which induce growth opportunities to develop strength. With regularity in practice, the mind eventually rights itself.

31. दुःखदौर्मनस्याङ्गमेजयत्वश्वासप्रश्वासा विक्षेपसहभुवः ।
duḥkha-daurmanasyāṅgamejayatva-śvāsa-praśvāsā vikṣepa-sahabhuvaḥ
Mental pain, depression, physical nervousness, and irregular breathing are the symptoms of a distracted state of mind.
These are outward manifestations of an internal state of being. They are the result of the above-mentioned obstacles to meditacion. They are also a way of life for many thousands who never undertake spiritual disciplines such as meditation and Yoga.But they can be thoroughly remedied by repetition of OM, surrender to the Lord, and regularity in practice.

Even during periods when one's original enthusiasm wanes, continuing in the daily schedule of spiritual practice strengthens the will and builds positive spiritual habits, or *samskaras*. In due time, each test is passed and meditation is approached with renewed vigor.

32. तत्प्रतिषेधार्थमेकतत्त्वाभ्यासः ।
tat-pratiṣedhārtham-eka-tattvābhyāsaḥ
In order to remove these obstacles, one should mediate on one aspect of Truth.
The seeker should choose one of the many forms of meditation in order to carry out his practice, focussing his mind on one specific object of concentration or embodiment of perfection. If he jumps from one object to another, steadiness of mind can never be developed. Not only must concentration be focussed on one object alone during any given sitting, but it should be the same object from year to year. This is the only way to gather the rays of the mind and to perfect one-pointedness.

33. मैत्रीकरुणामुदितोपेक्षाणां सुखदुःखपुण्यापुण्यविषयाणां भावनातश्चित्त प्रसादनम् ।
maitrī-karuṇā-muditopekṣāṇāṃ sukha-duḥkha-puṇyāpuṇya-viṣayāṇāṃ bhāvanātaścitta-prasādanam
The mind becomes clear through the cultivation of friendliness, kindness, contentment, and indifference toward happiness, vice and virtue.
Taming of the mind requires the development of goodwill and universal love toward all. Any kind of negative feeling or identification with the dualities of good and bad destroys peace of mind.

34. प्रच्छर्दनविधारणाभ्यां वा प्राणस्य ।
pracchardana-vidhāraṇābhyāṃ vā prāṇasya
It is also achieved by the expulsion and retention of the breath.

This is a reference to the practice of *pranayama* as a method of purification. Regulation of the breath gives control over the thought waves, for control of breath is directly related to control of mind. There are many *pranayama* exercices, each of which has a special effect on the autonomic nervous system and the psyche.

35. विषयवती वा प्रवृत्तिरुत्पन्ना मनसः स्थितिनिबन्धनी ।
viṣayavatī vā pravṛttirutpannā manasaḥ sthiti-nibandhanī
Steadiness of the mind is easily established when the higher senses come into operation.
Concentration on the higher objects of sensation, such as the *anahata*, or internal sound, quiets the mind.

36. विशोका वा ज्योतिष्मती ।
viśokā vā jyotiṣmatī
Or (by concentration on the internal) state of luminescence which is beyond sorrow.
Patanjali is here giving a series of methods that can be utilised for control of the vrittis, thought waves. One of the possible objects of meditation is a visualised light, either in the heart or the space between the eyebrows.

37. वीतरागविषयं वा चित्तम् ।
vīta-rāga-viṣayaṃ vā cittam
Or by fixing the mind on one who has transcended human passions and attachments.
Another highly regarded object of meditation is a saint or sage who has attained liberation. A picture of an inspiring soul, such as Swami Sivananda, Buddha or Jesus, may be kept on the altar or other place of meditation. He may be focussed on either visually or mentally.

38. स्वप्ननिद्राज्ञानालम्बनं वा ।
svapna-nidrā-jñānālambanaṃ vā
Or (by meditating upon) knowledge gained in dreams or deep sleep.

Many times the Truth is revealed by the superconscious during sleep. Usually this information is forgotten, and is only utilised by the subconscious. But if that knowledge is meditated upon consciously, great progress can be made upon the path.

39. यथाभिमतध्यानाद्वा ।
yathābhimatadhyānād-vā
Or by meditation on what is agreeable.
Patanjali has given only a few of the many techniques for meditation. An aspirant should choose one that suits his temperament, and stick to that method until reaching liberation.

40. परमाणुपरममहत्त्वान्तोऽस्य वशीकारः ।
paramāṇu-paramamahattvānto 'sya vaśīkāraḥ
(Thus a yogi's) mastery extends from the smallest atom to infinity.
That is, a yogi, when perfected, has no limitations. He is master of the universe, in all its forms.

41. क्षीणवृत्तेरभिजातस्येव मणेर्ग्रहीतृग्रहणग्राह्येषु तत्स्थतदञ्जनतासमापत्तिः ।
kṣīṇavṛtter-abhijātasyeva maṇer-grahītṛ-grahaṇa-grāhyeṣu tat-stha-tad-añjanatā samāpattiḥ
For the person who has controlled the vrittis though meditation, there is a merging of the perceiver, perceived and perception, just as a crystal assumes the color of the background.
When the mind waves are controlled, there is complete union between the subject, object and the relationship between the two. A crystal has no color of its own, yet when placed on a colored background, it assumes and reflects that same color. The pure mind, abandoning its own form, assumes the form of whatever object it meditates on.

42. तत्र शब्दार्थज्ञानविकल्पैः संकीर्णा सवितर्का समापत्तिः ।
tatra śabdārtha-jñāna-vikalpaiḥ saṅkīrṇā savitarkā samāpattiḥ
Savitarka samadhi *is that state in which the mind alternates*

between knowledge based on words, true knowledge, and knowledge based on sense perception or reasoning.

Savitarka samadhi is known as *samadhi* with reasoning. This is the lowest level of *samadhi* in which there is perfected concentration, but the meditator is focussing on natural elements and using his intellectual faculties. The purity of the various levels of knowledge is yet to be clarified.

43. स्मृतिपरिशुद्धौ स्वरूपशून्येवार्थमात्रनिर्भासा निर्वितर्का ।

smṛti-pariśuddhau svarūpa-śūnyevārtha-mātra-nirbhāsā nirvitarkā

Nirvitarka samadhi *is that state in which the memory is clarified and the mind, devoid of subjectivity, reflects true knowledge.*

Nirvitarka samadhi is *samadhi* that is beyond reason. It is meditation on an abstract object such as the *chakras*, or symbols. The mixing of the sources of knowledge ends. In *savitarka samadhi* there is some confusion between the element of reason and lower forms of knowledge. In *nirvitarka samadhi*, the element of reason, or intellectual argumentation, fades. In both cases there is a blissful experience, yet there is full awareness of subject and object.

44. एतयैव सविचारा निर्विचारा च सूक्ष्मविषया व्याख्याता ।

etayaiva savicārā nirvicārā ca sūkṣmaviṣayā vyākhyātā

By this (what is stated in the previous two sutras*),* samadhi *with inquiry,* samadhi *without inquiry, and that which is still more subtle is explained.*

Here Patanjali is distinguishing the various types of *samprajnata samadhi*. They include forms which may or may not involve inquiry, the mental process of reflection. Or they may include levels which involve meditation on one or more subtle objects.

45. सूक्ष्मविषयत्वं चालिङ्गपर्यवसानम् ।

sūkṣma-viṣayatvaṃ cāliṅga-paryavasānam

The state of samadhi *concerned with subtle objects extends as far as the unmanifested state.*

This is a way of saying that the degree if subtlety in objects of meditation is limitless. It extends as far as the unmanifest state itself. Yet, there remain objects separate from the meditator, and hence there is still duality.

46. ता एव सबीजः समाधिः ।
tā eva sabījaḥ samādhiḥ
These all constitute meditation with 'seed.'
All forms of *samadhi* that are arrived at through meditation on an external object remain *sabija*, with seed, meditation. No matter what the degree of subtlety, the meditator is still within the realm of *Prakriti*, where there is subject-object relationship.

47. निर्विचारवैशारद्येऽध्यात्मप्रसादः ।
nirvicāra-vaiśāradye 'dhyātma-prasādaḥ
On attaining the utmost purity in samadhi *without inquiry illumination dawns.*
Only when the meditator achieves that state of *samadhi* in which there is no longer the process of inquiry, and has purified himself, does Realisation dawn. The states of *samadhi* through which he passes before that final goal are very rewarding and blissful, and many powers manifest in those states. But the seeker must see even these rewarding experiences as obstacles for they too, though the most rewarding, must be trascended in order to merge with the Self.

48. ऋतम्भरा तत्र प्रज्ञा ।
ṛtambharā tatra prajñā
The knowledge that is attained in this state is Absolute Truth.
All duality, all relativity vanish. Intuitive cognition supersedes all other forms of knowledge.

49. श्रुतानुमानप्रज्ञाभ्यामन्यविषया विशेषार्थत्वात् ।
śrutānumāna-prajñābhyām anya-viṣayā viśeṣārthatvāt
Knowledge gained from inference and testimony is not equal

to that obtained in higher states of consciousness, because it is confined to a particular object.

This refers back to the seventh sutra, which defines correct knowledge. Even if knowledge is gained through intellectual process or thorugh the statement of a great sage, it is limited, and this is infereior to direct experience itself. In this case, the direct expereience is the intuitive limitless knowledge of *Purusha* or the Self.

50. तज्जः संस्कारोऽन्यसंस्कारप्रतिबन्धी ।
taj-jaḥ saṃskāro 'nya-saṃskāra-pratibandhī
The result (of that knowledge) is that samskaras *replace all others.*
Direct knowledge of the Lord obscures all other forms of knowledge, and in its light past *samskaras* replace all others.

51. तस्यापि निरोधे सर्वनिरोधान्निर्बीजः समाधिः ।
tasyāpi nirodhe sarva-nirodhān nirbījaḥ samādhiḥ
When even this is restrained, the 'seedless' state of samadhi *is entered.*
This is the climax of the evolution of *sadhana*, spiritual practice. When the last seeds of Karma are burnt, and even the *vritti* of direct cognition of the Lord is restrained, then *samadhi* is of the seedless type. This is the last phase of *asamprajnata samadhi*. The meditator, having spent many lifetimes perfecting himself, no longer has need of a physical form, and shortly enters *Mahasamadhi*, in which he merges with God.

13

Raja Yoga Sutras: Practice

Chalk out a program of life. Draw your spiritual routine. Stick to it systematically and regularly. Apply yourself diligently. Waste not even a single precious minute. Life is short. Time is fleeting. That tomorrow will never come. Now or never. Stand up with the firm resolve; I will become a Yogi in this very birth, this very moment. Do rigid, constant Yoga sadhana *or* abhyasa. *If you are really very sincere in your practice, and if your mind is filled with* vairagya *or dispassion and keen longing for Liberation, you will reach the goal of perfection within six years. There is no doubt about this.*

—Swami Sivananda

Sure Ways for Success in Life and God-Realisation

Although Pantanjali Maharishi is the author and compiler of the *Raja Yoga Sutras*, it is said in the *Yajnavalkya Smriti* that Hiranyagarbha was the original teacher of Yoga. Hiranyagarbha is the Cosmic Mind, or Cosmic Intelligence, also called Brahman. He is the sum total of all the subtle bodies,the highest created being through whom the supreme being projects the physical universe. Patanjali, as a realised sage whose intuitive abilities were developed to the highest degree, received the knowledge of Yoga directly and wrote it down for the benefit of all mankind.

While the first chapter of the *Sutras* explains the functions of the mind and the various levels of *samadhi*, the following chapters are more concerned with the specific practices that lead to that superconscious state. Patanjali covers all phases of Yoga from the very basics to levels of practice that are beyond the comprehension of all but liberated saints and sages. The last two chapters in particular deal with the vast realm that is experienced after attaining *samadhi*. While reading through them, it is best to bear in mind that realisation of the Self is attained only after many lifetimes of striving for that goal. And, as emphasised in the last pages of the previous chapter, even the attainment of powers and the experience of bliss during meditation are but stepping stones along the path. These are mere distractions when seen in light of the ultimate end merging with Divine.

साधनपादः Sādhana-Pādaḥ

Chapter Two: Yoga Sadhana

Pantanjali's second chapter sets forth the practice of Yoga, or *sadhana*. It discusses Kriya Yoga, which is purification through discipline, study, and self-surrender. It enumerates the five main afflictions, or causes for human suffering, and the methods for eliminating them. Finally, it discusses ther first five limbs of Raja Yoga—*yama*, *niyama*, asana, *pranayama, and pratyahara*—the foundations for meditation.

1. तपः स्वाध्यायेश्वरप्रणिधानानि क्रियायोगः ।
tapaḥ-svādhyāyeśvara-praṇidhānāni kriyā-yogaḥ
Austerity, self-study, and surrender to God constitute Kriya Yoga.
Austerity does not mean physical abuse or severe rigors. It refers to strict control of the senses in order to conserve energy for

higher pursuits. Austerity in this sense means fasting occasionally, rising early to meditate instead of sleeping late, and reducing certain physical comforts for the sake of greater control of mind. Study of the scriptures and other spiritual works keeps the mind flowing in the desired direction. In surrendering to God one also surrenders the fruit of work performed. This leads to Karma Yoga, the path of seelfless service, in which one regards oneself as the instrument of God, and serves humanity with no thoughts of either credit or blame.

2. समाधिभावनार्थः क्लेशतनुकरणार्थश्च ।
samādhi-bhāvanārthāḥ kleśa-tanu-karaṇārthāś ca
It alleviates afflictions and brings about samadhi.
By following the three practices of Kriya Yoga mentioned above, the student eliminates the source of his woes and eventually reaches the superconscious state.

3. अविद्याऽस्मितारागद्वेषाभिनिवेशाः क्लेशाः ।
avidyā 'smitā-rāga-dveṣābhiniveśāḥ kleśāḥ
Ignorance, egoism,attraction and aversion, and fear of death are the afflictions which cause suffering.
Ignorance, *avidya*, is the lack of awareness of Reality. It is identification with the temporal world rather than with the imperishable *Atman*, or Self. Egoism is the 'I-ness', and 'my-ness', which create the illusion that one person is different from another, bringing about conflict. *Raga-dvesha* translates as 'likes/dislikes;' when a person is swayed by feelings of attraction and aversion, he is identifying with the material world and setting himself up for the pain of loss and disapppointment. Fear of death, or clinging to life, is binding and stifling. Many who have been pronounced dead and were later revived have reported the experience of death as indescribably beautiful and peaceful. None can say when death will come. Fear of death is useless imagination, a waste of energy, and creates waves of pain which exist only in the mind.

4. अविद्या क्षेत्रमुत्तरेषां प्रसुप्ततनुविच्छिन्नोदाराणाम् ।
avidyā-kṣetram-uttareṣāṃ prasupta-tanu-vicchinno-dārāṇām
Ignorance is the cause of (the above-mentioned afflictions) which follow it, whether they be latent, weak suppressed or aggravated.
The suffering which comes from egoism, attraction and repulsion, and fear of death all stem from *avidya*, ignorance, regardless of the degree to which they manifest. As the root of the other obstacles, ignorance of the true nature of the Self is identification with the body mind. When *avidya* is replaced by Enlightenment, all other causes of pain automatically disappear.

5. अनित्याशुचिदुःखानात्मसु नित्यशुचिसुखात्मख्यातिरविद्या ।
anityāśuci-duḥkhānātmasu nitya-śuci-sukhātmakhyātir-avidyā
Ignorance mistakes the perishable, impure, painful and non-Self for the eternal, pure, good, and Self.
When in a state of ignorance, man mistakes what is mundane for what is Supreme. He cannont differentiate between that which will bring pain—the mind and body—and that which will bring immortality.

6. दृग्दर्शनशक्त्योरेकात्मतेवास्मिता ।
dṛg-darśana-śaktyor-ekātmatevāsmitā
Egoism is the identification of the Seer with the instrument of seeing.
The instrument of seeing in this case refers not only to the eyes but also to all the senses. Egoism is manifest when the individual cannot distinguish his Self from his senses and mind. He sees himself as separate from the rest of mankind, reacting to others with a sense of competition rather than cooperation.

7. सुखानुशयी रागः ।
sukhānuśayī rāgaḥ
Attraction is that which dwells on pleasure.
Most think of attraction and pleasure as positive things, but when associated with objects of the material world they inevitably bring

pain. Nothing in the physical world is permanent; hence the constant fear of loss and loss itself keep those seeking pleasure in an unhappy state. This is why the yogi learns to cultivate a dislike for worldly pleasures. He is never disappointed or unhappy. The result, ironically, is that by not seeking pleasure he is always happy.

8. दुःखानुशयी द्वेषः ।
duḥkhānuśayī dveṣaḥ
Aversion is that which attempts to avoid pain.
Just as attraction brings pain, so does aversion. The mental attitude of aversion is a negtive one, and often makes a neutral situation appear as if it were one to be avoided. It is not possible to avoid all distasteful circumstances. When there is *raga-dvesha*, or likes and dislikes, a person cannot be happy. He is dwelling on illusory pairs-of-opposites rather than learning to be content in all situations and surrendering to the Lord plan for his growth.

9. स्वरसवाही विदुषोऽपि तथा रूढोऽभिनिवेशः ।
svarasa-vāhī viduṣo 'pi tathā rūḍho 'bhiniveśaḥ
Fear of death is the continuous desire to live which is rooted even in the mind of the wise.
The fear of death is the fear of loss of identity, of letting go of the ego. Even when all else is given up, there is still the clinging to life. It is only when a sage reaches the very last stage of *asamprajnata samadhi* that he cares for nothing but merging with the Lord; and when this level is reached he remains in the body for only a few days.

10. ते प्रतिप्रसवहेयाः सूक्ष्माः ।
te pratiprasava-heyāḥ sūkṣmāḥ
Their subtle forms (of the pain-bearing afflictions) can be avoided by reabsorbing them into their causes.
When these various afflictions are a minor distraction to the aspirant they can be merged back into their cause by substituting the

opposite mental modificatins. For example, if egotistical thoughts arise, they can be combatted by focussing on the brotherhood of all mankind. If feelings of attraction or avoidance enter the mind, then contentment or acceptance can be substituted.

11. ध्यानहेयास्तद्वृत्तयः ।
dhyāna-heyās tad-vṛttayaḥ
Their active forms can be avoided through meditation.
If the afflictions are overt and a great distraction to the mind, they can be alleviated through regular meditation.

12. क्लेशमूलः कर्माशयो दृष्टादृष्टजन्मवेदनीयः ।
kleśa-mūlaḥ karmāśayo dṛṣṭādṛṣṭa-janma-vedanīyaḥ
Karma, whether worked out in this or future lives, has its roots in the pain-bearing afflictions.
The law of Karma states that every action brings about an equal and opposite reaction. Whatever is done to others will return to the doer in some form or another. Most people are continually creating new karmic situations. This is due to ignorance and its accompanying afflictions. Before final emancipaltion, all karmic debts must be worked out, whether one decides to do so in the present life or leaves this work for later lifetimes.

13. सति मूले तद्विपाको जात्यायुर्भोगाः ।
sati mūle tad-vipāko jātyāyur-bhogaḥ
As long as the root remains, the Karma must be fulfilled, resulting in various social situations, lifespans and experiences.
Each must reap what he sows. Various life experiences are due to the karmic situations that each has earned for himself by his thoughts, words and deeds.

14. ते ह्लादपरितापफलाः पुण्यापुण्यहेतुत्वात् ।
te hlāda-paritāpa-phalāḥ puṇyāpuṇya-hetutvāt
They have pleasure or pain as their fruit, according to whether their cause is virtue or vice.

Understanding this, the yogi strives to do only good actions and to accept peacefully the ill that comes his way so that all his seeds of Karma are burned and no new ones are sown.

15. परिणामतापसंस्कारदुःखैर्गुणवृत्तिविरोधाच्च दुःखमेव सर्वं विवेकिनः ।
pariṇāma-tāpa-saṃskāra-duḥkhair guṇa-vṛtti-virodhācca duḥkham eva sarvaṃ vivekinaḥ
To those who are discriminating, every action brings pain due to anticipation of loss, new desires, or conflicts arising out of the interaction between the mind and the three qualities of nature.
The wise man realizes that no happiness is to be found in the material world, for pain eventually arises from all actions. Where there is lack of discrimination, happiness is accompanied by the fear of its loss; and since change is a law of nature, loss is inevitable. When not concerned with loss, the mind is often conjuring up new ideas, and there is no happiness until those are satisfied, which is, again, immediately followed by fear of loss. The uncentered mind is never at rest for it is ever caught in the play of the qualities of nature-purity, activity and lethargy. Peace can only be found beyond the phenomenal world.

16. हेयं दुःखमनागतम् ।
heyaṃ duḥkham-anāgatam
The misery that has not yet manifested should be avoided.
Karma has been worked out, is being worked out, or is waiting to be worked out by one's actions. Karma that has already been incurred cannot be changed, but its misery can be avoided by positive thinking. Future pain can be avoided by carefully attending to present actions.

17. द्रष्टृदृश्ययोः संयोगो हेयहेतुः ।
draṣṭṛ-dṛśyayoḥ saṃyogo heya-hetuḥ
The cause of future Karma is the identification of the experiencer with the object that is being experienced.

When a person is identifying with this illusory world, the ego predominates, and he acts without wisdom, incurring new Karma for himself.

18. प्रकाशक्रियास्थितिशीलं भूतेन्द्रियात्मकं भोगापवर्गार्थं दृश्यम् ।
prakāśa-kriyā-sthiti-śīlaṃ bhūtendriyātmakaṃ
bhogāpavargārthaṃ dṛśyam
The universe, which is experienced through the interaction between the elements and the perceptions of the sense organs, is composed of sattwa, rajas, *and* tamas, *and exists solely for the purpose of (man's) experience and liberation.*
As has been explained, *Purusha* is absolute and without qualities. However, man sees not the Divine, but *Prakriti*, or nature, and its three *gunas*, or qualities. These are *sattwa*, purity; *rajas*, activity; and *tamas*, inertia. Through his senses he perceives and interprets nature and its elements. In life after life he gains experience in the realm of *Prakriti* until he finally realises that the qualities are nothing but his interpretation of Reality, and that in Truth, he is one with all. The purpose of life is to work through this physical plane, using its conditions to clear away Karma. Through constant purification and balancing of the mind, *sattwa*, *rajas* and *tamas* are brought into equilibrium, and man returns to the Source that is beyond the manifest world.

19. विशेषाविशेषलिङ्गमात्रालिङ्गानि गुणपर्वाणि ।
viśeṣāviśeṣa-liṅga-mātrāliṅgāni guṇa-parvāṇi
The states of the three gunas *are gross, fine, manifest and unmanifest.*
The three qualities pervade all of nature, whether in the elements of the earth or in the subtler matters of mind and spirit.

20. द्रष्टा दृशिमात्रः शुद्धोऽपि प्रत्ययानुपश्यः ।
draṣṭā dṛśimātraḥ śuddho 'pi pratyayānupaśyaḥ
The seer is pure consciousness only, and though pure, he appears to see through the mind.

The seer is the Self, or *Purusha*. It is untainted, pure, and without qualifications, but is reflected through the intellect of individual consciousnesses and is colored by *sattwa*, *rajas*, and *tamas*. It is veiled, appearing to have attributes, but in fact, it is Absolute Consciousness itself.

21. तदर्थ एव दृश्यस्यात्मा ।
tad-artha eva dṛśyasyātmā
The very existence of the seen is for the Seer.
The seen, *Prakriti*, exists for and is subordinate to the Seer, or Self. Its sole purpose is to provide experience for the growth and Self-Realisation of man.

22. कृतार्थं प्रति नष्टमप्यनष्टं तदन्यसाधारणत्वात् ।
kṛtārthaṃ prati naṣṭam-apyanaṣṭaṃ tad-anya-sādhāraṇatvāt
*Even though it (*Prakriti*) becomes non-existent for him who has fulfilled its purpose, it continues to exist for others for it is common to all.*
To one who has attained liberation, *Prakriti* ceases to exist, and its purpose has been carried out. But Nature, the phenomenal world, remains a common experience for those who have yet to realise the Self; it continues to exist for them.

23. स्वस्वामिशक्त्योः स्वरूपोपलब्धिहेतुः संयोगः ।
sva-svāmi-śaktyoḥ svarūpopalabdhi-hetuḥ saṃyogaḥ
The purpose of union of Purusha *and* Prakriti *is that the former gains awareness of his true nature and realises the power latent in him and in* Prakriti.
Here Patanjali answers the very basic questions as to why the soul must pass through the trials of worldly existence at all. *Purusha* here refers to the Soul which, though universal, has its individual manifestations. The Soul incarnates in order to experience *Prakriti*, to learn its lessons, and it comprehends and actualises its natural powers.

24. तस्य हेतुरविद्या ।
tasya hetur-avidyā
The cause (of this union) is avidya.
The soul, by its very nature, is eternal, omniscient and free. But it forgets its divinity through *avidya*, ignorance, and desires objects of the senses. So it must enter *Prakriti*, incarnating on earth to relearn all that in the material world is temporary and wrought in pain. This lesson is learned in time, depending on the desire for liberation, and the Soul returns to its Source.

25. तदभावात् संयोगाभावो हानं तद्दृशेः कैवल्यम् ।
tad-abhāvāt saṃyogābhāvo hānaṃ tad-dṛśeḥ kaivalyam
With the elimination of avidya *comes the disappearance of the association of* Purusha *and* Prakriti, *and the Seer is liberated.*
Ignorance is the reason for *Purusha* or Soul to associate itself with *Prakriti*. When ignorance is replaced by Illumination there no longer is need for the individual soul to exist in the material world, and it is liberated from the trials of earthly life.

26. विवेकख्यातिरविप्लवा हानोपायः ।
viveka-khyātir-aviplavā hānopāyaḥ
The meaning of destroying avidya *is unbroken discrimination.*
The word *viveka* is translated as discriminative cognition, awareness of the distinction between the Self and the non-Self, and awareness of Reality. So the remedy for ignorance is the constant unwavering awareness that the individual is but Brahman itself. This can only be achieved through many years of conditioning the mind to turn to divine thoughts each time worldly thoughts enter. This is the purpose of meditation and other forms of *sadhana*.

27. तस्य सप्तधा प्रान्तभूमिः प्रज्ञा ।
tasya saptadhā prānta-bhūmiḥ prajñā
Enlightenment is reached through seven steps.

Patanjali begins his explanation of the eight limbs of Raja Yoga. There are seven limbs before the aspirant reaches *samadhi.*

28. योगाङ्गानुष्ठानादशुद्धिक्षये ज्ञानदीप्तिराविवेकख्यातेः ।
yogāṅgānuṣṭhānād-aśuddhi-kṣaye jñāna-dīptirāviveka-khyāteḥ
By practicing the various steps of Yoga, impurities are destroyed and spiritual illumination arises, which develops into awareness of reality.
The theoretical aspects of Yoga have been dealt with, Patanjali now points out that following the practical steps is necessary.

29. यमनियमासनप्राणायामप्रत्याहारधारणाध्यानसमाधयोऽष्टावङ्गानि ।
yama-niyamāsana-prāṇāyāma-pratyāhāra-dhāraṇā-dhyāna-samādhayo 'ṣṭāvaṅgāni
Yama, niyama, *asana,* pranayama, pratyahara, dharana, dhyana *and* samadhi *are the eight limbs.*
Raja Yoga is sometimes called *Ashtanga Yoga*, or the Yoga of eight limbs. They translate, in the order given above, as self restraints, observance, postures, regulation of breath, withdrawal of the mind from sense objects, concentration, meditation and the superconscious state.

30. अहिंसासत्यास्तेयब्रह्मचर्यापरिग्रहा यमाः ।
ahiṃsā-satyāsteya-brahmacaryāparigrahā yamāḥ
The yamas *consist of non-injury, truthfulness, non-stealing, continence, and non-acquisitiveness.*
The *yamas*, or abstentions, make up the most basic of all spiritual practices. They are the injunctions common to every religion. These forms of self-restraint purify the individual and eliminate all of one's negative influences on others and environment.

Violence to others, whether in thought, word or deed, must be avoided. Non-injury means more than refraining from inflicting physical pain. Mental pain can be far more devastating. When one is established in complete harmlessness, even wild animals will approach in peace.

The function of truth is to maintain harmony through trust. It is better to be silent than to tell a truth that will cause pain or that springs from a wrong motive. A truthful person has power, for what he says comes to pass, and his word becomes law.

Brahmacharya, sexual abstinence, is necessary for rapid progress on the spiritual path. When sexual energy is under control, 99% of one's spiritual life is under control. This is very difficult, for, next to breathing, it is the body's strongest impulse. Be humble, pray for strength, and be regular in discipline, which will flatten out the sexual thought waves. With continence comes spiritual power. Ten months of control brings tremendous energy, and the chaste mind develops enormous willpower.

It is wise not to acquire possessions, for they often have strings attached, and tend to make the owner dependent. A person who has possessions is a prisoner of those objects, and must expend energy and time caring for them. The man who owns and desires nothing is absolutely free. Possessions satisfy the body, encouraging identification with it, and tend to muddy the mind.

31. जातिदेशकालसमयानवच्छिन्नाः सार्वभौमा महाव्रतम् ।
jāti-deśa-kāla-samayānavacchinnāḥ sārva-bhaumā mahā-vratam
These (abstentions) are not limited by social structure, location, time or circumstances, and they constitute the great (universal) vow.
These abstentions are universal, and are meant to be practiced at all times, regardless of the situation. Any inconvenience or pain that accrues as a result of their practice should be accepted as the result of karmic obligation.

32. शौचसन्तोषतपःस्वाध्यायेश्वरप्रणिधानानि नियमाः ।
śauca-santoṣa-tapaḥ-svādhyāyeśvara-praṇidhānāni niyamāḥ
The niyamas *consist of cleanliness, contentment, austerity, self-study and self-surrender.*
The *niyamas* are observances which cultivate positive qualities. They involve purification, stilling the mind, self-discipline,

inquiry into the nature of the Self, and surrendering the personal will, or ego, to the Supreme will.

Aside from cleanliness, one should cultivate indifference toward the body. Cleanliness means internal as well as external purification. A proper diet based on vegetarianism and natural foods, specialised yogic cleansing techniques, and the Yoga exercises keep the body internally pure and free from obstructions. Cleanliness also extends to the mind. Only when it is purified of all dross can it be a pure mirror for the reflection of the self.

Laughter comes from stimulation, but a smile comes from inner peacefulness. Satisfied with itself, the mind needs nothing else for its contentment, which grows in proportion to awareness of the inner self. The mind should not be affected by external objects. They may be possessed, but with detachment. Do not let them possess the mind.

Austerity means curtailing the insatiable demands of the senses. Drink water instead of coffee, practice silence instead of talking, control greed by eating bland food, and counteract sleep by getting up early. When the mind learns that its demands for pleasure will not be met through the senses, it stops its useless wandering and turns inward. Control of the senses clears the way for such powers as telepathy and clairvoyance.

Study of spiritual works and the scriptures helps to keep a person on the right path. Books alone, however, can only take one so far, and can lead to intellectual pride. Surrender to the will of God is necessary, for ultimately everything depends upon His grace.

33. वितर्कबाधने प्रतिपक्षभावनम् ।
vitarka-bādhane pratipakṣa-bhāvanam
When negative or harmful thoughts disturb the mind, they can be overcome by constant pondering over their opposites.

The yogi is ever alert, always watching his mind. When he sees useless thought waves arising, he immediately replaces them with positive thoughts, thus creating new mental habits that are conducive to spiritual growth.

34. वितर्का हिंसादयः कृतकारितानुमोदिता लोभक्रोधमोहपूर्वका मृदुमध्याधिमात्रा दुःखाज्ञानानन्तफला इति प्रतिपक्षभावनम् ।
vitarkā hiṃsādayaḥ kṛta-kāritānumoditā lobha-krodha-moha-pūrvakā mṛdu-madhyādhimātrā duḥkhājñānānanta-phalā iti pratipakṣa-bhāvanam
Negative thoughts and emotions, such as violence, whether committed, abetted, or caused through greed, anger or delusion, and whether present in mild, medium or great intensity, result in endless pain and ignorance. Thus there is the necessity for pondering over the opposites.
All thoughts, emotions and actions that are in the opposition to the basic tenets of the *yamas* and *niyamas* bring about the Karma of further pain and ignorance. This is true whether the action is actually carried out, remains in thought form, or is incited in others. Whatever the cause, whatever the degree of involvement, Karma is still incurred, That is why it is necessary to substitute positive and sublime thoughts the moment negative ones are caught arising in the mind.

35. अहिंसाप्रतिष्ठायां तत्सन्निधौ वैरत्यागः ।
ahiṃsā-pratiṣṭhāyāṃ tat-sannidhau vaira-tyāgaḥ
When non-violence is firmly established, hostility vanishes in the yogi's presence.
One who is firmly rooted in non-violence radiates this conviction to others. He is so powerful that not even violent thoughts can exist in his presence.

36. सत्यप्रतिष्ठायां क्रियाफलाश्रयत्वम् ।
satya-pratiṣṭhāyāṃ kriyā-phalāśrayatvam
When truth is firmly established, the yogi attains the result of action without acting.

The words of a person who has practiced truth to the highest degree will manifest, for the words of such a person reflect the Truth of *Atman*.

37. अस्तेयप्रतिष्ठायां सर्वरत्नोपस्थानम् ।
asteya-pratiṣṭhāyāṃ sarva-ratnopasthānam
When non-stealing becomes firmly established, all wealth comes to the yogi.
The more a yogi flees from material objects, the more they seem to come to him. The purpose of this natural law is twofold. The first is so that he may be tested and confirmed in his renunciation. The second is so that he, as a wise person, may appropriately dispense the wealth to benefit mankind.

38. ब्रह्मचर्यप्रतिष्ठायां वीर्यलाभः ।
brahmacarya-pratiṣṭhāyāṃ vīrya-lābhaḥ
When brahmacharya, or sexual continence, is firmly established, vibrant vitality is gained.
When sexual energy is sublimated and preserved it is converted into *ojas*, or spiritual energy. This *ojas* is such a radiant force that it uplifts all who come into contact with the *brahmachari*.

39. अपरिग्रहस्थैर्ये जन्मकथन्तासंबोधः ।
aparigraha-sthairye janma-kathantā-saṃbodhaḥ
When non-acquisitiveness is established, an understanding of the purpose of birth is gained.
When the yogi no longer desires to have possessions he frees himself from the material world. This gives him a perspective of the purpose of his birth, both in this life and in past ones. He gains comprehension of the law of Karma and understands what lessons remain to be learned before attaining Realisation.

40. शौचात्स्वाङ्गजुगुप्सा परैरसंसर्गः ।
śaucāt svāṅga-jugupsā parair-asaṃsargaḥ
From purification comes disgust for one's own body and a disinclination to come into physical contact with others.

Cleanliness, both internal and external, and mental purification help to turn the mind toward the Divine. Through purification one sees quite clearly that beauty is only skin-deep and that real beauty exists in the spirit only. When the body is kept immaculately clean, it becomes more easily apparent that it is but an instrument for carrying out the work of advancing toward God-Realisation.

41. सत्त्वशुद्धिसौमनस्यैकाग्र्येन्द्रियजयात्मदर्शनयोग्यत्वानि च ।
sattva-śuddhi-saumanasyaikāgryendriya-jayātma-darśana-yogyatvāni ca
From purification also comes clarity of mind, cheerfulness, one-pointedness, control of the senses, and fitness, for realisation of the Self.
From internal and external cleansing come all of the above, that is, a prevailing sense of *sattwa*, the quality of purity and light.

42. सन्तोषादनुत्तमः सुखलाभः ।
santoṣād-anuttamaḥ sukha-lābhaḥ
From contentment comes supreme happiness.
Man is ever searching for happiness in external objects, but it can only be attained when the mind is satisfied with what has been allotted and is no longer looking. When the mind is stilled and contented, happiness is automatic.

43. कायेन्द्रियसिद्धिरशुद्धिक्षयात्तपसः ।
kāyendriya-siddhir aśuddhi-kṣayāt tapasaḥ
The destruction of impurities through austerities brings about powers to the body and senses.
When austerities, self-imposed discipline, are practiced, great will is developed, and the abilities of the physical body and senses are extended beyond what is considered normal.

44. स्वाध्यायादिष्टदेवतासंप्रयोगः ।
svādhyāyād iṣṭa-devatā-saṃprayogaḥ
Through study that leads to knowledge of the Self comes union with the desired ishta devata.

Intense self-inquiry and study lead one to communion with his personal deity, or *ishta devata*. However a person conceives of God, that is how he encounters Him. This *sutra* also alludes to the use of Mantra. Constant repetition of the name of Deity will bring His grace.

45. समाधिसिद्धिरीश्वरप्रणिधानात् ।
samādhi-siddhir īśvara-praṇidhānāt
From surrender to Ishwara *comes the accomplishment of attaining* samadhi.
Only by surrendering one's will, one's ego, one's life, to God is the superconscious state attained.

46. स्थिरसुखमासनम् ।
sthira-sukham-āsanam
Asanas should be steady and comfortable.
Having thoroughly explained the *yamas* and *niyamas*, Patanjali now moves on to the next limb of Raja Yoga, the asanas, or postures. This is the whole subdivision of Raja Yoga known as Hatha Yoga, which works directly with the *prana* and kundalini, the more subtle energy currents of the body. Hatha Yoga postures, always done in a specific order, massage the endocrine glands and release energy blockages in the system so that a meditative state is brought about physically rather then sitting and watching the mind. Hatha Yoga is best practiced in conjunction with meditation for the asanas are a vital aid, but not the end, on the path to *samadhi*.

It is said that the asana should be steady and comfortable. Whether the posture is a simple cross-legged meditation position or part of a set of Hatha Yoga exercises, it is important that the practitioner not be strained. He should be able to relax in the position, yet hold it perfectly still for a given amount of time. Fidgeting and loss of concentration only waste energy. Just as in meditation, the mind and body must remain one-pointed.

47. प्रयत्नशैथिल्यानन्तसमापत्तिभ्याम् ।
prayatna-śaithilyānanta-samāpattibhyām
Posture is mastered by releasing the tension and meditation on the Unlimited.
There should be no strain, but only a firm and relaxed maintaining of the position. Then with the mind focussed on the Infinite, one's limitations are more easily extended, and the asana is mastered.

48. ततो द्वन्द्वानभिघातः ।
tato dvandvānabhighātaḥ
From that (mastery of asana), no assaults come from the pairs of opposites.
When asanas are mastered, the yogi is not touched by the play of duality. His will and concentration are developed to such an extent that heat and cold, pleasure and pain, good and bad, and all other worldly influences do not touch him.

49. तस्मिन्सति श्वासप्रश्वासयोर्गतिविच्छेदः प्राणायामः ।
tasmin sati śvāsa-praśvāsayor-gati-vicchedaḥ prāṇāyāmaḥ
The next step is pranayama, *which is the control of the inhalation and exhalation of breath.*
The fourth limb of Raja Yoga is *pranayama*, which includes specific breathing exercises for heating and cooling the body, raising its energy levels, or relaxation.

Prana, the vital energy, may be obtained from food and water, but the primary source is the air that is breathed. Control of it is directly linked with control of the mind. Because of its power, the techniques should be practiced under the guidance of a teacher. The awakening of the kundalini as a means of Self-Realisation depends on control over the breath and therefore the *prana*.

50. बाह्याभ्यन्तरस्तम्भवृत्तिर्देशकालसंख्याभिः परिदृष्टो दीर्घसूक्ष्मः।
bāhyābhyantara-stambha-vṛttir deśa-kāla-saṅkhyābhiḥ paridṛṣṭo dīrgha-sūkṣmaḥ
Pranayama *is inhalation, exhalation or retention of breath; it is*

regulated by place, time and number, and (becomes progressively) prolonged and subtle.
Here all the variations in *pranayama* are given, each yielding a different result. With practice, each breath and retention are prolonged and made more silent, and the yogi develops more control and concentration.

51. बाह्याभ्यन्तरविषयाक्षेपी चतुर्थः ।
bāhyābhyantara-viṣayākṣepī caturthaḥ
The fourth type (of pranayama*) goes beyond the sphere of inhalation and exhalation.*
Beyond inhalation, exhalation and retention is the fourth type of *pranayama*, which involves actually directing the subtle *prana*, rather than the breath itself. When this is achieved, the flow of external breathing stops, and the yogi is able to move his *prana* in such a way as to awaken the great psychic force of *kundalini*.

52. ततः क्षीयते प्रकाशावरणम् ।
tataḥ kṣīyate prakāśāvaraṇam
That unveils the light.
The fourth type of *pranayama*, that which activates the kundalini, brings Illumination. It clears the mind so that the Inner Light can shine.

53. धारणासु च योग्यता मनसः ।
dhāraṇāsu ca yogyatā manasaḥ
And makes the mind fit for dharana *(concentration).*
Pranayama is the link between the physical and mental mind—calm, lucid and steady.

54. स्वविषयासंप्रयोगे चित्तस्वरूपानुकार इवेन्द्रियाणां प्रत्याहारः ।
sva-viṣayāsaṃprayoge citta-svarūpānukāra ivendriyāṇām pratyāhāraḥ
Pratyahara *is the imitation of the mind by the senses, which comes by withdrawing the senses from their objects.*

In meditation the mind is withdrawn from external stimulation so that it can be at peace. *Pratyahara*, the fifth limb of Yoga, involves the same thing with the senses. Whatever objects are agitating to the senses are simply eliminated from sensory contact. The eyes do not watch a stimulating film. The ears are not given an opportunity to hear music that raises feelings of discontent. The tongue is given no opportunity to taste food that is detrimental. In this way the mind is much less likely to take on thought forms which are detrimental since the sense organs arise. A good portion of the more difficult aspects of discipline can be dealt with in this way, and the mind is more easily stilled.

55. ततः परमा वश्यतेन्द्रियाणाम् ।
tataḥ paramā vaśyatendriyāṇām
From that comes the highest mastery over the senses.
The senses are a man's connection to physical plane. When it is decided that it is time to transcend the distractions of the the world, the most difficult undertaking is mastery of the senses. Through perfection of *pratyahara* the greatest obstacles to Enlightenment are overcome.

विभूतिपादः Vibhūti-Pādaḥ

Chapter Three: Divine Manifestations of Power

Chapter three of *Raja Yoga Sutras* elucidates the last three limbs of Raja Yoga, *dharana*, *dhyana* and *samadhi*. These three highest levels of meditation practiced together are called *samyama*, which is also explained in detail. Patanjali also describes many of the *siddhis*, or powers, that are attained through the protracted practice of meditation.

1. देशबन्धश्चित्तस्य धारणा ।
deśa-bandhaś cittasya dhāraṇā
Dharana *is fixing the mind on one object.*

The object of *dharana*, concentration, may be external or it may be an internal plexus. It may also be a Mantra. If there is difficulty in keeping the mind within a limited area of focus in the early stages of practice, one may keep it moving within a broader circumscribed area of focus which is narrowed as greater control is gained. When the mind can be limited to one point, it is concentrated.

2. तत्र प्रत्ययैकतानता ध्यानम् ।
tatra pratyayaika-tānatā dhyānam
An unbroken flow of perception between the mind and objects is dhyana, *meditation.*
In meditation the mind is not distracted but holds steadily to the object of concentration. No other thoughts enter the mind.

3. तदेवार्थमात्रनिर्भासं स्वरूपशून्यमिव समाधिः ।
tad evārtha-mātra-nirbhāsaṃ svarūpa-śūnyam iva samādhiḥ
When consciousness of subject and object disappears and only the meaning remains, it is called samadhi.
Samadhi is a merging of the mind into the essence of the object of meditation. Nothing exists but that pure awareness.

4. त्रयमेकत्र संयमः ।
trayam ekatra saṃyamaḥ
(The practice of) these three together is samyama.
When concentration, meditation and *samadhi* flow in an unbroken sequence on one object, the process is called *samyama.* This flow cannot be forced. Any such attempt means that thought waves are being summoned to control thought waves, which is self-defeating, for the aim is to still all thought waves. The ability to practice *samyama* comes from years of practice and purification.

5. तज्जयात्प्रज्ञालोकः ।
taj-jayāt-prajñālokaḥ
By mastering it (samyama) *comes the light of direct knowledge.*

When *samyama* is mastered, higher consciousness is attained. All intuitive knowledge becomes available.

6. तस्य भूमिषु विनियोगः ।
tasya bhūmiṣu viniyogaḥ
Its (of samyama*) application (should be) in stages.*
Even though a person must be highly evolved in order to be able to achieve *samyama*, a caution is still given here that progress should be gradual. *Samyama* is very powerful, and its application requires great wisdom.

7. त्रयमन्तरङ्गं पूर्वेभ्यः ।
trayam-antaraṅgaṃ pūrvebhyaḥ
These three are more internal than the preceding ones.
Dharana, *dhyana* and *samadhi* are internal; they are practices of the mind. This is in contrast to the first five limbs of Raja Yoga which work through the physical system.

8. तदपि बहिरङ्गं निर्बीजस्य ।
tad api bahir-aṅgaṃ nirbījasya
But even these are external (compared) to the 'seedless' state.
In *nirbija samadhi*, mentioned in the last *sutra* of the first chapter, there is absolutely nothing remaining but union with the Lord. So, it is said that *samyama* is but an externalisation in relation to that ultimate state.

9. व्युत्थाननिरोधसंस्कारयोरभिभवप्रादुर्भावौ निरोधक्षणचित्तान्वयो निरोधपरिणामः ।
vyutthāna-nirodha-saṃskārayor abhibhava-prādurbhāvau nirodha-kṣaṇacittānvayo nirodha pariṇāmaḥ
Through the constant replacement of disturbing thought waves by ones of control, the mind is transformed and gains mastery of itself.
Reaching the superconscious state is a matter of practice. If useless thoughts are eliminated the moment they appear, they are gradually weeded out.

10. तस्य प्रशान्तवाहिता संस्कारात् ।
tasya praśānta vāhitā saṃskārāt
Its flow becomes undisturbed through repetition.
Mastery of control of the mind comes through creating new habits. When the *samskaras* of restraint are reinforced often enough, the mind becomes tranquil.

11. सर्वार्थतैकाग्रतयोः क्षयोदयौ चित्तस्य समाधिपरिणामः ।
sarvārthataikāgratayoḥ kṣayodayau cittasya samādhi-pariṇāmaḥ
The transformation (leading to the ability to enter) samadhi *comes gradually through the elimination of distractions and the rise of one-pointedness.*
Both control of the mind, as described in *sutra* nine, and entering *samadhi* are gradual transformations. This is being explained because of the inherent responsibility involved in entering the higher levels of consciousness.

12. ततः पुनः शान्तोदितौ तुल्यप्रत्ययौ चित्तस्यैकाग्रतापरिणामः ।
tataḥ punaḥ śāntoditau tulya-pratyayau cittasyaikāgratā-pariṇāmaḥ
One-pointedness of the mind occurs when the contents of the mind that rise and fall at two different moments are exactly the same.
Vrittis are called thought waves, for they are rising and falling moment by moment. In normal thinking, there are literally thousands of different waves within just a few minutes. As one *vritti* falls, another rises—one after another in succession, for the mind can only have one thought at a time. One-pointedness occurs when the *vritti* that is falling and the *vritti* that is arising both carry the same thought.

13. एतेन भूतेन्द्रियेषु धर्मलक्षणावस्थापरिणामा व्याख्याताः ।
etena bhūtendriyeṣu dharma-lakṣaṇāvasthā-pariṇāmā vyākhyātāḥ
By this (what has been said in the previous sutras*) changes in the form, time, and condition of the elements and sense organs are explained.*

The preceding *sutras* have dealt with the gradual gaining of control of the mind. By mastering the mind, its relation to the elements and sense organs changes. The changes are explained in the following series of aphorisms.

14. शान्तोदिताव्यपदेश्यधर्मानुपाती धर्मी ।
śāntoditāvyapadéśya-dharmānupātī dharmī
There's a substratum that remains consistent through all changes, past, present and future.
All things, whether of the physical or etheric world, have an underlying essence. While they may go through change, as water becomes ice or steam, they still retains their basic Reality.

15. क्रमान्यत्वं परिणामान्यत्वे हेतुः ।
kramānyatvaṃ pariṇāmānyatve hetuḥ
The cause of various transformations is the different natural laws.
Whether change is brought about in the normal course of events, or it is due to the will of the yogi, it still proceeds from natural laws. Science is just beginning to discover and work with the many forces beyond gross physical perception that have been utilised by yogis for many thousands of years.

16. परिणामत्रयसंयमादतीतानागतज्ञानम् ।
pariṇāma-traya-saṃyamād atītānāgata-jñānam
By performing samyama *on the three kinds of changes (form, time and condition) comes knowledge of the past and future.*
Beginning with this *sutra*, the remaining aphorisms in the third chapter deal with the various *siddhis*. While the word *siddhi* is usually taken to mean power, it actually refers to the accomplishments of an advanced yogi. It is of paramount importance that the student understand that yogic powers are not, and should not be, considered a goal in themselves. They are the by-product of the struggle toward God-Realisation. Those who strive for the powers alone are bound to the ego and

eventually suffer because of this lack of purification. There is often a fascination on the part of the beginning student with yogic powers, but this is replaced in time with the understanding that power corrupts, and that these inevitable accomplishments are but distractions and temptations to the sincere yogi.

On the other hand, it is best that it be clearly understood that these *siddhis* do exist. It takes a most highly advanced spiritual person to perform them, yet one who is so near God-Realisation knows that he is wasting spiritual energy and abusing the powers by displaying them to the idly curious. These abilities are due to natural laws, as mentioned in the fifteenth *sutra*, although science has only begun to investigate them. In the past, science has dealt mostly with laws of the physical plane. Yogic *siddhis* work directly with the more subtle and powerful aspects of Nature. Research is now beginning in the West, although Russia and other East European countries have done extensive work in recent years.

In this particular *sutra*, it is explained that knowledge of the past and future are achieved by practicing *samyama* on form, or physical properties; on time, or changing characteristics; and on condition, or the temporary state in which an object exists at any given time. Sometimes this *sutra* is interpreted to mean that one may gain knowledge not of the past and future, but of the *nature* of past and future. In other words, all things must change, and this knowledge is a fundamental attainment because it brings acceptance and contentment.

17. शब्दार्थप्रत्ययानामितरेतराध्यासात् संकरस्तत्प्रविभागसंयमात्
सर्वभूतरुतज्ञानम् ।
śabdārtha-pratyayānām itaretarādhyāsāt saṃkaras-tat-
pravibhāga-saṃyamāt sarva-bhūta-ruta-jñānam
Sound, meaning and corresponding ideas are usually confused together in the mind; but when samyama is performed on the

sounds, their meaning and ideas, comprehension is gained of the sound of all living beings.

This is most easily understood through the use of Mantra, in which constant meditation on the Lord's name brings realisation of His qualities and even the experience of His presence. Generally, however, the *sutra* refers to any word of any language, and even to the sounds of animals.

18. संस्कारसाक्षात्करणात् पूर्वजातिज्ञानम् ।
saṃskāra-sākṣātkaraṇāt pūrva-jāti-jñānam
By perceiving samskaras *comes knowledge of the previous birth.*

When *samyama* is performed on the *samskaras*, or habitual impressions of one's mind, knowledge of past births comes. This is because the Karma that must be worked out in this life depends on the impressions carried over from past lives that were not dealt with at the time.

19. प्रत्ययस्य परचित्तज्ञानम् ।
pratyayasya para-citta-jñānam
(By performing samyama *on) another's mind, its mental images are known.*

20. न च तत्सालम्बनं तस्याविषयीभूतत्वात् ।
na ca tat sālambanaṃ tasyāviṣayī-bhūtatvāt
But other mental factors which are not the subject of samyama *cannot be known.*

21. कायरूपसंयमात् तद्ग्राह्यशक्तिस्तम्भे चक्षुःप्रकाशासंप्रयोगेऽन्तर्धानम् ।
kāya-rūpa-saṃyamāt tad-grāhya-śakti-stambhe cakṣuḥ-prakāśāsaṃprayoge 'ntardhānam
Samyama performed on one's physical body suspends the ability of another to see it; the reflected light (from the body) does not come into contact with another's eyes, hence the power of invisibility.

22. एतेन शब्दाद्यन्तर्धानमुक्तम् ।
etena śabdādyantardhanam uktam

From this can also be explained the disappearance of sound and other physical phenomena.

23. सोपक्रमं निरुपक्रमं च कर्म तत्संयमादपरान्तज्ञानमरिष्टेभ्यो वा ।
sopakramaṃ nirupakramaṃ ca karma tat saṃyamād-aparānta-jñānam ariṣṭebhyo vā
Karma may be either dormant or active; by performing samyama *on both, and through omens, the* yogi *may know the time of death.*

24. मैत्र्यादिषु बलानि ।
maitryādiṣu balāni
(By performing samyama*) on friendliness (mercy, love, etc.), their strengths are gained.*

25. बलेषु हस्तिबलादीनि ।
baleṣu hasti-balādīni
(By performing samyama*) on strengths (of various animals) comes the power of an elephant (or any other species).*

26. प्रवृत्त्यालोकन्यासात् सूक्ष्मव्यवहितविप्रकृष्टज्ञानम् ।
pravṛttyāloka-nyāsāt sūkṣma-vyavahita-viprakṛṣṭa-jñānam
(By performing samyama*) on light comes intuitive knowledge of that which is subtle, hidden or distant.*

27. भुवनज्ञानं सूर्ये संयमात् ।
bhuvana-jñānam sūrye saṃyamāt
By performing samyama *on the sun comes knowledge of the world.*

28. चन्द्रे ताराव्यूहज्ञानम् ।
candre tārā-vyūha-jñānam
(By performing samyama*) on the moon comes knowledge of the stars.*

29. ध्रुवे तद्गतिज्ञानम् ।
dhruve tad-gati-jñānam
(By performing samyama*) on the Pole Star comes knowledge of the movement of the stars.*

30. नाभिचक्रे कायव्यूहज्ञानम् ।
nābhi-cakre kāya-vyūha-jñānam
(By performing samyama*) on the navel center comes knowledge of the organisation of the body.*

31. कण्ठकूपे क्षुत्पिपासानिवृत्तिः ।
kaṇṭha-kūpe kṣut-pipāsā-nivṛttiḥ
(By performing samyama*) on the hollow of the throat comes cessation of thoughts of hunger and thirst.*

32. कूर्मनाड्यां स्थैर्यम् ।
kūrma-nāḍyāṃ sthairyam
(By performing samyama*) on the nerve centers which control* prana, *steadiness is achieved.*

33. मूर्धज्योतिषि सिद्धदर्शनम् ।
mūrdha-jyotiṣi siddha-darśanam
(By performing samyama*) on the light at the crown of the head comes the power to perceive perfected Beings.*

34. प्रातिभाद्वा सर्वम् ।
prātibhād vā sarvam
Through intuition, all knowledge is available.

35. हृदये चित्तसंवित् ।
hṛdaye citta-saṃvit
(By performing samyama*) on the heart, understanding of the nature of the mind is gained.*

36. सत्त्वपुरुषयोरत्यन्तासंकीर्णयोः प्रत्ययाविशेषो भोगः परार्थात् स्वार्थसंयमात् पुरुषज्ञानम् ।
sattva-puruṣayor atyantāsaṃkīrṇayoḥ pratyayāviśeṣo bhogaḥ parārthāt svārtha-saṃyamāt puruṣa-jñānam
Enjoyment is the result of a lack of discrimination between Purusha *and* sattwa. *Knowledge of* Purusha *comes from performing* samyama *on the interests of the Self rather than on the individual's interest.*

Purusha is absolute Divinity, which is beyond qualities. *Sattwa* is purity, but it remains a quality of Nature. From *sattwa* comes joy and light, but as mentioned previously, these qualities must be transcended for the final merging with the Self. This distinguishes between the purity of the Absolute and the purity of Nature. Is is further explained that knowledge of *Purusha* is gained by perfected meditation on the interests of the Self rather than on individual interests.

37. ततः प्रातिभश्रावणवेदनादर्शास्वादवार्ता जायन्ते ।
tataḥ prātibha-śrāvaṇa-vedanādarśāsvāda-vārtā jāyante
From that comes intuitional hearing, thought, sight, taste, and smell.
Whatever is given up, automatically comes to the renunciate. By performing *samayama* on the interests of the Self rather than on individual interests, all intuitional knowledge becomes available.

38. ते समाधावुपसर्गा व्युत्थाने सिद्धयः ।
te samādhāvupasargā vyutthāne siddhayaḥ
These are obstacles to the state of samadhi, *though they are considered powers to the mind which is worldly.*
Here Patanjali makes it very clear that all of the *siddhis* that have been described above are but Temptation sand distractions from the superconscious state. They only appear attractive to those who are steeped in worldliness, egoism, and the desire for power.

39. बन्धकारणशैथिल्यात् प्रचारसंवेदनाच्च चित्तस्य परशरीरावेशः ।
bandha-kāraṇa-śaithilyāt pracāra-saṃvedanāc-ca cittasya para-śarīrāveśaḥ
When the cause of bondage has been eliminated, the mind can enter another's body through knowledge of its channels.
When the highly advanced yogi has given up attachment to life and has developed intuitive knowledge of the physical body, he gains the ability to use another's body for the purpose of helping and teaching others. This is not the same as possession by the lower astral entities. The perfected yogi acts purely through

the Self, which is common to all, and is thus merely directing Divine energy.

40. उदानजयाज्जलपङ्ककण्टकादिष्वसङ्ग उत्क्रान्तिश्च ।
udāna-jayāj-jala-paṅka-kaṇṭakādiṣvasaṅga utkrāntiś-ca
By mastery of udana *comes levitation and the ability not to come into contact with water, mire, thorns, etc.*
Udana is one of the type of *prana*, which is concerned by the pull of gravity. This power is available to the yogis in the last phases of their earthly lives before merging in the Self. It is not to be confused with 'hopping,' the ability to bounce about a foot above ground during certain powerful *pranayama* exercises. Some spiritual groups teach these exercises to beginners. However it is physically and psychically dangerous and is not recommended because it causes the *prana* to move too quickly in the body. Problems can result for those who have not been practicing asanas and more simple *pranayama* for a number of years.

41. समानजयाज्ज्वलनम् ।
samāna-jayāj-jvalanam
By mastery of samana *comes blazing fire.*
Samana is another type of *prana*, which relates to digestion. From control of *samana* comes radiance.

42. श्रोत्राकाशयोः संबन्धसंयमाद्दिव्यंम् श्रोत्रम् ।
śrotrākāśayoḥ saṃbandha-saṃyamād divyaṃ śrotram
By performing samyama *on the relationship between the* akasha *and the ear, comes superphysical hearing.*
Akasha means ether, or that medium through which sound energy travels.

43. कायाकाशयोः संबन्धसंयमाल्लघुतूलसमापत्तेश्चाकाशगमनम् ।
kāyākāśayoḥ saṃbandha-saṃyamal-laghu-tūla-samāpatteś-cākāśa-gamanam
By performing samayama *on the relationship between the* akasha

and the body and on the buoyancy of lightweight objects comes the ability to pass through space.

44. बहिरकल्पिता वृत्तिर्महाविदेहा ततः प्रकाशावरणक्षयः ।
bahir-akalpitā vṛttir-mahā-videhā tataḥ prakāśāvaraṇa-kṣayaḥ
(By performing samyama *on) mental modifications that are beyond the ego and intellect comes the ability to remain outside the physical body. Hence, all that hides the illumination is removed.*
Man's mind is not limited by his physical body, although he usually thinks it is. But it is the intellect and the ego that bind him there. By practicing *samyama* on those thoughts that are beyond worldly imagination, the yogi connects with Universal Mind, and his own mind is not bound by time, space or causation. All ignorance disappears.

45. स्थूलस्वरूपसूक्ष्मान्वयार्थवत्त्वसंयमाद् भूतजयः ।
sthūla-svarūpa-sūkṣmānvayārthavattva-saṃyamād bhūta-jayaḥ
By performing samyama *on the elements on their gross, constant, subtle, pervasive and functional states, they can be controlled by the yogi.*

46. ततोऽणिमादिप्रादुर्भावः कायसंपत् तद्धर्मानभिघातश्च ।
tato 'ṇimādi-prādurbhāvaḥ kāya-saṃpat tad-dharmānabhighātaś-ca
From that (ability to control the elements) come the eight siddhis, *such as making the body as small as possible and the perfection and invincibility of the body.*
Patanjali is referring to what are called the *Maha Siddhis*, or Great Powers. These are attainment of: 1) minute size, 2) colossal size, 3) weightlessness, 4) great weight, 5) any desire or knowledge, 6)) entering the body of another, 7) unhampered will, and 8) Divine Power.

47. रूपलावण्यबलवज्रसंहननत्वानि कायसंपत् ।
rūpa-lāvaṇya-bala-vajra-saṃhananatvāni kāya-saṃpat
Perfection of the body is beauty, fine complexion, strength, and absolute firmness.

48. ग्रहणस्वरूपास्मितान्वयार्थवत्त्वसंयमादिन्द्रियजयः ।
grahaṇa-svarūpāsmitānvayārthavattva-saṃyamād-indriya-jayaḥ
Mastery of the sense organs is attained by performing samyama *on their power of perception, true nature, relation to the ego, pervasiveness and function.*

49. ततो मनोजवित्वं विकरणभावः प्रधानजयश्च ।
tato manojavitvaṃ vikaraṇa-bhāvaḥ pradhāna-jayaś-ca
From that proceeds immediate ability to have knowledge without the use of the senses, and complete mastery over Prakriti.

50. सत्त्वपुरुषान्यताख्यातिमात्रस्य सर्वभावाधिष्ठातृत्वं सर्वज्ञातृत्वं च ।
sattva-puruṣānyatā-khyāti-mātrasya sarva-bhāvādhiṣṭhātṛtvaṃ sarva-jñātṛtvaṃ ca
Only through realisation of the difference between sattwa *and* Purusha *come omnipotence and omniscience.*
In the very final phases of a sage's last life he directly experiences the difference between the quality of purity and *Purusha*. Here, the yogi leaves the realm of *Prakriti*, Nature, and becomes one with *Purusha*, the Universal Soul. Then the powers of *Purusha*, omnipotence and omniscience, are his.

51. तद्वैराग्यादपि दोषबीजक्षये कैवल्यम् ।
tad-vairāgyād-api doṣa-bīja-kṣaye kaivalyam
By non-attachment to even that (the omnipotent and omniscience of Purusha*) comes destruction of the final seed of bondage, and liberation is attained.*
Absolutely everything must be given up in order to reach God-Realisation, even the powers that come with God-Realisation.

52. स्थान्युपनिमन्त्रणे सङ्गस्मयाकरणं पुनरनिष्टप्रसङ्गात् ।
sthānyupanimantraṇe saṅga-smayā-karaṇaṃ punar-aniṣṭaprasaṅgāt
On being invited by a celestial being, the yogi should not feel pleasure or pride, for there is danger of a revival of evil.

The higher the level attained by the yogi, the greater the temptations. Ego is the cause of any attachment or pride that might arise when the yogi attains the ability to commune with celestial beings, and this would be his downfall.

53. क्षणतत्क्रमयोः संयमाद्विवेकजं ज्ञानम् ।
kṣaṇa-tat-kramayoḥ saṃyamād-vivekajaṃ jñānam
By performing samyama *on a moment and its succession comes discrimination.*
The yogi cannot be tempted by celestial beings if he is fully concentrated on the moment at hand. This is what is meant by the phrase 'Be here now.' His full awareness is being applied to each second that passes, so no time is left for temptations and distractions.

54. जातिलक्षणदेशैरन्यतानवच्छेदात् तुल्ययोस्ततः प्रतिपत्तिः ।
jāti-lakṣaṇa-deśair-anyatānavacchedāt tulyayos-tataḥ pratipattiḥ
It (discrimination) also leads to knowledge of the difference between two similar objects, when their difference cannot be ascertained by class, characteristics or location.
Samyama performed moment to moment brings awareness of Reality that cannot possibly be discerned by any ordinary forms of perception. This *sutra* is not dealing with normal differences of objects but in the subtle distinctions of the highest level of *Prakriti* and *Purusha*. Only a liberated sage can see such differences.

55. तारकं सर्वविषयं सर्वथाविषयमक्रमं चेति विवेकजं ज्ञानम् ।
tārakaṃ sarva-viṣayaṃ sarvathā-viṣayaṃ-akramaṃ ceti vivekajaṃ-jñānam
The highest knowledge, born of discrimination, transcends all; it perceives all simultaneously in time and space, and transcends all, even the World process.
When discrimination is perfected, the yogi transcends time, space and causation. There are no barriers for him. All of eternity and

infinity are available to him. This is why he is said to be God-Realised.

56. सत्त्वपुरुषयोः शुद्धिसाम्ये कैवल्यम् ।
sattva-puruṣayoḥ śuddhi-sāmye kaivalyam
Kaivalya *(liberation) is attained when there is equality between* sattwa *and* Purusha.
Liberation takes place when the mind has the same purity as *Purusha* itself. The purified mind recognises its nature as *Purusha*. The essence of this nature is, and always has been, bliss, freedom, peace, Self-sufficiency and perfection.

कैवल्य-पादः Kaivalya-Pādaḥ

Chapter Four: Liberation

The final chapter of Patanjali's *Raja Yoga Sutras* discusses *kaivalya*, liberation or independence. The full-blown develops perfect discrimination, or the ability to distinguish the real from the unreal. He is no longer affected by the three *gunas* of nature, and can distinguish *Purusha* from *Prakriti*.

1. जन्मौषधिमन्त्रतपःसमाधिजाः सिद्धयः ।
janmauṣadhi-mantra-tapaḥ-samādhijāḥ siddhayaḥ
Siddhis *are attained as a result of birth, medicinal herbs, Mantras, austerities or* samadhi.
Siddhis that are brought to present life by birth indicate their attainment in a previous life, but it does not guarantee that the individual is making proper use of them in this life. Those gained through chemical means are not necessarily associated with any level of spirituality at all, and can be easily governed by the ego. *Siddhis* achieved by Mantras, repetition or *tapas*, austerities, are generally of a very high order as long as they are performed for attaining God-Realisation rather than personal or material gain.

Powers that come from *samadhi* are the purest, for they come to the aspirant without being desired. It must be remembered that *siddhis* are not the aim but a by-product of the path of God-Realisation.

2. जात्यन्तरपरिणामः प्रकृत्यापूरात् ।
jātyantara-pariṇāmaḥ prakṛtyāpūrāt
All evolutionary transformations are due to the fulfilling of Nature's tendencies.
All powers come in direct correlation with the evolution of the individual toward perfection through his many incarnations. Any attempt to force their manifestation will stunt spiritual growth. It is man's purpose to achieve Union with the Divine. This is a natural progression which can be aided through self-discipline and self-inquiry.

3. निमित्तमप्रयोजकं प्रकृतीनां वरणभेदस्तु ततः क्षेत्रिकवत् ।
nimittaṃ-aprayojakaṃ prakṛtīnāṃ varaṇa-bhedas-tu tataḥ kṣetrikavat
An apparent cause is not necessarily instrumental in bringing about natural tendencies; it only removes obstacles, as a farmer (clears some stones to create an irrigation passageway).

4. निर्माणचित्तान्यस्मितामात्रात् ।
nirmāṇa-cittānyasmitā-mātrāt
Minds are created only from egotism.
The mind is not the Self. It proceeds out of ego, or separation from the Self, and must be transcended to return to the Self.

5. प्रवृत्तिभेदे प्रयोजकं चित्तमेकमनेकेषाम् ।
pravṛtti-bhede prayojakaṃ cittaṃ-ekaṃ-anekeṣām
Although the pursuits of the many (created minds) vary, they are controlled by the one Mind.
The many individual minds are scattered and pursue various activities, but they are all subordinate to and ultimately under

the control of the one Universal Mind, which is Self, absolute Consciousness.

6. तत्र ध्यानजमनाशयम् ।
tatra dhyānajaṃ-anāśayam
Of these, the mind born of dhyana *is free from past tendencies,* samskaras.
Of the many individual minds, those which are tempered and directed by meditation become free from useless habits and scattering activity.

7. कर्माशुक्लाकृष्णं योगिनस्त्रिविधमितरेषाम् ।
karmāśuklākṛṣṇaṃ yoginas-trividhaṃ-itareṣām
For a yogi, Karma is neither white nor black; for others it is threefold.
For a yogi, Karma is objectively worked out—there is no positive or negative about it. For others it is threefold—black, white and gray—meaning there are subjective reactions to the work that must be carried out, and this in turn creates new Karma.

8. ततस्तद्विपाकानुगुणानामेवाभिव्यक्तिर्वासनानाम् ।
tatas-tad-vipākānuguṇānāṃ-evābhivyaktir-vāsanānām
From these (threefold Karma) is manifested fruition that corresponds to the desires or tendencies.
Each person enters a life situation according to his past Karma. His reaction to the situation is determined by his desires or tendencies. If he wants power or material wealth he will eventually receive them, but he must then suffer the pain that goes with them. If he wants only liberation, he must go through the discipline to achieve it, and that goal will be achieved.

9. जातिदेशकालव्यवहितानामप्यानन्तर्यं स्मृतिसंस्कारयोरेकरूपत्वात् ।
jāti-deśa-kāla-vyavahitānāṃ-apyānantaryaṃ smṛti-saṃskārayor-ekarūpatvāt
There is an immediate succession (desire followed by appropriate karmic situation), that is due to memory and samskaras, *even though it may be interrupted by social class, location and time.*

The law of Karma is absolute. The effect of a desire or tendency must definitely be reaped, although it may be in a different lifetime and under different circumstances. Those who experience what seems to be undeserved suffering are only working out previously incurred Karma.

10. तासामनादित्वं चाशिषो नित्यत्वात् ।
tāsāṃ-anāditvaṃ cāśiṣo nityatvāt
There is no beginning to them (desires), for the will to live is eternal.
This gives a a scope of how long man has been through birth and rebirth. He has been reincarnating as long as there has been desire. It is desire that brings him to the physical plane, and there is no beginning to desire.

11. हेतुफलाश्रयालम्बनैः संगृहीतत्वादेषामभावे तदभावः ।
hetu-phalāśrayālambanaiḥ saṃgṛhītatvād-eṣāṃ-abhāve tad-abhāvaḥ
Desires are held together by cause, effect, support and objects; and when these disappear, so do the desires.
What gives momentum to desires is cause and effects, or past Karma; support, or the activity of the mind which creates them; and the objects of the desires. When these foundations are removed, so are the desires.

12. अतीतानागतं स्वरूपतोऽस्त्यध्वभेदाद्धर्माणाम् ।
atītānāgataṃ svarūpato 'styadhva-bhedād-dharmāṇām
The past and future exist in their own right; the difference in properties are due to different paths.
The world exists apart from man. But it is the various paths of the individual that create what appears to be the different properties and characteristics of the world, separating *Prakriti* from *Purusha*.

13. ते व्यक्तसूक्ष्मा गुणात्मानः ।
te vyakta-sūkṣmā guṇātmānaḥ
They, whether manifest or unmanifest, exist in the three gunas.

The properties or characteristics of the world, as man sees them, are actually manifestations of the qualities of *Prakriti—sattwa, rajas* and *tamas*.

14. परिणामैकत्वाद्वस्तुतत्त्वम् ।
pariṇāmaikatvād-vastu-tattvam
The reality of an object is due to the uniqueness in change (of the gunas*).*
Each object on the material plane can be identified and called a reality because it is made up of its own unique combination of the three qualities of nature, just as any color is a combination of the three primary colors—red, yellow and blue.

15. वस्तुसाम्ये चित्तभेदात्तयोर्विभक्तः पन्थाः ।
vastu-sāmye citta-bhedāt-tayor-vibhaktaḥ panthāḥ
The object being the same, the apparent difference (between two perceptions) is due to different minds' separate paths.
The object remains the same, but when it is perceived by more than one mind, there immediately arise varying views of that object. This is due to the different paths of each individual. The word 'path' alludes to the fact that all are traveling toward realisation of the Self, and it is the individual attitudes or karmic situations that determine how a person sees something.

16. न चैकचित्ततन्त्रं वस्तु तदप्रमाणकं तदा किं स्यात् ।
na caika-citta-tantraṃ vastu tad-apramāṇakaṃ tadā kiṃ syāt
An object is not dependent on one's mind, for it still exists whether or not it is perceived by that mind.

17. तदुपरागापेक्षित्वाच्चित्तस्य वस्तु ज्ञाताज्ञातम् ।
tad-uparāgāpekṣitvāc-cittasya vastu jñātājñātam
An object is either known or unknown to the mind because of the coloring of the mind.
What is perceived or cognized by an individual is entirely dependent upon the orientation and tendencies of that mind and not on the object itself.

18. सदा ज्ञाताश्चित्तवृत्तयस्तत्प्रभोः पुरुषस्यापरिणामित्वात् ।
sadā jñātāś-citta-vṛttayas-tat-prabhoḥ puruṣasyāpariṇāmitvāt
The modification of the minds are always known to the Self due to the unchanging nature of Purusha.
The Soul, *Purusha*, observes all of the changes through which the mind goes because it is the Eternal Witness. All true knowledge exists permanently in the Self, while the mind is constantly being modified by thought waves.

19. न तत्स्वाभासं दृश्यत्वात् ।
na tat-svābhāsaṃ dṛśyatvāt
Nor is it self-luminous, for it is in the realm of perception.
The mind is something that can be perceived as an object, and not the source of knowledge, just as the moon is not a source of light but a reflection of the sun.

20. एकसमये चोभयानवधारणम् ।
eka-samaye cobhayānavadhāraṇam
It cannot perceive two things at once.
Even though thoughts are formed in but a split second, still only one thought-form can exist in the mind at one time. So it is impossible for the mind to be perceiving itself while it perceives something else.

21. चित्तान्तरदृश्ये बुद्धिबुद्धेरतिप्रसङ्गः स्मृतिसंकरश्च ।
cittāntara-dṛśye buddhi-buddher-atiprasaṅgaḥ smṛti-saṃskaraś-ca
If one mind could perceive another, then there would be cognition of cognition, as well as confusion of memory.
The mind can neither perceive itself nor perceive another mind, for if this were the case there would be complete confusion of the knowledge and memory of the different minds. The mind is but an instrument; all knowledge comes from beyond it.

22. चितेरप्रतिसंक्रमायास्तदाकारापत्तौ स्वबुद्धिसंवेदनम् ।
citer-apratisaṃkramāyās-tad-ākārāpattau svabuddhi-saṃvedanam
Knowledge of itself comes through the self-cognition which occurs when the mind is stilled.
Patanjali has thus developed the explanation that the mind cannot perceive itself. It is *Purusha*, the Self, that perceives the mind.

23. द्रष्टृदृश्योपरक्तं चित्तं सर्वार्थम् ।
draṣṭṛ-dṛśyoparaktaṃ cittaṃ sarvārtham
The mind that is colored by the Seer (the Self) and the seen (mind) understands everything.
When the mind is stilled and allowed perception of itself through the Self, knowledge gained by the Self is then also known by the mind. Only then does the mind have full knowledge. Obviously then, it is not intellectualisation but meditation that brings Self-knowledge.

24. तदसंख्येयवासनाभिश्चित्रमपि परार्थं संहत्यकारित्वात् ।
tad-asaṃkhyeya-vāsanābhiś-citraṃ-api parārthaṃ saṃhatya-kāritvāt
The mind, though filled with innumerable tendencies and desires, acts for the Self, for they act in conjunction.
The mind is directly associated with the Self, so it acts for the Self even while it is still full of worldly thoughts.

25. विशेषदर्शिन आत्मभावभावनाविनिवृत्तिः ।
viśeṣa-darśina ātma-bhāva-bhāvanā-vinivṛttiḥ
He who sees this distinction ceases to see the mind as Atma.
Through discrimination, the yogi understands that the Soul and the mind are not the same.

26. तदा विवेकनिम्नं कैवल्यप्राग्भारं चित्तम् ।
tadā viveka-nimnaṃ kaivalya-prāgbhāraṃ cittam
With an inclination toward discrimination, the mind graviates toward kaivalya.

The mind which can distinguish the difference between mind and Atma has the power of discrimination, and moves automatically toward liberation.

27. तच्छिद्रेषु प्रत्ययान्तराणि संस्कारेभ्यः ।
tac-chidreṣu pratyayāntarāṇi saṃskārebhyaḥ
Thoughts that arise as interruptions to discrimination are due to past samskaras.
Before liberation is attained, remaining habitual thoughts and tendencies arise in the mind from time to time to interrupt the growth of discrimination.

28. हानमेषां क्लेशवदुक्तम् ।
hānam-eṣāṃ kleśavad-uktam
Their removal is achieved in the same way as the removal of the afflictions, as previously described.
The methods of the removal of the interruptions of discrimination are the same as for removal of the afflictions, or causes of misery, described in the second chapter, *sutras* 10, 11, and 26.

29. प्रसंख्यानेऽप्यकुसीदस्य सर्वथा विवेकख्यातेर्धर्ममेघः समाधिः ।
prasaṃkhyāne 'pyakusīdasya sarvathā viveka-khyāter-dharma-meghaḥ samādhiḥ
For one who has given up even the desire for the highest state of awareness, and who exercises discrimination, Dharma-Megha-Samadhi *comes.*
Even the desire of liberation must be given up, for it is a *vritti* as is any other desire. With this renunciation and discrimination comes *samadhi* of 'cloud of virtue', *Dharma-Megha-Samadhi*, that which burns the seeds of all past *samskaras*, bringing full liberation.

30. ततः क्लेशकर्मनिवृत्तिः ।
tataḥ kleśa-karma-nivṛttiḥ
From that follows freedom from all miseries and karma.

31. तदा सर्वावरणमलापेतस्य ज्ञानस्यानन्त्याज्ज्ञेयमल्पम् ।
tadā sarvāvaraṇa-malāpetasya jñānasyānantyāj-jñeyaṃ-alpam
Then, with the removal of all distractions and impurities, (it becomes obvious that) what can be known by the mind is miniscule compared to Infinite Knowledge (of Enlightenment).

32. ततः कृतार्थानां परिणामक्रमसमाप्तिर्गुणानाम् ।
tataḥ kṛtārthānāṃ pariṇāma-krama-samāptir-guṇānām
The three gunas, *having fulfilled their purpose, which is the process of change, cease to exist.*
For the person who has transcended *Prakriti*, the qualities of nature come to an end, for they have fulfilled their purpose which is to push him through growth and to create the field for transformations on the path to Self-Realisation.

33. क्षणप्रतियोगी परिणामापरान्तनिर्ग्राह्यः क्रमः ।
kṣaṇa-pratiyogī pariṇāmāparānta-nirgrāhyaḥ kramaḥ
The process of the succession of moments becomes apparent at the end of the transformation (of the gunas*).*
The lessons of the physical plane appear to occur in time, but in fact, they are a succession of separate moments in which there are varying plays of nature's qualities, *sattwa, rajas, tamas*. This is much like a movie in which there appears to be a continuity, but it is only the effect of seeing many single frames in succession. Each frame—each lesson—is an entity, but this can only be seen when the film stops—when the individual is no longer looking through *Prakriti*.

34. पुरुषार्थशून्यानां गुणानां प्रतिप्रसवः कैवल्यं स्वरूपप्रतिष्ठा वा चितिशक्तिरिति ।
puruṣārtha-śūnyānāṃ guṇānāṃ pratiprasavaḥ kaivalyaṃ svarūpa-pratiṣṭhā vā citi-śaktir iti
Kaivalya *is that state in which the* gunas *(attain equilibrium and) merge in their cause, having no longer a purpose in relation to*

Purusha. *The Soul is established in its True Nature, which is Pure Consciousness. End.*

Liberation occurs when the *gunas* no longer have an effect. The three qualities of nature rest in balance, ceasing to go through change, for their purpose has been fulfilled. Then, the yogi can no longer be called an individual, for he is *Purusha* itself.

14

Electronic Meditation

The body is internally associated with the mind; rather, the body is a counterpart of the mind; it is a gross visible form of the subtle, invisible mind. Every change in thought makes a vibration in your mental body and this, when transmitted to the physical body, causes activity in the nervous matter of your brains. This activity in the nervous cells causes many electrical and chemical changes in them. It is thought activity which causes these changes. When the mind is turned to a particular thought and dwells on it, a definite vibration of matter is set up and often, more of this vibration is caused, the more does it tend to repeat itself to become a habit, to become automatic. The body follows the mind and imitates its changes.

—Swami Sivananda
Thought Power

In recent years, with the advent of finer electronic technology, printed circuits, solid-state circuitry, and so on, has come a new and increasingly popular phenomenon known as biofeedback. In the early days of its history, it was pretty much confined to the research laboratories of various medical and psychological institutes. Now, because of advances in electronics, a simple, inexpensive biofeedback monitor can be purchased by anyone.

These machines have become more and more familiar ever since their thrust into the popularity stream of the 1960s. According to Nicholas and June Regush in their book *Mind Search*, 'Biofeedback is one of the more recent and significant advances in medicine. It is being used to learn how to control an array of disorders such as headaches, high blood pressure and poor circulation. Through the use of instruments which record the body's minute electrical signals and feed them back in amplified form through a tone or some visual indicator on the machine, it's possible to be aware of certain changes in the internal body processes, to act on them and change the signal . . . High tones indicate considerable tension, lower tones, more relaxation. The aim is to reduce the tone by relaxing. As you listen to signals and try to relax by giving yourself positive suggestions, you learn to connect the feelings of being relaxed to the corresponding tone. Feeling internal changes as they occur is the key to biofeedback.'

It is important to note here that these machines are used for the purpose of learning relaxation techniques and in no way can they propel one into higher states of consciousness. A journalist reporting on biofeedback instruments claimed he 'was able to meditate to unusual states of intensity' after he had simply 'fooled around with the gadget for about a week to see what it would do.' Although it is conceivable that such a claim is valid, it could only apply to a person who had strong and deep *samskaras*, or a nature inherently suited to deep meditation. The average user cannot expect to achieve such results.

What Is Biofeedback?

Ordinarily, life functions are carried on automatically without the individual's conscious control or knowledge. Biofeedback, stated simply, is a process by which those automatic inner activities are brought to conscious awareness. One of the earliest devices, long before they were used for meditation, was the polygraph, better known as the lie detector. The polygraph has been used for years, not only in psychology but also in the area of physiological research. To use this machine, various receivers are attached to specific areas of the body. As the body responds emotionally and physically to certain stimuli, the sensors pick up these changes and record them on the machine, where they are transformed into a more readily identifiable form, such as lines drawn on a sheet of graph paper.

The pneumatic bellows is the first attachment. This tubular device is strapped across the subject's chest or stomach, and detects changes in the volume of the chest during normal respiration. The respiratory cycle is never constant and can be influenced by a variety of factors, including the emotions. Respiration occurs in a complicated manner in which the brain sends rhythmic impulses to respiratory muscles like the diaphragm or the intracostal muscles. When relaxed, breathing is slow and regular; when excited, it becomes rapid and shallow. Scientists agree with Yoga that there is probably no other bodily function which is so closely connected with the mind and the nerves as breathing.

The second attachment is a wide air bladder which is wrapped around the subject's upper arm or wrist, and inflated. This attachment detects changes in blood pressure and pulse, both of which are intimately connected with the workings of the subconscious.

The third is the galvanic skin response, or general skin resistance, commonly abbreviated GSR. This sensor functions because of the physiological relationship between the sweat glands and a person's emotional level. It has been proved that there is a direct relationship. When a person is relaxed and calm, the sweat glands function minimally and the skin remains relatively dry; yet when he is excited and nervous, the sweat glands become active and the hands become moist. This provides another accurate indication of changes in a person's emotional level.

Two small electrodes are placed on the subject's hand, and a minute electrical current is passed between them. This current is totally harmless; in fact, it is so small that it cannot even be felt. As the surface of the skin becomes more moist or dry, depending on the emotional changes within the subject, a corresponding change in the electrical resistance across the surface of the skin occurs. The machine measures the charge transmitted across the electrodes and compares it to that which was discharged. In this way, it creates a 'normal' or 'average' level of resistance. Athough this varies with each individual, it remains constant during any one sitting. As the subject's skin becomes drier or more moist, this change is registered as a deviation from the normal resistance. The standard polygraph read-out is indicated by means of pen tracings along a moving graph paper. However, on less sophisticated and inexpensive machines, these changes may be indicated by blinking lights or different sounds.

A polygraph is both expensive to own and complicated to operate. It requires a second person to attach the receivers correctly and monitor the read-out. However, the third attachment, the GSR, has been adapted by many companies and put onto the market at reasonable prices. When the individual experiments with biofeedback on his own, one of these portable, compact GSR units is probably what he uses. To use it, one simply attaches two electrodes, one to either of any two fingertips, and turns the machine on. A high-pitched sound indicates mental and physical activity, while a low-pitched sound indicates relaxation. By associating the feelings which accompany the low-pitched sound with relaxation, and attempting to recall these feelings, the subject learns to relax his body and mind.

Almost equally as popular as the GSR is the EEG, electroencephalograph. The EEG, rather than measuring the activity of the body's nervous system, actually measures the electrical output of the brain by means of electrodes placed on the skin around the region of the scalp. The sensors do not deliver any electrical charge but are receivers only. Every brain emits waves of energy, much like radio waves, of which the length and amplitude can be measured. A wavelength in excess of 13 cycles per second (cps) corresponds to the normal waking state, and is called the beta state. A wavelength with 7.5 cps–13 cps is the alpha state, indicating the mind is extremely relaxed or contemplative. The delta state, 3.5–7.5 cps, is a much deeper state than alpha. It is a state at which much creative thought takes place. There is still a good deal to be learned about this state, as well as about the theta state. At 0.5–3.5 cps, theta is the state of deep sleep, where there is no consciousness.

Measurement of Brain Waves

While these various states are based on cycles per second, or length of brainwave, the magnitude of the energy output can also be measured. A reading of 30–40 microvolts is common for experienced meditators, and advanced yogis have recorded mental outputs in excess of 100 microvolts at will in the alpha state. Brainwaves will have an amplitude no matter what the wavelength, or brain state (see graph on facing page).

Beyond Relaxation

Self-awareness is the consciousness or knowledge of one's condition or state of being and of the changes that occur in body, mind and environment. Because the biofeedback machine translates the changes that occur in the body into forms that can

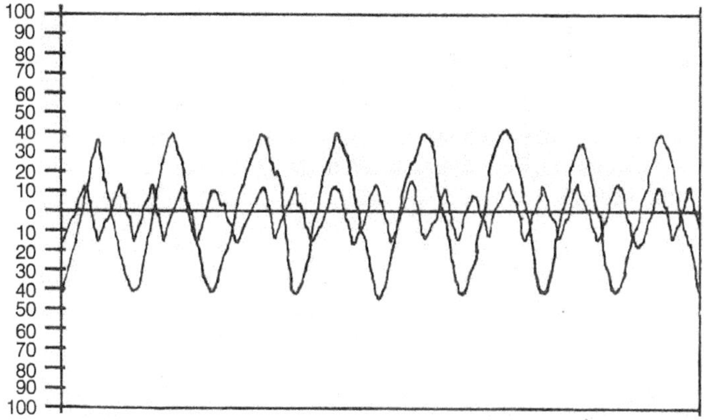

Measurement of Brain Waves
Amplitude (power of brainwaves)
measured in microvolts—one second

Cycles per second—cps
number of cycles (brainwaves) in one second

The shorter line indicates an amplitude of 15 microvolts, an output that is common in a normal waking state. It also registers that there are 18 cycles per second, which is low beta.

The taller line indicates an amplitude of 40 microvolts, which is a considerably high output for most meditators.

be seen or heard, the subject can increase his self-awareness as a by-product of the use of the biofeedback machine. At least up to a certain point.

A trained and alert yogi is completely aware of the various subconscious processes which take place in his mind and body, and is able to control his autonomic nervous system through the power of concentration. The average person cannot do this because he lacks the necessary physical and mental training and discipline. He has not spent the time on internal intunement. For thousands of years, yogis taught and practiced that one can control the involuntary functions of the body through concentration and meditation, while traditional science paid no attention. Now, with the revelations of biofeedback research, many are convinced that the yogic theory is not only true but is also possible for anyone with only a minimal amount of training.

But control of the mind is not that simple. Too often, those who make claims about a fast and easy method have very little knowledge of internal awareness, themselves; nor has their method stood the test of time. Mind control takes not only personal experience, but years of self-study and introspection. Yogis know that the autonomic nervous system, which controls and regulates the involuntary functions of the body, is under the control of the subconscious mind, and, for them, the subconscious is under the control of the conscious mind. A yogi can directly command his subconscious through suggestion and by mentally visualising all the internal functions.

In biofeedback, electronic instruments are used for getting results from the subconscious, but its uses are limited. For example, if a person connected to a GSR machine, for reading skin resistance, is touched, a large change will occur in the instrument read-out. In fact, a substantial reaction can be produced merely by bringing one's hand slow toward the person. The GSR takes its reading directly from the activity of the sweat glands, which themselves are under the control of the sympathetic nervous system. The sympathetic nervous system is that subdivision of the autonomic nervous system which is sometimes called the 'fight or flight' mechanism. In times of great emotional activity, it increases the heart rate and supply of blood to the brain, increases oxygen intake and pumps adrenaline into the blood. The nervous system carries impulses to all internal organs and tissues, not just the sweat glands. If a person becomes excited *in any way*, his sympathetic nervous system activates physical and chemical changes throughout the body. As Barbara B. Brown states in her book *New Mind and New Body*, one of the greatest difficulties with biofeedback research is that its use necessitates control measures to insure that the experiments are not affected by unrelated influences. Ms. Brown goes on to say that this is a very difficult job for the psychologist, as opposed to the physicist or chemist, because those influences which work on human behavior are not as easy to isolate and analyze as those which affect conventional laboratory experiments.

At best, the biofeedback machines are rough indicators of biological functions. Those monitoring instruments used for relaxation or concentration serve as an indirect measure of sympathetic nervous system activity. Biofeedback can only be used to detect unspecified functioning of the autonomic nervous system and to visualise how much one is able to change its activities. Beyond a little relaxation and the reduction of certain metabolic activities like blood pressure, the biofeedback systems can provide little aid to meditation. One should not confuse the inner peace of the superconscious state achieved by yogis with the relaxation achieved through biofeedback conditioning.

In every person there is a certain power of concentration which can be used to attain a relaxed state of mind. One may concentrate on the lights or sounds of a biofeedback monitor, or on a beautiful sunset at the beach, and experience a relaxed state of body and mind in either case. But this must not be confused with delving deeply into the inner being and finding awareness and union with the Source of perfection. Biofeedback can only give quantitative information on certain bodily functions; it does not give any indication of the quality or depth of the meditative experience.

Externals vs Internals

Despite the aid to relaxation which can be gained through experiments with biofeedback machines, their use cannot be substituted for a healthy and balanced lifestyle. A scientific instrument may monitor reduced blood pressure—but it can do nothing for arteries that have been clogged with calcium deposits and cholesterol. It cannot be imagined that the brain is getting more oxygen and nourishment through observation techniques when the body is weak and full of toxins. Scientists are now beginning to understand the relationship between sense organs, like the skin, and the mind. In fact, the whole theory of Western psychology is externally oriented. It is based on the study of observable behavior patterns and the physiological output of the brains of others. This is a far cry from the study of one's own mind, as is done in meditation. Traditional psychological techniques often provide more insight for the psychologist than they do for the individual seeking inner growth.

Many scientists still do not distinguish between brain functions and the mind. Although both the brain and mind have intimate connections with the physical functioning of the body, the mind can exist separate from the body and can have knowledge and experience without sensory contact. The mind, which is located in the astral body, has three functions, which are sensation, thought and volition. It has three mental processes—and these are cognition, desire and will. It also has three aspects, the subconscious mind, the conscious mind, and the superconscious mind. The brain, however, is part of the physical body. It acts as a computer, carrying out the thoughts of the mind and transmitting electrical impulses within the body to maintain and control the different life functions. In this differentiation between brain and mind, biofeedback research is still incomplete.

For a yogi, the sensory experiences of pleasure and pain that come from objects, such as delicious food or soft clothing, are recognised as unreal, for they are a result of the internal state of the mind and are not a quality of the externals. A businessman may go to a party to enjoy himself. He takes pleasure in the conversation, and the food and beverage. Imagine he suddenly hears news that there has been a great upset in the stock market. He will immediately forget his drink and sandwich, not because they have lost their taste, but because he no longer has a taste for them. There is no more enjoyment. The drink and sandwich have not changed. What has changed is the direction of the mind. The mind is now concerned with the value of the stocks which at *this particular time* is an unpleasant subject. Consequently, there is no pleasure in what was pleasurable a minute ago.

A yogi believes that all experiences of sorrow and pleasure, victory and defeat, hot and cold are in the mind only. One should strive to be happy at all times despite external influences. Yoga goes beyond the mind and reaches a state of experience where there are no changing dualities. Traditional Western philosophy has been to accept the sensory experiences as real; traditional Eastern philosophy has been to accept those experiences in relative terms without giving them any permanent value.

Moreover, the scientific conclusions arrived at by studying behavior patterns only bring about false theories, distorted by the limitations of the objective mind and the tools used. Often there are conflicting theories based on experiences of the senses and the information given by the apparatus used. Consider what happens when one hand has been immersed in 110 °F hot water and the other hand, in 35 °F cold water, and after some time both are dipped in 70 °F water. One hand will feel warm and the other hand will feel cold. Simultaneously, there are two interpretations of the same experience for the mind, and neither of them can be called absolutely real.

The yogi studies the subjective state of mind by inner contemplation; biofeedback techniques use conditioning to observe changes in observable behavior. The data collected under this latter form of study is subject to individual interpretations, which may not correspond to reality. Consider the story about the professor who was interested in learning 'frog psychology.' He trained a frog to jump using the method of conditioned learning, that is, reward and punishment techniques. If the frog jumped on command, he got a reward of food; if he did not, he received a mild electric shock. After some time, the frog was conditioned to perform just by hearing the command 'Jump!' Then the professor wanted to find out more about frog psychology, mostly, what made the frog jump in the first place. Therefore, he removed one leg from the frog and commanded it to jump. The frog jumped with three legs, though not perfectly. One by one, all the legs were removed and the frog was commanded, 'Jump!' But the frog did not jump; he just sat on the table and croaked. The conclusion which the professor reached was that the frog did not jump because it couldn't hear when all its legs had been removed.

This anecdote indicates the dangers of relying upon individual interpretations of external phenomena. Yoga psychology utilises a different approach. The yogi studies his mind through meditation. This experience, mystical in nature, is very different from the sensory experience. Yogic science is not merely a study of the behavior patterns of mind over matter, but it is a direct perception of life's principles. Eventually, the experimenter, subject and results—knower, knowledge known—merge into one.

Supernormal phenomena take place naturally when, owing to innate faculties or abilities developed through proper training, one functions simultaneously on two planes. The external study of these phenomena along lines of ordinary science can only lead to limited results. Traditionally, science has been involved in a constantly closer examination and analysis of phenomena or sensations. As a result of this analysis, laws are framed and made to agree with the activity of man's thoughts. Human science studies the surface of our sensible world, the surface on which our thought reflects itself. Yogic science studies that force which is at the center of life, and brings a union between the external and internal worlds. It studies the inner thoughts, working from inner planes toward planes nearer the center, getting closer and closer to that Reality from which all life emanates.

Yogic science is not a matter of erudition; its roots lie in action. It must be lived to be learned. It is in oneself, and not in others, that the rich source of spiritual development must be sought. For the true initiate, dogma must be replaced by direct perception or intuitive knowledge of the higher planes. Conditioned learning is but a mechanical means to help concentrate the mind. The techniques used in biofeedback may help one to recognise some facts about mind control, but we must not be deluded by the mechanics of our contemporary society. Machines cannot replace experience; meditation and mind control are experiential. A child can use a calculator to solve all his arithmetic homework, but he will not learn to add. Biofeedback machines will give rough quantitative feedback to one's initial efforts to control the mind, but one can learn meditation only by practice of attunement to the inner Self, not to a machine.

15

Obstacles to Meditation

Watch your mind very carefully. Be vigilant. Be on the alert. Do not allow the waves of irritability, jealousy, hatred and lust to disturb you. These dark waves are enemies of peaceful living, meditation and wisdom. To some it is very difficult to keep the mind unruffled and pure, the causes being deep-rooted worldly Samskaras, *unfavorable surroundings, and the predominance of extrovert tendencies. To some, of course, evil thoughts are not a problem at all. They appear occasionally as a passing phase without doing much havoc. The very fact that evil thoughts give you mental suffering is a sign of spiritual progress; for many do not have that much of sensitiveness.*

—Swami Sivananda
Religious Education

The obstacles and stumbling blocks on the path toward Realisation can be easily overcome once an intelligent and comprehensive understanding of them has been reached. It should always be borne in mind that failures are but stepping stones to success. Just as a pilot guides a ship along a dangerous coastline having knowledge of its reefs, so the aspirant is guided through the ocean of spiritual endeavor by knowing about the various obstacles and the methods of overcoming them. One must train the mind properly and not be discouraged, for the journey to perfection was never completed overnight.

Cessation of Practice

The mind wants variety in the practice of meditation as much as it wants variety in anything else. It rebels against monotony. When this happens, the student can give the mind a little relaxation and variety by changing the schedule of the practice, but it should never be given up completely. Cessation of practice is a grave mistake; *sadhana*, spiritual practice, should never be given up under any circumstances. The beginner, fun of enthusiasm and zeal, often hopes to acquire psychic powers in short time. When he does not achieve them, he becomes discouraged and wants to give up. He may lose faith in the efficacy of his practice and, often, even considers forgetting about it completely. The practice of meditation must be continued, but without any expectation. Growth comes, but it is gradual. Sincerity, regularity and patience will insure eventual advancement.

Health and Diet

This body is the only vehicle man has for attaining Self-Realisation, and as such it is best kept strong and healthy. Just as the axe must be kept sharp to cut a tree, so the goal can be reached sooner when the body is in excellent condition. A man may practice Yoga, or any other discipline or religion, and die before attaining perfection. Then he is born in another life, practices for some years more and dies again. In this way, much time is lost in recurring birth and death. Although one should not be attached to the body, it is essential that it be kept strong, clean, and able to withstand rigorous practice.

A healthy mind is also important. Because body and mind are intimately connected, it is important to maintain a cheerful frame of mind at all times. Cheerfulness and good health walk hand in hand. The wise aspirant keeps his body healthy with regular exercise, Yoga postures and breath control, a moderate diet, rest, and plenty of fresh air. One should avoid drugs and medicines as much as possible and, when necessary, resort to natural cures.

At the other extreme, there are some aspirants who refuse to take medicine even though they are seriously ill. These people necessarily torture the body; they allow disease to strike deep and ruin their health. Soon they become physically unfit to continue their practice. It is much better to take medication for a couple of days and resume practice quickly than to allow a disease to reach advanced stages, thereby causing great difficulty and delay in resuming regular practice. It is worth noting that the most effective cure for many ailments is fasting, during which the digestive system is given a rest, and poisons are eliminated from the body.

Just as clouds screen the sun, the clouds of sickness screen one from continued practice and self-discipline. Even if seriously ill, *Japa* and light meditation can still be practiced. Meditation is the best medicine for any disease, for it energises and purifies every cell and tissue in the body.

Improper diet is another hindrance to spiritual progress. All foods have distinct energies. Just as the physical body is formed from the gross physical portion of the foods that are eaten, so the mind is formed from the more subtle portions. If the food is impure, the mind also becomes impure. Cigarettes, liquor, narcotics, and stale or aged food are most detrimental. Meals should be simple, light and nutritious. The processed, adulterated preparations found on many supermarket shelves have no place in a yogic diet.

Many people eat far more than is necessary, merely out of habit or for sense gratification. An immoderate diet is the cause of the great majority of diseases encountered in modern society. If one is suffering from stomach ache or the inevitable sleepiness caused by overloading the stomach, then meditation is impossible. It is important not to eat for two hours before practicing meditation. If meditation is practiced in the early morning hours, the evening meal should be light.

Moderation is the keynote in one's daily habits. The body may become more susceptible to disease because of too much or too little sleep, eating the wrong foods, exposure to crowds, laborious mental work, excessive sexual activity, or lack of regular exercise. If a student of meditation becomes sick, he may be inclined to blame the practice rather than his own indiscretions and excesses. The mind is always looking for an excuse to avoid discipline, but it must never be stopped, even for one day. Listen to the inner voice of the Self rather than to the complaints of the mind.

Laziness and Sleep

Laziness, drowsiness and sleep are universal obstacles on the spiritual path, and sleep is the most powerful. Like food, it has become an overindulged habit of long standing for most people. However, the amount of sleep necessary can be cut down drastically through regular practice of meditation. Sleep is a psychological need and may be reduced gradually and slowly. The brain needs rest for only a short time every day; if denied, there is no doubt that one feels tired and is incapable of either working or meditating. Through the various yogic practices, a calm and steady mind is developed. Energy is no longer wasted on emotions and useless desires. The mind spends more time in a relaxed state, so it does not require great amounts of rest. One will have more and more time for *sadhana* once a new and more pleasant pattern has been established.

Often during meditation one will begin to wonder if the mind has slipped into its old habit of sleeping or if meditation is actually occurring. This can be easily determined for during meditation the body feels light and the mind is cheerful, while during sleep the body and eyelids are heavy and the mind is dull. If sleep does become a problem during meditation, splashing cold water on the face, doing breathing exercises, or standing on the head for five minutes will return the mind to an alert state.

Lethargy and depression often afflict the beginner in meditation. Sometimes the cause is physical, such as poor eating habits, indigestion, bad company or poor weather. When this is the case, the cause should be removed, or perhaps a change of physical activity substituted.

Lethargy frequently sets in when the student's life is too unbalanced. Only a very small minority are fit for full-time meditation; others must lead a controlled and balanced life. Young students, full of enthusiasm and ideas of independence and romanticism, need to regulate their energies. Instead, they sometimes disdain discipline and wander from one teacher to another. Sitting cross-legged for half an hour, they mistake lethargy for purity, assume they are beyond doing service for others, and imagine that Realisation has been achieved. Or having become bored, some have turned to drugs to supply a poor substitute for the experience they could not find. A serious student, however, establishes for himself a daily program of meditation, exercise and study. If lethargy becomes an obstacle, some brisk work or charitable activity vigorously pursued will rectify the situation. Physical activity provides the necessary balance for the practice of meditation, and hard work should be an integral part of each day's discipline.

Complications of Daily Life

Unfavorable environments, uncongenial atmosphere and other obstacles do not necessarily lead to defeat of one's efforts. Rather, they can serve as trials and aids in the development of such strong powers as discrimination, empathy, will and endurance. The struggle through difficult situations brings rapid progress.

On the other hand, undesirable company is highly disastrous, for such contact fills the mind with useless ideas. To avoid being pulled into negativity, the meditator should protect himself carefully from any distracting influences. People who lie and steal, or are greedy, or indulge in backbiting and pass the time with idle gossiping have no place in the life of a spiritual person. The healthiest approach is to strictly avoid them.

The term undesirable company includes more than just people; it's anything that gives rise to negative thoughts or vibrations. Raucous surroundings, books and songs that create discontent, movies and television programs centering on violence and sensuality, all lead the mind astray and fill it with desires it would not normally have. One should even consider curtailing the reading of newspapers, for their intent as well as effect is to tantalise the mind with waves of unrest and sensationalism. All these distractions draw the mind outward rather than focus it inward. They foster the illusion that this world is a solid reality and obscure the Supreme Truth which underlies all names and forms.

The world is full of avarice, hypocrisy, flattery, untruth, double-dealing and selfishness, and those who profess to be friends are often one's greatest enemies. Beware of self-proclaimed friends who come for money and other comforts when circumstances are affluent, then disappear when the tide has turned. These fair-weather friends give their own brand of advice, waste precious time in useless chatter, and pull one off the spiritual path and down to their own level. Of course, most people do not like to think that this is true. Most would like to feel that their relationships are based on selfless love, but in fact many are based on the fear of being alone and the desire for diversion. One should cut off connections that are not beneficial and trust only the Inner Voice that dwells in one's heart. Associate only with those whose own aspirations for perfection are uplifting and encouraging.

Useless Conversation

Spiritual power is lessened by many bad habits, not the least of which is useless and excessive talking. Diarrhea of the tongue wastes much energy that could be utilised for personal development. Too much talking makes a person restless and unfit for the practice of meditation. The wise speak only a few words, and those only when necessary, for by their very economy they will carry the most force. To help calm, center, and discipline the mind, *mouna*, silence, can be observed for about two hours daily, in addition to the time spent in meditation. In order to be of the most practical value, silence is best practiced at those times when there is great temptation to talk.

People of an intellectual nature are often prone to unnecessary discussions and controversies. A person who is unable to remain quiet easily becomes involved in heated debates, too many of which lead to enmity, hostility, and energy drain. When intellectual reasoning, which is normally concerned only with investigation of the physical plane, is used for metaphysical inquiry, it can lead the student to the threshold of intuition. Past this point, however, it is of no use, for transcendental matters are beyond the reach of reason. Then one must give up arguing, become silent, and look within.

Fault-finding is, likewise, a most detrimental habit. The mind of the person who is always poking his nose into the affairs of others is always outgoing and out of controL No one can be introspective when the mind is engaged in activity of this sort. Diligent application to spiritual practice allows no time for managing the affairs of others. Forget the shortcomings of other people and work to improve yourself first. Life is precious and short. No one knows when it will be taken away. Every minute should be used for much higher purposes than gossiping and judging others.

Self-justification is another behavioral weakness to be overcome, along with its associated characteristics—self-assertion, obstinacy, dissimulation and lying. Once these weaknesses become established in the framework of the personality, it is very difficult to eliminate them, for the ego never admits its own faults. One lie covers another in an endless succession of vain attempts at self-justification. Improvement comes quickly and rapidly only when one learns to readily admit one's faults, mistakes and weaknesses.

Petty-mindedness is closely associated with backbiting and trying to pull down other people. All evils are caused by jealousy and ignorance. They can easily be combated and eradicated by always rejoicing in the welfare of others.

Uprooting the Ego

It must be evident by now that meditation involves far more than sitting with eyes closed in concentration. It demands rigorous introspection and an overhauling of one's personality, life patterns and values. Behavior correction and the uprooting of weaknesses are relatively easy adjustments to make. The more serious obstacles to meditation and spiritual practice, which lie deep within, are the emotional imbalances and personality defects that nurture outward bad habits.

The petty obstinate egoism behind the mask of human personality is one of the biggest hurdles to overcome, for it veils the divine Self, supports surface thoughts, and perpetuates its own habitual feelings and actions. This lower self-arrogating nature must be whittled down, for if it persists in retaining its limited, false values, no amount of *sadhana*, spiritual practice, will bear fruit.

Too often a student says he wants to study and practice meditation, yet he is unwilling to eradicate the lower nature and change old habits. Clinging to them, he refuses even to admit the need for change. This type of student will never make any real progress because brief spiritual experiences, without radical transformation of the lower nature, lead nowhere.

It is not easy to change deeply ingrained habits, and the sincere beginner often feels helpless against them. By regular *sadhana*, untiring selfless service, association with spiritually minded people and strong determination to eradicate egoism, a powerful but selfless will is developed. One must introspect and discover all weaknesses and defects. This is considerably easier for those living under the guidance of a guru, who points them out and indicates suitable ways to eradicate them. The transmutation of lower nature to higher nature demands full and heartfelt dedication. To make the transition to the highest goal, a willingness to surrender the ego is needed. Then only, with persistent endeavor, real change comes about.

Sometimes the old personality attempts to re-establish itself, even after years of meditation. Obstinately self-assertive, and supported by the lower mind and will, it can make the aspirant incorrigible, unruly, arrogant and impertinent. Identifying with the ego, he breaks all rules and disciplines, revolts against all things, and is ever ready to fight with those who are unwilling to accept his views and opinions.

The ego cherishes its own ideas and impulses, and refuses to follow beneficial instruction. Dissimulation, hypocrisy, exaggeration and secretiveness are the traits of a dominant ego.

One who is in its grip may even lie in order to cover up his errant ways, to maintain his position, and to indulge in his own ideas and bad habits. Wallowing in self-justification, and denying faults and defects, the student may be unaware of the effects of his actions, for the intellect has been clouded by impurities. Not knowing what he means and not meaning what he says, he is too self-willed and self-satisfied to see the error of his ways.

One who is not straightforward and cannot keep discipline or open his heart to others, cannot be helped by any teacher. Nothing can help one who deliberately shuts his eyes to the Truth. Such an aspirant, instead of making progress along the path, remains stuck in the mire of his own creation.

If there is any recognition that something is wrong, the slightest attempt to improve, or even a slightly receptive attitude, then the errors can be corrected. One who is frank with his teacher and himself, begins to realise the nature and source of his defects; he is soon on the way to improving his life.

Power, name, fame and wealth, which strengthen and reinforce the ego, are all renounced and sacrificed by the serious aspirant. For westerners who are taught to revere individuality, the need to surrender the ego is especially difficult to understand. But there are no half-measures; discipline of senses and constant meditation must be cultivated in order to make progress.

The Emotions

Of all the emotional barriers the most devastating is anger, the greatest enemy of peace, for it is the most negative. It is a modification of lust for when one's desires are not gratified, one becomes angry. The mind then becomes confused, memory and understanding are lost, and things are said and done without awareness or control. Anger does great damage to one's own physical and psychic bodies, as well as those of others. The whole nervous system is shattered by one fit of anger. Occasionally a spiritual teacher expresses a little anger outwardly in order to correct a student, but this should not be confused with an emotional outburst. Though he may appear hot and indignant on the outside, the true master remains cool within, for his motive is the growth of his disciples. Only when anger is the outcome of selfish or petty motives is it wrong.

Anger is very difficult to control when it has been allowed to grow and become habitual. It is much more easily controlled when it is a small ripple in the subconscious mind. One should watch the mind carefully for any signs of irritability; then control is no problem. Frequent irritation over trifling matters is a sign of mental weakness. This can be overcome by carefully developing its positive counter-force, the virtue of patience.

Just as heat and light can be transformed into electricity, anger can be transformed into spiritual energy. All vices, unwanted qualities, and wrong actions stem from anger; when anger has been controlled, all others die by themselves. This is half the student's battle.

Anger gains strength with repetition, and in checking it one gradually strengthens the will. The practice of meditation itself helps to eliminate the causes of anger, for it slowly changes values and perspectives. By learning to remain silent even in the face of insult and abuse, it becomes easier to check the impulses and emotions before they take form. Always speak moderately, and if there is a possibility of a burst of anger during conversation, stop speaking and do something else. Words should be soft and arguments hard, for if the words are hard they will create discord. Drinking cool water or taking a brisk walk are excellent aids in combatting the onslaught of anger, as is *mouna*, the practice of maintaining silence for long periods of time. Smoking, eating meat and drinking are irritants which aggravate the problem, and are best avoided.

Fear is the most debilitating emotion. The student must always be willing to risk everything including his very life in the quest for spiritual perfection. Timidity makes one absolutely unfit for the spiritual path. A criminal who is fearless, and totally indifferent and unattached to his body, is more fit for Realisation than a nervous or overcautious person. His energies only need to be rechanneled. Fear is a product of the imagination, but nonetheless it assumes real forms, and can be troublesome in a variety of ways.

Fear manifests in many shapes, such as: fear of death, fear of disease, fear of solitude, fear of company. Taking hold of the mind, imagination works havoc and makes one prey to all sorts of fear. Fear of public criticism especially stands in the way of a student's meditative progress. Yet even in the face of persecution, one must stick to his convictions. Then only can one grow. Fear can be overcome by self-inquiry, devotion to a higher cause, and the cultivation of the opposite of fear, courage. Positive always overcomes negative, and courage always overcomes timidity.

Discouragement

The meditator sometimes begins to doubt the existence of an Absolute Source, his own capacity to succeed in Realisation and the efficacy of his practice. Lack of faith is discouraging and is a dangerous obstacle in the path of personal development. when these thoughts crop up, the student is in danger of slackening his efforts and giving up his practice altogether. This would be a great mistake. It must be remembered that there will always be periods when one's progress is more or less apparent. Whenever doubts arise, the student should at once seek the company of spiritually elevating people and remain under their influence for some time. Conversing with people of firm and clear faith and practice clears all doubts.

When a student's expectations are too unrealistic, doubt is eventually bound to raise its head. The beginner often thinks that kundalini will be awakened within six months, and he will thereupon blossom out with clairvoyance, clairaudience, thought reading and flying in the air. Many strange ideas are sometimes entertained, and when these expectations fail to materialise, doubt sets in. This confusion can be removed by study of religious books, right inquiry and reasoning, in addition to spiritual company. Doubt will rise up again and again to mislead the aspirant. It must be destroyed beyond recovery by certainty of conviction, unshakable faith based on reason, and the understanding that difficulties are bound to manifest from time to time. It should always be borne in mind that these are but challenges that help to strengthen the practice.

Loss of the Vital Energy

For serious progress toward the highest goal of Realisation, the observance of brahmacharya is essential. The word brahmacharya comes from Sanskrit and means knowledge of Brahman. It refers to the total control of all senses, and, more particularly, to celibacy. Celibacy is a concept that is almost foreign to the Western mind. It is a difficult one for many to fully understand, especially when people are becoming more comfortable with their own inner feelings and are striving to make their relationships more open and free. But celibacy is an ancient and timeless aspect of all the religious traditions of the world. Each has its group of aspirants who have renounced all worldly desires and sensual pleasures. They are known as monks and nuns, and in the Yoga tradition, as swamis, or *sanyasis*. Although it should not be thought that a purely celibate life is recommended for all, a complete understanding of spiritual life is not possible without a basic knowledge of the practice and purpose of brahmacharya.

It might be said that 99% of the goal of spiritual life has been attained when one has control over sensual experiences. This is difficult, not merely because of the gratification derived from the senses, but because it is the inherent nature of all living things to procreate, to continue the species. The most powerful impulse in nature, after breathing, is procreation. So of all that a yogi must master before he achieves the ultimate goal, control of his sexuality is the most difficult.

Cosmic energy, which forms and perpetuates the galaxies and world, is the same energy which is continuously vibrating in man's body and mind. This life energy, or universal *prana*, manifests on the gross physical level as sexual energy. When it has been controlled and sublimated, it is transformed into *ojas shakti*, or spiritual energy. Sexual energy moves in a downward direction, but *ojas* moves upward away from the sexual centers and is stored in the brain. *Ojas* is the creative power, the vital energy, the vigor in a person who has converted sensuality into spirituality.

In the sexual experience, energy is dissipated and lost. But through brahmacharya, the same energy is preserved. Through constant *sadhana*, spiritual practice, this energy is eventually converted into the most powerful force of all, the kundalini *shakti*. The kundalini lies dormant at the base of the spine in the *muladhara chakra* until it reaches the *sahasrara* at the crown of the head. It is in the rising of the kundalini that the higher meditative experiences occur. If energy is always being dissipated downward in sexual activity, it cannot be stored, nor can it build enough power to push upward through the *chakras*.

Aside from the consideration of kundalini, there are other practical reasons for sublimation of the sexual drive. Celibacy is a form of *pratyahara*, control of the senses. For those sincerely seeking to advance in meditation, total control of all cravings of the body is necessary. A strong will is developed by slowly gaining mastery over the sexual desire, as well as the desire for savory, exotic food, luxurious surroundings, and so forth. As the mind is turned inward, the advanced student gradually ceases to identify with experience of the physical world.

The greatest drive in man is procreation. One can see how powerful it is by the extent to which it has been exploited by the advertising media. There are precious few products that are not sold on the promise that, on one level or another, they will bring sexual fulfillment. The pull to unite with the opposite sex is so strong that it often overpowers all wisdom and reason. But the dedicated yogi cares more for control of the mind than pleasures of the body. Lord Buddha is said to have told his disciples that if there were any other obstacle as powerful as the sexual drive, he could not have reached enlightenment.

Of course, repression of the sexual urge is not suggested, for it would only lead to backlash or ill health. But a gradual reduction in sexual activity helps to develop the will, strengthen the spirit, and turn the mind from external to internal. Its energy can be put to positive and constructive use. This is the nature of sublimation. When the ultimate Union, with the Lord Himself, becomes the most important thing to a person, desire for sexual gratification falls away, for it is an experience far inferior to that of God-Realisation.

The Mind Itself

The mind itself offers many impediments to meditation. In the beginning of practice, layer after layer of impure and negative thoughts arise from the subconscious mind as soon as one sits for meditation. Students occasionally abandon practice because of this without understanding why it happens. There is an old adage that if you kill one mosquito twenty more come to the funeral. Even so, negative thoughts assail and attack with doubled force when the meditator tries to rid himself of them. This is the natural law of resistance.

Eventually they will all perish for negative thoughts cannot stand before positive thoughts. The very fact that undesirable thoughts create a feeling of uneasiness when they arise during meditation indicates growth and maturity, for at one time these thoughts were welcomed into the mind. They cannot be driven out forcibly or suddenly, or they will turn against the meditator with increased energy. They wither away of their own accord when the student persists in his practice with tenacity and diligence.

The mind must be watched, particularly when it is relaxed. The dark waves of irritability, jealousy, anger and hatred are the enemies of meditation, peace and wisdom. They must be countered immediately with positive thoughts, for ill thoughts are destroyed by good thoughts. Just as it is easiest to stop an intruder at the gate, so it is easiest to check a negative thought as soon as it arises. It can be nipped in the bud by sustained *sadhana*, good actions and awareness of the misery which arises from negativity. When the state of purity is attained, the problem no longer exists.

Hatred, like anger, is one of the fiercest foes of the serious student. Like greed or lust, it is insatiable. Though it may temporarily subside, it can burst out again with redoubled force. It is like a contagious disease which infects one person after another. If a father has a quarrel with someone, his children may also hate that person, although he has done them no harm. Contempt, prejudice and ridicule are all various modes of hatred.

If an Englishman hates an Irishman, an Irishman hates an Englishman; if a Catholic hates a Protestant, a Protestant hates a Catholic. Prejudice of this or any other kind must be rooted out vigorously. Prejudiced and bigoted people confine themselves in small circumscribed groups. Because of their jaundiced vision, they fail to see the good in others whom they treat with contempt.

But it is possible to stick to one's own principles and still pay equal regard to the viewpoints of others. Truth is not the sole monopoly of any person, group or spiritual system. Universal peace and brotherhood are possible only when hatred, prejudice and bigotry have been replaced with love. Because its branches go out in so many directions in the subconscious mind, hatred needs prolonged and intense treatment. Constant selfless service combined with meditation for many years will remove this rank weed from the heart.

Infatuation and attachment are serious obstacles because they are subtle as well as powerful. When millions of people are killed during a war, a man does not weep, yet he weeps when his wife dies. This is because infatuation creates the idea of 'mine,' and the greater the attachment, the greater the pain. When a person speaks of 'My wife,' 'My son,' or 'My home,' he reveals an attitude of separation from the rest of mankind. So long as there is identification with the ephemeral physical world, little progress can be made on the path of meditation.

Greed, which is closely linked with infatuation, is insatiable, and it agitates the mind. Even though a man may be a millionaire, he schemes to become a billionaire. Greed assumes various subtle forms. If a man thirsts for name and fame, this also is greed. infatuation, attachment and greed are destroyed by vigorous self-inquiry, prolonged meditation and constant *sadhana*.

Another impediment to meditation is memory or recalling past events. To understand this, assume for a moment that one is meditating quietly in a solitary country setting. If memories of a past holiday in Las Vegas arise and the mind is allowed to dwell on them, for the moment one will actually be living in Las Vegas in a past time. This applies also to daydreams. Looking back to past experience gives life to the memory picture, reinforces it and pulls the mind away from its true nature. A sage never looks back; he concentrates only on identification with the Absolute.

Obstacles for the Experienced Meditator

Pitfalls still await the meditator even after the practice has been well established. The aspirant sometimes becomes puffed up with moral and spiritual pride after acquiring a few experiences or powers. He may separate himself from others and treat them with contempt. This kind of arrogance poses a serious obstacle to Self-Realisation and must be completely removed. As long as there is pride and boastfulness, it is impossible to relinquish the ego and realise Divinity.

Religious hypocrisy, a related frailty, manifests in those who have made some progress but have not yet thoroughly purified the lower nature. Pretending to be what they are not, these people make an elaborate outward show of their vaunted religiosity. For aspirants travelling the spiritual path and dedicating all actions to God, there is no greater crime than using religion to take advantage of trusting people. In fact religious hypocrisy is much worse than ordinary hypocrisy, for the religious hypocrite makes a mockery of spirituality and God. He needs to undergo a long and drastic course of treatment, imposed upon him by somebody else for he himself is too egoistic and devious to apply self-cure or even to want it.

Sometimes during meditation, visions of terrifying forms may appear. Whether projected from the depths of the subconscious or actual materialisations of lower astral entities, they can cause no harm. Appearing simply as a test of strength and courage, they cannot remain in the presence of pure and divine thoughts. The aspirant must stand firm and not let fear or nervousness upset the practice of meditation. Other visions and experiences also come and go, but these are not the goal of meditation. One who attaches importance to them becomes distracted from the path. Avoid all thoughts of these visions; remain indifferent and substitute higher thoughts. The final and true goal of meditation is intuitional and direct experience of the Supreme.

In time, a number of psychic powers also come to the student. They should not be given much thought, however, for there is nothing special or miraculous about them besides their novelty; yogis recognise them as perfectly natural. Just as an aborigine is astonished the first time he sees an airplane, so also most people are amazed and impressed by a display of psychic powers. But powers such as clairvoyance and clairaudience are not worth striving after because far greater illumination and peace are possible beyond them. Furthermore, the desire for them may upset and extinguish a student's spiritual propensities.

If one regularly practices concentration and meditation, psychic powers are bound to come. But they must not be used for selfish or materialistic purposes, for every wrong action will have a deleterious reaction, and misuse results in both psychic and spiritual loss. The powers are strong intoxicants; the intellect becomes turbid and understanding becomes cloudy. The practitioner becomes a victim of his own ignorance.

During meditation practice, the mind can assume various states of quietude and peace which are often confusing or misleading. There is a supersensual bliss that comes with the very lower stages of *samadhi* which once experienced leads the student to imagine that the final goal has been reached. Thereupon he gives up further practice. One should never be satisfied with these lower experiences but continue onward toward the experiences of the ancient sages as described in the Upanishads and other religious texts. Meditation is a lifelong practice, for there will never be a point where there is nothing more to be gained or learned.

At times the mind rests in a silent, neutral equilibrium that is mistaken for *samadhi*, or it lapses into a state of stupefaction following a deep meditative experience. In neither of these cases is there perfect awareness; rather, the mind becomes inert, unfit for active use. Do not be misled by these two states for, when they prevail, the body is light and the mind is dull rather than sharp.

Careful introspection and continued practice helps to transcend these stages.

An intelligent student, who practices meditation daily, learns to recognise the different states into which the mind passes. While the beginner may sometimes find meditation a tedious affair, with advancement more understanding is gained of the mind and its operations; the entire meditative experience becomes very absorbing. More meditation means more gain of mental control and understanding. As control of the mind is gained, a corresponding growth of inner spiritual strength occurs.

There is one last obstacle that all who meditate must face. When all the other obstacles have been overcome by painstaking, dauntless effort, and all the internal enemies have perished, one faces what appears to be a great void. This too must be crossed by the meditator. It is accompanied by an overpowering feeling of being stripped bare and left totally alone. There is nothing that can be seen or heard. The aspirant is beyond seeking solace in others, and confronts the necessity of depending entirely upon himself. Presence of mind is needed at this critical juncture. By drawing courage and strength from within, a triumphant leap to the final goal is made.

Here, set out, are the major obstacles to meditation. A careful study and understanding of them prepares the seeker to face and overcome them. Time and energy should not be wasted. With diligence and determination one can become a spiritual giant. The path of meditation is strewn with difficulties, but each hindrance serves only as a challenge to goad the student on to higher achievements.

16

Experiences in Meditation

This final chapter is excerpted from Swami Sivananda's book Concentration and Meditation. *The experiences in meditation that Master Sivananda describes are his own; but, owing to traditions and true humility he would never admit that he had experienced these various states. Swami Sivananda always wrote from his own experience; he would never discuss that which he had not tested for himself yet he would never describe his experiences in the first person.*

Various Experiences in Meditation

1. In the beginning of meditation, lights of various colours, such as red, white, blue, green, a mixture of red and green lights, etc., appear in front of the forehead. They are elemental lights. Every element has its own hue. Earth has yellow colour. Water has white colour. Fire has red colour. Air has green colour. Space has blue colour. The coloured lights are due to these Tattvas only.

Sometimes a big sun or moon, or lightning-like flashes appear in front of the forehead during meditation. Do not mind these appearances. Shun them. Try to dive deep into the source of these lights.

Sometimes Gods, Sages, Saints will appear in meditation. Receive them with honour. Bow to them. Get advice from them. They appear before you to help and give you encouragement.

In the beginning of meditation and concentration you will see in the centre of the forehead a resplendent, flashing light. This will last for half or one minute and then disappear. The light will flash either from above or sideways. Sometimes a sun of 6 inches or 8 inches in diameter with or without rays will be seen. You will see the form of your Guru or image of worship also.

When you get glimpses of the Self, when you see the blazing light, when you get some other extraordinary spiritual experiences, do hot fall back in terror. Do not give up the Sadhana. Do not mistake them for a phantom. Be brave. March boldly with joy.

2. What sort of dreams do you get? What kind of thoughts arise in your mind as soon as you wake up, when you are alone in the room, when you walk in the streets? Are you able to keep up the same state of mind you have during meditation in a closed room when you walk in the street also? Introspect and closely watch your mind. If the mind is perturbed when you walk in the streets, you are still weak, you have not advanced in meditation, you have not grown in spirituality. Continue the meditation vigorously. An advanced student will have thoughts of Brahman even in dream.

Understand the power of silence. The power of silence is infinitely greater than lectures, talks, orations and discourses. Lord Dakshinamurti taught the four youths, Sanaka, Sanandana, Sanatana and Sanatkumara through silence. The language of silence is the language of God. The language of silence is the language of heart. Sit silently and restrain the mental modifications. Sit silently and send out the inner spiritual force to the whole world. The whole universe will be benefited. Live in silence. Become silent. Rest in silence. Know the Self and be free.

When you sit for meditation in the morning send out your love and peace to all living beings. Say: *Sarvesham Santir Bhavatu.* May peace be unto all: *Sarvesham Svasti Bhavatu.* May prosperity be unto all: *Lokah Samastah Sukhino Bhavantu.* May happiness be unto the whole world.

In the peace all the pains are destroyed; for the intellect of the tranquil-minded soon becomes steady. When the mental peace is attained, there is no hankering after sense-objects. The Yogi has perfect mastery over his reason. The intellect abides in the Self. It is quite steady. The miseries of the body and the mind come to an end.

During meditation you will have no idea of time. You will not hear any sounds. You will have no idea of environments. You will forget your name and all sorts of relationship with others. You will enjoy peace and bliss. Gradually you will rest in *Samadhi.*

In the beginning, the aspirant remains in a state of bliss for some time. He comes down. By constant practice of incessant meditation, he continues to remain in that exalted state for ever. Later on, the body-idea completely vanishes.

When you enter into deep meditation, you will have no consciousness of your body or surroundings, you will have equanimity of mind. You will not hear any sound. There will be stoppage of upgoing and down-going sensations. The consciousness of egoism will also gradually vanish. You will experience inexplicable joy and indescribable happiness. Gradually, reasoning and reflection also will cease.

When you enter the silence through deep meditation, the world outside and all your troubles will drop away. You will enjoy supreme peace. In this silence is Supreme Light of lights. In this silence is undecaying Bliss. In this silence is real strength and joy.

When you practise rigorous meditation, Kevala Kumbhaka or natural retention of breath without Puraka (inhalation) and

Rechaka (exhalation) will come by itself. When Kevala Kumbhaka comes, you will enjoy immense peace and you will have one-pointed mind.

The visions of the Rishis concerning the soul and such other transcendental matters, manifest themselves to one who is devoted to the constant duties prescribed by the scriptures, who is unselfish and who seeks to know the supreme Brahman.

During deep meditation, the aspirant forgets the external world first and then the body.

That feeling of rising up during meditation is a sign that indicates that you are going above body-consciousness. You will feel a peculiar Ananda (bliss) also when you experience this feeling. In the beginning this feeling of rising up will last for a minute only. After a minute you will feel that you have come back to normal consciousness again.

You will enjoy a sort of higher type of indescribable peace during your meditation. But it will take a long time to get real spiritual experiences or merge the mind in your Lakshya or chosen object of meditation or get over body-consciousness completely. Be patient. Preserve. You will succeed.

The attainment of cosmic consciousness is permanent in realised souls. It is like a glimpse in the beginning. Through steady meditation, it becomes permanent or natural.

3. Concentration is fixing the mind on any point, external or internal. During meditation the mind becomes calm, serene and steady. The various rays of the mind are collected and focussed in the object of meditation. The mind is centered on the Lakshya. There will be no tossing of the mind. One idea occupies the mind. The whole energy of the mind is concentrated on that one idea. The senses become still. They do not function. Where there is deep concentration, there is no consciousness of the body and surroundings. He who has good concentration can visualise the

picture of the Lord very clearly within the twinkling of an eye.

Do not try to drive away the unimportant thoughts. The more you try, the more they will return, and the more they will gain strength. You will tax your energy. Become indifferent. Fill the mind with divine thoughts. They will gradually vanish.

All *Vrittis* or mental modifications such as anger, jealousy, hatred, etc., assume subtle forms when you practise meditation. They are thinned out. They should be eradicated in toto through *Samadhi* or blissful union with the Lord. Then only you are quite safe. Latent *Vrittis* will be waiting for opportunities to assume a grave and expanded form. You should be very careful and vigilant.

When your meditation becomes deep, you will lose consciousness of the body. You will feel that there is no body. You will experience immense joy. There will be mental consciousness. Some lose sensation in the legs, then in the spinal column, the back, the trunk and the hands. When the sensation is lost in these parts, they feel that the head is suspended in the air. The mind may try to run back in the body.

Do not mistake a little concentration or one-pointedness of mind for *Samadhi*. Simply because You have risen a little above body-sensation on account of a little concentration, do not think that you have attained *Samadhi*.

Samadhi or superconscious state is the highest goal which one can attain through meditation. It is not a thing that can be attained through a little practice. To attain *Samadhi* one should observe strict Brahmacharya, dietetic restrictions and must have purity of heart. If these are not attained there is no possibility of attaining that state. These preliminary qualifications should be grasped well and then only one must try to enter the portals of *Samadhi*. None can enter *Samadhi* unless he is himself a great devotee of the Lord. Otherwise the so-called *Samadhi* becomes insensiate to him.

The state of *Samadhi* is beyond description. There is no means or language to give expression to it. Even in worldly experience, you cannot express the taste of an apple to one who has not tasted it nor the nature of the colour to a blind man. The state is All-bliss, Joy and Peace. This much only can be said. One has to feel this himself.

When you practise meditation, worldly thoughts, cravings and Vasanas are suppressed. If you are irregular in meditation and if your dispassion wanes, they try to manifest again. They persist and resist. Therefore, be regular in meditation and do more vigorous Sadhana. Cultivate more dispassion. They will be gradually thinned out and eventually destroyed.

You can ford over the boisterous ocean of the world through meditation. Meditation will save you from all sorrows. Therefore be regular in your meditation.

Anahata Sounds

Anahata sounds (or the melody) are the mystic sounds heard by the Yogi at the beginning of his cycle of meditation. This subject is termed Nada-Anusandhana or an enquiry into the mystic sounds. This is a sign of purification of the Nadis or astral currents, due to Pranayama. The sounds can also be heard after the uttering of the Ajapa Gayatri Mantra, '*Hamsah Soham*', a lakh of times. The sounds are heard through the right ear with or without closing the ears. The sounds are distinct when heard through closed ears. The ears can be closed by introducing the two thumbs into the ears through the process of Yoni Mudra. Sit in Padma or Siddha Asana, close the ears with right and left thumbs, and hear the sounds very attentively. Occasionally, you can hear the sounds through the left ear also. Practise to hear from the right ear only. Why do you hear through the right ear only or hear distinctly through the right ear? Because of the solar Nadi (Pingala) which is on the right side of the nose. The Anahata sound is also called Omkara Dhvani. It is due to the vibration of Prana in the heart.

Ten Kinds of Sounds

Nada that is heard is of 10 kinds. The first is Chini (like the sound of the word Chini); the second is Chini-Chini; the third is the sound of bell; the fourth is that of conch; the fifth is that of Tantri (lute); the sixth is that of Tala (cymbals); the seventh is that of flute; the eighth is that of Bheri (drum); the ninth is that of Mridanga (double drum) and the tenth is that of clouds, viz., thunder.

Before thou settest the foot upon the ladder's upper rung, the ladder of the mystic sounds, thou hast to hear the voice of thy inner God (Highest Self) in 7 manners. The first is like the nightingale's sweet voice chanting a song of parting to its mate. The second comes as the sound of a silver cymbal of the Dhyanis, awakening the twinkling stars. The next is as the melodious plaint of the ocean-sprite imprisoned in its shell. And this is followed by the chant of Veena. The fifth sound of bamboo-flute shrills in thine ear. It changes next into a trumpet-blast. The last vibrates like the dull rumbling of a thunder-cloud. The seventh swallows all the other sounds. They die, and then are heard no more.

Lights in Meditation

Various kinds of lights manifest during meditation owing to concentration. In the beginning, bright white light, the size of a pin's point will appear in the forehead in the Trikuti, the space between the two eyebrows, which corresponds tentatively to the Ajna-Chakra of the astral body. You will notice, when the eyes are closed, different coloured lights, white, yellow, red, smoky, blue, green, mixed lights, flashes like lightning, like fire, burning charcoal, fire-flies, moon, sun, stars. These lights appear in the mental space, Chidakasa. These are all elemental lights. Each element has its own specific colour. Prithvi (earth) Tanmatra has a yellow-coloured light; Apas (water) Tanmatra has a white-coloured light; Agni (fire) Tanmatra has a red-coloured light; Vayu (wind) Tanmatra has a smoky light; Akasa (sky) Tanmatra has a blue light. Yellow and white lights are very commonly seen. Red and blue lights are rarely noticeable. Frequently there is a combination of white and yellow lights. In the beginning, small balls of white light float about before the mind's eye. When you first observe this, be assured that the mind is becoming more steady and that you are progressing in concentration. After some months, the size of the light will increase and you will see a full blaze of white light, bigger than the sun. In the beginning, these lights are not steady. They come and disappear immediately. They flash out from above the forehead and from the sides. They cause peculiar sensations of extreme joy and happiness and there is an intense desire for a vision of these lights. When you have steady and systematic practice of two to three hours in the morning, and two to three hours at night, these lights appear more frequently and remain steadily for a long time. The vision of the lights is a great encouragement in Sadhana. It impels you to stick steadily to meditation. It gives you strong faith also in superphysical matters. The appearance of the light denotes that you are transcending the physical consciousness. You are in a semi-conscious state when the light appears. You are between two planes. You must not shake the body when these lights manifest. You must be perfectly steady in the Asana. You must breathe very, very slowly.

Triangle (Light) in the Face

One whose food is moderate, whose anger has been controlled, who has given up all love for society, who has subdued his passions, who has overcome all pairs (heat and cold, etc.), who has given up his egoism, who does not bless anyone nor take anything from others—such a man during meditation obtains it (the triangle) in the face:

Light from Sushumna

'*Vishoka Va jyotismati*' (Chap. I, Sutra 36. Patanjali-Yoga-Sutras).

'You can attain *Samadhi* by meditation on the Effulgent One who is beyond all sorrow.

Sometimes, during meditation you will see a brilliant dazzling light. You will find it difficult to gaze on this light. You will be compelled to withdraw your mental vision from this light. This dazzling light is the light emanating from the Sushumna (central psychic-canal) in the heart.

Forms in the Lights

You will see two kinds of forms (1) lustrous forms of Devatas, (2) physical forms. You will see your Ishta Devata or tutelary deity (guiding Devata) in handsome dress and with various, valuable ornaments, flowers, garlands, with four hands and weapons. Saints, Sages, etc., appear to encourage you. You will find a huge collection of Gods and celestial ladies with various musical instruments in their hands. You will see beautiful flower-gardens, fine palatial buildings, rivers, mountains, golden temples, sceneries so lovely and picturesque as cannot be adequately described.

Dazzling Lights

Sometimes, during meditation, you will get very powerful, dazzling lights, bigger than the sun. They are white. In the beginning, they come and fade away quickly. Later on, they are steady, they become fixed for 10 or 15 minutes or half an hour according to the strength and degree of concentration. For those who concentrate on the Trikuti, the space between the two eyebrows, the light appears in the forehead in the Trikuti, while for others who concentrate on the top of the head, Sahasrara Chakra, the light manifests on the top of the head. The light is so powerful and dazzling sometimes, that you have to withdraw yourself from looking at it and break the meditation. Some people are afraid and do not know what to do and how to proceed further. They come to me for instructions. I tell them that this is a new sensation which they have not hitherto experienced. By constant practice, the mind engaged in concentration will be used to it, and the fear will vanish. I ask them to go on with the practice. Some people concentrate on the heart, some on Trikuti, and some on the top of the head. It is a question of personal taste. It is easy to control mind by concentrating on the Trikuti. If you are used to fix on the Trikuti, stick to it always. Don't make frequent changes. Steadiness is very necessary. The beings and objects with whom you are in touch during the early period of meditation belong to the astral world. They are similar to human beings minus a physical overcoat. They have desires, cravings, love, hatred, etc., just as human beings have. They have fine bodies. They can move about freely. They have powers of materialisation, dematerialisation, multiplying, clairvoyant vision of an inferior order. The lustrous forms are higher Devatas of mental or higher planes who come down to encourage you. Various Shaktis manifest in lustrous forms. Adore them. Worship them. Do mental worship as soon as you behold them. Angels are beings of mental or higher planes. They also appear before your mind's eye.

Sometimes, you will feel an invisible help, possibly from your Ishta Devata when you are actually pushed from the physical body into the new plane. That invisible power assists in your separating from the body and going above body consciousness. You will have to mark carefully all these operations.

Don't waste your time in looking at these visions. This is only a curiosity. These are all encouragements to convince you of the existence of superphysical, metaphysical realities and the solid existence of Brahman. Drive these pictures. Fix yourself on the goal—Lakshya. Advance. Proceed seriously and energetically.

As soon as you retire for sleep, these lights manifest themselves without any exertion on your part. Just when you are going to transcend the physical consciousness, just when you are drowsy, these lights appear without your effort. Also in the morning, before you get up, in the transitional stage, half-asleep, half-awake, you will get again these lights by themselves without attempt.

Sometimes, during meditation, you will see an infinite blue sky, ethereal space. You will see yourself in the blue space as a black dot. Your form will appear in the centre of the light sometimes. Sometimes, you will notice highly vibratory, rotating particles in the light. You will see physical forms, human forms, children, women, adult males, Rishis with beards, and lustrous forms. Visions are either subjective or objective, your own mental reactions or of realities on finer planes of matter. Universe consists of planes of matter of various grades of density. Rhythmical vibrations of elements in various degrees, give rise to the formation of various planes. Each plane has its beings and things. Visions may be of these things or beings. They may be purely imaginary. They may be crystalisation of your own intense thinking. You must discriminate in Yogic practices. Reason and common sense must be used throughout.

Mystic Experiences of Sadhakas

'I had some peculiar sensation near my solar plexus in my meditation some three years back, that is to say, I noticed the whirling sensation of a flywheel rotating around. Then I came across some peculiar sights. I saw with the physical eyes a sort of white or blue hue of light all around the people's head and also on the surface of the buildings. When I gaze at the open, grand expanse of sky in daytime I notice a living wormlike white light moving hither and thither. When I work intently in my office, white shining lights flash across my eyes. Sometimes little sparks of light are noticed on my books. This gives me a peculiar joy and I begin to chant the name of the Lord: "*Sri Ram, Jaya Ram, Jaya Jaya Ram*". Nowadays when I am cycling to my office a round light-like ball is seen and is visible till I reach my destination. The same thing appears at times when I gaze at the beautiful Akasa.' . . . . 'S'.

'I meditated for five hours daily for a month in Gangotri. One day I had a great deal of dejection for two hours. I could not find any peace. I found it difficult to bear the mood of dejection. I then sat on the banks of Ganga and began to meditate upon Mahatma Gandhiji. It gave me solace then. After a few days I sat meditating on Sri Ramachandra for one and a half hours. This *Saguna* meditation automatically turned into a Nirguna type. I felt perfect Shanti for 10 minutes. My mind was fully engrossed in the meditation on OM. This continued for half an hour. One day I had a different kind of experience. I opened my eyes after meditation. I found everything as Brahman without the help of reasoning. I had this mood the whole day. A celibate spoke to me for one hour on that day. I was only hearing but my mind did not attend to his speech. It remained in the same mood. I could not recollect even a word of his speech.

'On another occasion I meditated for half an hour. I had a very ecstatic mood. But owing to some distraction from sounds from outside, the ecstatic mood dropped down. Again I began to meditate. I saw a beautiful light at the bottom of my heart. As soon as that light disappeared, I began to weep unconsciously. Somebody came to me and called me by my name. I did not know anything. He shook my body. I stopped weeping a little and looked at his face and wept again and again for 25 minutes' 'V'.

'I observed silence as a trial for the first time from 26-2-32 to 4-3-32.

'*Mistakes*:—Occasionally I had to express my ideas by gestures. On the last three days I uttered the words "Yes", "enough", "what" absent-mindedly. I had the wrong imagination as if there was pain in the jaws. I had a great curiosity for speaking.

'Benefits:—I was able to do more work, reading, Japa and meditation for a longer period than usual. I could not sleep before midnight. The ideas of books were rolling on till midnight. No room for anger and irritability. I was not able to get anything by heart. I tried to get by heart a few verses but could not. It was due to my previous habit of uttering once or twice loudly.' . . . . 'Ram'.

'I did Pranayama for a month and then began to hear some sweet melodious sounds, viz., flute, violin, bell-sound, Mridang, sound from cluster of bells, conch sound, drum sound, sound of thunder, sometimes from right ear only, while at other times from both the ears.' . . . . 'N'.

'During concentration I used to smell extraordinary sweet fragrance and good smell' 'R'.

'I used to see during meditation in my Trikuti a blazing sun, a dazzling light and brilliant star. The vision was not steady at all.' . . . . 'G'.

'I used to have vision of some sages in my Trikuti during the course of concentration. I used to see my chosen deity, Lord Krishna, with flute in his hands.' . . . 'S'.

'I used to see at times coloured lights, red, green, blue and white in Trikuti during my meditation. Sometimes I used to see a blue expansive sky. I myself appeared as a dot in that blue sky.' . . . . 'V'.

'During meditation I used to see several gods and goddesses with lustrous effulgent bodies with beautiful ornaments.' . . . . 'R'.

'Sometimes during meditation I used to see a big void only.' . . . . 'T'.

'During concentration I used to see my own face in the centre of a big light. Sometimes I used to see the faces of my friends. I could clearly recognise them' . . . . 'R'

'I used to feel a current of electricity passing from my Muladhara to the back of the neck when I sat for meditation. Even at ordinary times I used to feel this' . . . . 'K'.

'During meditation some astral entities with ghastly hideous faces and long teeth, black in colour used to threaten me. But they did not do any harm.' . . . . 'A'.

'When I sat for meditation I used to get jerks of the legs and hands. Sometimes my body used to jump from one place to another.' . . . . 'M'.

'I used to see palatial buildings, rivers, mountains and gardens during my meditation.' 'S'.

'I used to meditate with open eyes. One night I saw in front of me a brilliant light. In the centre of the light I saw Lord Krishna with flute in hand. My hair stood on end. I became speechless. I was struck with awe and wonder. It was 3 a.m.' 'S'.

'One day I had deep meditation. I separated myself actually from the physical body. I actually saw it as a slough thrown out. I was floating in the air. I had a peculiar sensation of a mixture of extreme joy and extreme fear. I stayed in the air for a couple of minutes only. Owing to great fear I suddenly entered back into the physical body. I slowly glided with a peculiar sensation into the physical body. The experience was thrilling' . . . . 'S'.

Uddalaka's Experience

The sage Uddalaka was not able to master Samadhi which leads one into the blissful realm of Reality, because the monkey-mind jumped speedily from one branch to another of sensual objects.

He seated himself in Padmasana and uttered Pranava (OM) with high-sounding intonation. Then he started his meditation.

He forcibly controlled his mind. With great difficulty he separated the senses from the objects. He dissociated himself completely from all external objects. He closed the avenues of the body. He fixed his mind on the heart. His mind was freed from all tossing. He destroyed all thoughts of objects just as a warrior kills with his sword his foes who rise against him again and again.

He saw before him a radiant light. He dispelled Moha: He passed through the stage of darkness, light, sleep and infatuation. He eventually reached the stage of Nirvikalpa Samadhi and enjoyed perfect calmness. After six months, he woke from his Samadhi. He would spend in one sitting, days, months and even years in deep Samadhi and then wake up.

In the Hours of Meditation

Brahman, Self, Purusha, Chaitanya, Consciousness, God, *Atman*, Immortality, Freedom, Perfection, Peace, Bliss, Bhuma or the Unconditioned, are synonymous terms. If you attain Self-realisation alone, you will be freed from the round of births and deaths and its concomitant evils. The goal of life is the attainment of final beatitude or Moksha. Moksha can be attained by constant meditation in the heart that is rendered pure and steady by selfless service, *Japa*, etc.

Reality or Brahman can be realised by man. Many have attained Self-realisation. Many have enjoyed the Nirvikalpa Samadhi. Sankara, Dattatreya, Mansoor, Shams Tabriez, Jesus, Buddha were all realised souls who had direct perception of the Truth or cosmic vision. But one who has known cannot communicate it to others for want of means. Even the knowledge acquired by the five senses, which are common to all, cannot be communicated to others. You cannot tell the taste of sugar candy to a man who has never tasted it; you cannot communicate the idea of colour to one born blind. All that the teacher can do is to tell his disciple the method of knowing the Truth or the path that leads to the unfoldment of intuitional faculty.

These are the signs that indicate that you are growing in meditation and approaching God. You will have no attraction for the world. The sensual objects will no longer tempt you. You will become desireless, fearless, 'I'-less and 'mine'-less. Attachment to the body will gradually dwindle. You will not entertain the ideas, 'She is my wife; he is my son; this is my house.' You will feel that all are manifestations of the Lord. You will behold God in every object.

The body and mind will become light. You will always be cheerful and happy. The name of the Lord will always be on your lips. The mind will be ever fixed on the lotus feet of the Lord. The mind will be ever producing the image of the Lord. It will be ever seeing the picture of the Lord. You will actually feel that purity, light, bliss, knowledge and divine love are ever flowing from the Lord to you and filling up your heart.

You will have no body-consciousness. Even if there be body-consciousness, it will be in the form of a mental retentum. A drunkard may not have full consciousness that he has a cloth round his body. He may feel that something is loosely hanging from his body. Even so, you will have a feeling of the body. You will feel that something is sticking to you like a loose cloth or loose shoes.

You will have no attraction for the sex. You will have no sex-idea. Woman will appear to you as manifestation of the Lord. Money and gold will appear to you as pieces of stone. You will have intense love for all creatures. You will be absolutely free from lust, greed, anger, jealousy, pride, delusion, etc. You will have peace of mind even when people insult you, beat you and persecute you. The reason why you are not perturbed is that you get immense spiritual strength from the Indweller or the Lord. Pain or pleasure, success or failure, honour or dishonour, respect or disrespect, gain or loss are alike to you.

Even in dreams, you are in communion with the Lord. You will not behold any worldly pictures.

You will converse with the Lord in the beginning. You will see him in physical form. When your consciousness becomes cosmic, conversation will stop. You will enjoy the language of the silence or the language of the heart. From Vaikhari (vocal speech), you will pass on to subtle forms of sounds and eventually you will rest in soundless Omkara or soundless Brahman.

Dispassion and discrimination, serenity, self-restraint, one-pointedness of mind, Ahimsa, Satyam, purity, forbearance, fortitude, patience, forgiveness, absence of anger, spirit of service, sacrifice, love for all, will be your habitual qualities. You will be a cosmic friend and benefactor.

During meditation you will have no idea of time. You will not hear any sound. You will have no idea of the environments. You will forget your names and all sorts of relationship with others. You will enjoy perfect peace and bliss. Gradually you will rest in Samadhi.

Samadhi is an indescribable state. It is beyond the reach of mind and speech. In Samadhi or the superconscious state the meditator loses his individuality and becomes identical with the Supreme Self. He becomes an embodiment of bliss, peace and knowledge. So much only can be said. You have to experience this yourself through constant meditation.

Contentment, unruffled state of the mind, cheerfulness, patience, decrease in the excretions, sweet voice, eagerness and steadiness in the practice of meditation, disgust for worldly prosperity or success and company, desire to remain alone in a quiet room or in seclusion, desire for association with Sadhus and Sannyasins, one-pointedness of mind are some of the signs which indicate that you are growing in purity, that you are prospering in the spiritual path.

You will hear various kinds of Anahata sounds, of a bell, a kettle drum, thunder, conch, Veena or flute, the humming sound of a bee, etc., during meditation. The mind can be fixed in any of these sounds. This also will lead to Samadhi. You will behold various kinds of colours and lights during meditation. This is not the goal. You will have to merge the mind in that which is the source of these lights and colours.

A student in the path of Vedanta ignores these sounds and lights. He meditates on the significance of the great utterances of the Upanishads by negating all forms. 'The sun does not shine there, nor do the moon and the stars, nor does this lightning shine and much less this fire. When He shines, everything shines after Him; by His light all these shine'. He meditates, also like this: 'The air does not blow there. The fire does not burn there. There is neither sound nor touch, neither smell nor colour, neither mind nor Prana in the homogeneous essence. I am blissful Siva, I am blissful Siva'.

Be a spiritual hero in the worldly battle-field. Be a brave, undaunted, spiritual soldier. The inner war with the mind, senses, Vasanas and Samskaras is more terrible than the external war. Fight against the mind, senses, evil tendencies, Longings, Vrittis and Samskaras boldly. Use the machine-gun of self-inquiry to explode the mind efficiently. Dive deep and destroy the undercurrents of passion, greed, hatred, pride and jealousy, through the submarine or torpedo of Japa of OM or Soham. Soar high in the higher regions of bliss of the Self with the help of the aeroplane of the thought of God. Use the 'mines' of chanting of OM to explode the tendencies that are hidden in the sea of subconscious mind. Sometimes move the 'tanks' of discrimination to crush your ten enemies, the ten turbulent senses. Start the Divine League and make friendship with your powerful allies viz., dispassion, fortitude, endurance, serenity, self-restraint, to attack your enemy-mind. Throw the bomb of 'Sivoham Bhavana' to destroy the big mansion of body and the idea 'I am the body', 'I am the doer' and 'I am the enjoyer'. Spread profusely the gas of 'Purity' to destroy your internal enemies viz., Passion and Ignorance quickly. 'Black-out' the mind by destroying the thoughts or imaginations by putting out all the lights or bulbs of sensual objects so that the enemy 'mind' will not be able to attack you. Fight closely against your enemy 'mind' with the bayonet of one-pointedness (Samadhana) to get hold of the priceless treasure or Atomic pearl. The joy of Samadhi, the bliss of Moksha, the peace of Nirvana are now yours, whoever you may be, in whatever clime you are born. Whatever might be your past life or history, work out your salvation. O beloved Rama, with the help of these means come out victorious right now, this very second.

Vision of God

You will sometimes see a vast bright golden light. Within the light you will see your Ishta Devata in front. Sometimes you will see yourself within the light. You will see a golden-coloured light all around.

You may see your Ishta Devata as big as a mountain shining like the sun. You may see the figure during eating, drinking and working. When you enjoy the bliss of this vision, you will experience no taste for food while eating. You will simply swallow the food. You will hear continuous ringing of the Veena. You may see the blazing light of the sun.

The object of your meditation will come before you much quicker if you practise regular meditation. You will feel as if you are covered by the object on which you meditate. You will see as if the whole space is illumined. Sometimes you will experience the sound of ringing bells. You will feel the inner peace of the Soul.

You will see all sorts of beautiful colours. Sometimes you will behold a beautiful garden with charming scenery. Sometimes you will see saints and sages. Full-moon and crescent moon, sun and stars, will appear. You will see light on the wall.

When you get these experiences, when you behold these visions, you will feel peculiar indescribable bliss. Do not get false contentment. Do not stop your spiritual practice and meditation thinking that you have attained the highest realisation. Do not attach much importance to these visions. You have attained only the first degree of concentration. The highest goal or realisation is profound Silence or Supreme Peace, wherein all thoughts cease and you become identical with the Supreme Self.

He who does Japa, Pranayama and meditation, feels lightness of the body. Passion and Inertia are decreased. The body becomes light.

The sudden jerks in meditation come especially when the Prana becomes slow and the outward vibrations make the mind come down from its union with the Lord to the level of physical consciousness.

The mind becomes very subtle by the practice of Japa, Kirtan, meditation and Pranayama. The power of thinking also gets developed.

You will hear the melodious sound of OM during meditation. You will see the form of your Guru.

May you attain this final beatitude or ineffable Brahmic seat of eternal splendour and everlasting bliss through constant meditation.

Feeling of Separation

During the course of practice, one day you will feel that you have separated yourself from the body. You will have immense joy mixed with fear, joy in the possession of a new, light, astral body, fear owing to the entry in a foreign, unknown plane. At the very outset, the new consciousness is very rudimentary in the new plane, just as in the case of a pup with newly opened eyes in the eighth or tenth day on the physical plane. You will only feel that you have a light airy body and will perceive a rotating, vibratory limited astral atmosphere with illumination of golden lights, objects, beings, etc. You may feel you are rotating or floating in the air and consequently there is the fear of falling.

You will never fall; but the new experience of subtlety generates novel feelings and sensations in the beginning. How you leave the body, remains unknown at the outset. You are suddenly startled, when you have completely separated, and when you enter into the new plane, sometimes with blue-coloured sphere around, sometimes with partial illumination (Prakasha) mixed with darkness while at other times with extremely brilliant golden, yellow diffused illumination. The new joy is inexpressible and indescribable in words. You will have to actually feel and experience yourself (Anubhava). You will have to eat yourself. You are unaware of how you have left the body, but you are fully conscious of your returning. You gently feel as if you glide on a very smooth surface; as if you enter smoothly, gently through a small whole of fine tube with an airy, light body. You have an airy, ethereal feeling. Just as air enters through the crevices of a window, you enter with the new astral body into the physical body. I think I have expressed the idea lucidly. When you have returned, you can markedly differentiate the life in the gross and subtle planes. There is an intense craving to regain the new consciousness and to remain in that state always. You are not able to stay for a period longer than 3, 5 or 10 minutes in the new region. Further, you can hardly leave the body at will, through simple willing, in the beginning. By chance, through efforts, you are able to separate from the body in a month in the course of Sadhana. If you plod on with patience, perseverance and firmness, you will be able to leave the body at will and stay for a longer time in the new plane with the new subtle body. You are quite safe from identification with the body. You have made conquest, only if you can leave the body at will and only if you are able to stay in the new region for 2 or 3 hours. Your position is quite secure then and not otherwise. Mouna or the vow of silence, solitude, living alone are *sine qua non* to achieve this end. If circumstances prevent you to observe Mouna, strictly avoid long talk, big talk, tall talk, all unnecessary talks, all sorts of vain discussions, etc., and withdraw yourself from society as much as possible. Too much talk is simply wastage of energy. If this energy is conserved by Mouna, it will be transmuted into Ojas or spiritual energy which will help you in the Spiritual practice. Speech is Tejomaya Vak according to Chhandogya Upanishad. The gross portion of fire goes to constitute bone, the middle portion to form marrow; and the subtle portion of fire to form speech. So speech is a very powerful energy. Remember this, remember this, remember this always. Observe Mouna for 3 months, 6 months or 1 year. If you cannot do for months continuously, observe for a day in a week, just as Sri Mahatma Gandhiji did. You must draw inspiration from Mahatmas like Sri Krishna Ashramji Maharaj who is now living absolutely nude for the last many years in the icy regions of Himalayas, near the origin of the Ganga, Gangotri. He is observing Kashta Mouna, a rigid vow of silence for many years. (In Kashta Mouna you do not communicate your thoughts to others even in writing or by signs.) Why not you also become a Krishna Ashram of wide repute and glory? After continuous, hard practice, you will be able to separate yourself from the body, very frequently. There is established a habit. As soon as you silence the thought, and calm the mind, the mental habit of slipping from the physical body supervenes automatically. There is no difficulty then. The mind enters the new groove and appears on a new stage or platform.

Astral Journey

You can simply by mere willing travel to any place you like with the astral body (astral travel, astral journey) and there materialise by drawing the necessary materials either from Asmita (Ahamkara) or the universal storehouse-ocean of elements. The process is very simple to occultists, and Yogins who know the rationale, the detailed technique of the various operations, albeit it seems extraordinary to poor mundane creatures with diverse emotions, passions and attachment. Thought-reading, thought-transference also can be quite easily performed by those who can function with the astral body. Concentrated mental rays can penetrate opaque walls, just as X-rays pass through bones.

Materialisation

You first separate yourself from the body, then you identify yourself with the mind and then you function on the mental plane, with this fine body, just as you do on this earth plane. Through concentration, you rise above body-consciousness; through meditation, you rise above mind; and finally through Samadhi, you become one with Brahman. These are the three important, Antaranga Sadhanas (internal means), in the achievement of final beatitude.

Cosmic Consciousness

This exalted, blissful experience comes through intuition or Samadhi. The lower mind is withdrawn from the external, objective world. The senses are abstracted in the mind. The individual mind becomes one with the cosmic mind or

Hiranyagarbha or the Oversoul, the Soul of the Universe, the one common thread-soul. The function of the intellect, the objective mind and the senses are suspended. The Yogi becomes a living soul and sees into the life of things through his new divine eye of intuition or wisdom.

The state of Cosmic Consciousness is grand and sublime. It is beyond description. The mind and speech return from it baffled, as they are not able to grasp and describe it. The language and words are imperfect. It induces awe, Supreme Joy and Highest Unalloyed Felicity, free from pain, sorrow and fear. This is divine experience. It is a revelation of the Karana Jagat, the causal world wherein the types are realised directly.

Sri Sankara, Dattatreya, Shams Tabriez, Madalasa, Yajnavalkya, Ram Das, Tulsi Das, Kabir, Mira, Lord Jesus, Lord Buddha, Lord Mohammed, Lord Zoroaster, had experience of Cosmic Consciousness.

The yogi who has experience of Cosmic Consciousness acquires many kinds of Siddhis or powers, which are described in Srimad Bhagavata and Raja Yoga of Patanjali Maharshi.

Arjuna, Sanjaya and Yasoda had the experience of Cosmic Consciousness. Yasoda saw the whole universe within the mouth of Bala Krishna.

Gita describes the state of cosmic consciousness through the mouth of Arjuna in these words: 'Thy mighty form with many mouths and eyes, long-armed, with thighs and feet innumerable, vast-bosomed, set with many fearful teeth, radiant, Thou touchest heaven, rainbow-hued, with open mouths and shining vast-orbed eyes on every side, all-swallowing, fierytongued, Thou lickest up mankind devouring all into Thy gaping mouths, which are tremendous-toothed and terrible to see. Some caught within the gaps between Thy teeth, are seen with their heads to powder crushed and ground.'

In France, Professor Bergson preached about intuition which transcends reason but did not contradict it.

This new experience bestows new enlightenment which places the experiencer on a new plane of existence. There is an indescribable feeling of elation and indescribable joy and Bliss. He experiences a sense of universality, a Consciousness of Eternal Life. It is not a mere conviction. He actually feels it. He gets the eye Celestial.

The Jivahood has gone now. The little 'I' has melted. The differentiating mind that splits up has vanished. All barriers, all sense of duality, differences, separateness have disappeared. There is no idea of time and space. There is only eternity. The ideas of caste, creed and colour have gone now. He has the feeling of AptaKama (one who has obtained all that he desires). He feels, 'There is nothing more to be known by me.' He feels perfect awareness of superconscious plane of Knowledge and intuition. He knows the whole secret of Creation. He is omniscient. He is a Sarva-Vit or Knower of all details of Creation.

Absolute fearlessness, desirelessness, thoughtlessness, I-lessness, mine-lessness, angerlessness, Brahmic aura in the face, are some of the signs that indicate that the man has reached the state of superconsciousness. He is also always in a state of perfect bliss. You can never see anger, depression, cheerlessness and sorrow in his face. You will find elevation, joy and peace in his presence.

Cosmic consciousness is perfect awareness of the oneness of life. The Yogi feels that the universe is filled with one life. He actually feels that there is no such thing as blind force or dead matter and that all is alive, vibrating and intelligent. This is the experience of scientist Bose also. He has demonstrated it through laboratory experiments.

He who has cosmic consciousness feels that the universe is all his. He is one with the supreme Lord. He is one with the Universal knowledge and Life. He experiences bliss and joy beyond understanding and description. In the moment of illumination or great spiritual exaltation he has the actual divine universal vision. He is conscious of being in the presence of God. He sees the light of God's countenance. He is lifted above the ordinary plane of consciousness. He reaches a higher state of consciousness. He has a cosmic or universal understanding. He has developed the cosmic sense. The human soul is revolutionised.

He does not worry about death or future, about what may come after the cessation of the life of the present body. He is one with Eternity, Infinity and Immortality!

During illumination the floodgate of joy breaks. The Yogi is inundated with waves of indescribable ecstasy. Bliss, Immortality, Eternity, Truth, Divine Love become the core of his being, the essence of his life, the only possible reality. He realises that the deep, everlasting fountain of joy exists in every heart, that the immortal life underlies all beings, that this eternal, all-embracing, all-inclusive love envelops, supports and guides every particle, every atom of creation. Sin, sorrow, death are but words now for him without meaning. He feels that the elixir of life, the nectar of immortality is flowing in his veins.

He feels no need for food or sleep. He is absolutely desireless. There is a great change in his appearance and manner. His face shines with a radiant light. His eyes are lustrous. They are pools of joy and bliss. He feels that the entire world is bathed in a sea of satisfying love, or immortal bliss which is the very essence of life.

The whole world is home to him. He could never feel strange or alien to anyplace. The mountains, the distant lands which he had never seen would be as much as his own, as the home of his boyhood. He feels that the whole world is his body. He feels that all hands, all feet are his.

Fatigue is unknown to him. His work is like child's play, happy and care-free. He beholds only God everywhere. Chair, table, tree have a Cosmic significance. His breath will stop completely sometimes. He experiences Absolute Peace. Time and space vanish.

Cosmic Consciousness is an inherent, natural faculty of all men and women. Training and discipline are necessary to awaken the consciousness. It is already present in man. It is inactive, or non-functioning in the majority of human beings on account of the force of Avidya or ignorance.

May you all attain the State of Cosmic Consciousness, your birthright, centre, ideal and goal, through association with the sages, purity, love, devotion and Knowledge!

Blissful Experience

Samadhi or blissful divine experience arises when the ego and the mind are dissolved. It is a state to be attained by one's own effort. It is limitless, divisionless and infinite, an experience of being and of pure consciousness. When this experience is realised, the mind, desires, actions and feelings of joy and sorrow vanish into a void.

The ultimate Truth or Brahman or the Absolute can be experienced by all persons by regular practice of meditation with a pure heart. Mere abstract reasoning and study of books will not do. What is wanted is direct experience. The direct experience is the source for higher intuitional knowledge or divine wisdom. This experience is superconscious or transcendental. There is neither the play of the senses nor the intellect here. This is not an emotional experience. The senses, mind and intellect are at perfect rest. They do not function a bit. This experience is not an imaginary experience of a visionary dreamer. It is not a reverie. It is not a hypnotic trance. It is a solid living Truth like the Amalaka fruit on the palm of your hand. The third eye or the eye of wisdom (Jnana Chakshus) is opened in the experiencer. The extraordinary experience comes from cognition through the spiritual eye or the eye of intuition. This eye of wisdom can be opened when the senses, mind and intellect cease functioning. The Jnana Chakshus can only be opened by eradicating completely all desires, wrath, greed, pride, egoism and hatred.

There is neither darkness nor void in this experience. It is all light. There is neither sound nor touch nor form here. It is a magnanimous experience of unity or oneness. There is neither time nor causation here. You become omniscient and omnipotent. You become a Sarvavit or all-knower. You know everything in detail. You know the whole mystery of creation. You get immortality, higher knowledge and eternal bliss.

All dualities vanish here. There is neither subject nor object. There is neither meditation nor Samadhi. There is neither Duality nor non-duality. There is neither tossing of the mind nor one-pointedness. There is neither meditator nor the meditated. There is neither gain nor loss. There is neither pleasure nor pain. There is neither east nor west. There is neither day nor night.

Samadhi is of various kinds. The Samadhi that is induced by the practice of Mudra and Pranayama (Retention) is Jada Samadhi. There is no awareness here. The Yogi can be buried for six months in a box beneath the earth. It is like deep sleep. The Yogi does not return with superintuitional knowledge. The Vasanas are not destroyed by this Samadhi. The Yogi will be born again. This Samadhi cannot give liberation.

Then there is the Chaitanya Samadhi. The Yogi has perfect awareness. He comes down with divine knowledge. He gives inspired talks and messages. The hearers are much elevated. The mental tendencies are destroyed by this Samadhi. The Yogi attams Kaivalya or perfect freedom.

The Samadhi experienced by a Bhakta is Bhava Samadhi. The devotee attains the state through Bhava and Mahabhava. The Raja Yogi gets Nirodha Samadhi through destruction of imagination (chittavrittinirodha). The Vedantin attains Bhava Samadhi through negation of the illusory vehicles, or Upadhis such a body, mind, senses, intellect, etc. For him the world and body are unreal. He passes through the stages of darkness, light, sleep, and infinite space and eventually attains infinite consciousness.

Again there are two other varieties of Samadhi, viz., Savikalpa or Sabija or Samprajnata and Nirvikalpa or Nirbija or Asamprajnata Samadhi. In the first variety there is the triad, viz., knower, knowledge, knowable or seer, sight and seen. The Samskaras are not destroyed. In the latter the Samskaras are totally fried or destroyed. There is no triad in Nirvikalpa. Savikalpa, Savichara, Saananda are varieties of Savikalpa *Samadhi*.

When you are established in the highest Nirvikalpa *Samadhi* you have nothing to see, nothing to hear, nothing to smell and nothing to feel. You have no body-consciousness. You have full Brahmic Consciousness only. There is nothing but the Self. It is a grand experience. You will be struck with awe and wonder.

A Bhakta who meditates on the form of Lord Krishna will see Krishna and Krishna only everywhere when he is established in Samadhi. All other forms will disappear. This is one kind of spiritual experience. He will see himself also as Krishna. Gopis of Vrindavan, Gauranga and Ekanath had this experience. Those who meditate on the all-pervading Krishna will have another kind of cosmic experience. Arjuna had this kind of experience. He had consciousness of the whole of Creation. He had cosmic consciousness.

If you meditate on Hiranyagarbha, you will become identical with Hiranyagarbha. You will have knowledge of Heavenly planes. You will also have cosmic consciousness. The experience of Savikalpa Samadhi of a devotee and Raja Yogi is the same.

The transcendental experience is also called by the name Turiya or the fourth state. The first three states are 'waking', 'dreaming' and 'dreamless sleep' and the fourth state is 'Turiya'. The first three states are common to all. The fourth is latent in every human being. When you are established in the fourth state, when you experience the transcendental state of Brahmic consciousness, the Truth, which had been before but as an intellectual abstraction, becomes a living reality definitely experienced by you.

Various names such as Nirvana, Turiyatita, Brahma Sakshatkara, Nirvikalpa Samadhi, Asamprajnata Samadhi, are given to this transcendental state, but all of them unmistakably point to the same goal. Real spiritual life begins after one enters into this state of superconsciousness.

You will realise at all times and under all circumstances that you are identical with the invisible existence, knowledge and bliss; that you pervade all persons and objects; and that you are beyond all limitations. If you have the knowledge of the Self or Brahman at all times without any break, then you are established in the Self. This is a state to be experienced within but cannot be expressed in words. This is the final state of Peace, the goal of life. This experience will give you freedom from all forms of bondage.

Some aspirants mistake 'deep sleep state' and the state of Tandri or 'half sleep' state for Nirvikalpa Samadhi. This is a terrible mistake. If you experience Samadhi of any kind, you will have supersensuous knowledge. If you do not possess any intuitional knowledge, be sure that you are far from Samadhi. You can experience Samadhi only when you are established in Yama, Niyama and when you have a very pure heart. How can the Lord be enthroned in an impure heart? Samadhi comes only after constant and protracted practice of meditation. Samadhi is not a commodity that can be obtained easily. Those who can really enter into Samadhi are very very rare.

In Samadhi or Superconsciousness the Yogic practitioner gets himself merged in the Lord. The senses, the mind and the intellect cease functioning. Just as the river joins the ocean, the individual soul mixes with the Supreme Soul. All limitations and differences disappear. The Yogi attains the highest knowledge and eternal bliss. This state is beyond description. You will have to realise this yourself.

Taste the immortal sweetness of the beautiful life in the Self within. Live in *Atman* and attain the blessed immortal State. Meditate and reach the deeper depths of eternal life, the higher heights of divine glory and eventually attain the full glory of union with the Supreme Self. Now your long wearisome journey terminates. You have reached your destination, your sweet original home of everlasting peace, the Param Dhama.

Mind Moves

After a short practice of meditation you will feel that body gets lighter in a short time, say 15 or 30 minutes after you have taken your seat in Padma, Siddha, or Sukhasana, according to taste and temperament. You may be semi-conscious of the body also. There is great deal of happiness owing to concentration. This is happiness resulting from concentration—concentration-Ananda—which is quite different from sensual pleasures. You must be able to differentiate these two pleasures through the intellect, rendered subtle by constant practice, meditation. Dharana and Dhyana have a power to sharpen the intellect. A trained intellect can comprehend subtle, philosophical, abstruse problems beautifully well. A disciplined intellect that can carefully differentiate concentration-Ananda and meditation-happiness, will naturally run daily to enjoy this kind of new happiness. Such a mind will loathe sensual pleasures. There will be extreme abhorrence, and positive aversion to objects. It is but natural, because this kind of happiness is more lasting, sustained, self-contained and real, as it emanates from *Atman*. You can distinctly feel that the mind is moving, that it is leaving its seat in the brain, and that it is trying to go to its original seat. You know that it has left its old groove and is now passing the new groove in the avenue. As a result of meditation, new channels are formed in the brain, new thought-currents are generated and new brain-cells are formed. There is a transformed psychology altogether. You have got a new brain, a new heart, new feelings, new sentiments and new sensations.

Bhuta-Ganas

Sometimes, these elementals appear during meditation. They are strange figures, some with long teeth, some with big faces, some with big bellies, some with faces on the belly, some with faces on the head. They are supposed to be the attendants of Lord Siva. They have terrifying forms. They do not cause any harm at all. They simply appear on the stage. They come to test your strength and courage. They can do nothing. They cannot stand before a pure, ethical aspirant. Repetition of a few Omkaras will throw them at a distance. You must be fearless. A coward is absolutely unfit for the spiritual line. Develop courage by constantly feeling you are the *Atman*. Negate the body-idea that is inveterate. Practice, practice, Nididhyasana, Meditation always, all the 24 hours. That is the secret. That is the key. That is the master-key to open the treasury of Sat-Chid-Ananda. That is the cornerstone of the edifice of Bliss. That is the pillar of the edifice of Bliss. That is the pillar of the mansion of Ananda.

Glimpses of the Self

By experiences, pleasant and painful, man gathers materials and builds them into mental and moral faculties.

As a merchant closing the year's ledger and opening a new one does not enter in the new one all the items of the old but only its balances, so does the spirit hand over to the new brain judgments on the experiences of a life that is closed, the conclusions to which he has come, the decisions to which he has arrived. This is the stock handed over to the new life, the mental furniture for the new dwelling, a real memory.

The mind which ever rises and falls with the ebb of desires, fancies this illusory universe to be true through its ignorance; but it should be informed of the real nature of this world, then it will cognise it to be Brahman itself.

During meditation you may experience that you are rising from your seat. Some experience that they fly in the air.

Various persons get various spiritual experiences. There cannot be a common experience for all. It depends upon the temperament, mode of Sadhana, place of concentration, and various other factors. Some hear melodious sounds in the ears. Some see lights. Some get Ananda (spiritual bliss).

If there is any error in Sadhana (meditation), at once consult the senior Sannyasins or realised souls and remove the mistake. If your general health is sound, if you are cheerful, happy and strong physically and mentally, if the mind is peaceful and unruffled, if you get Ananda in meditation and if your will is growing strong, pure and irresistible, think that you are improving in meditation and everything is going on all right.

The Divine Light comes not through open doors but only through narrow slits. The aspirant sees the ray as a sunbeam passing through a chink into a dark room. It is like a 'flash of lightning.' This sudden illumination chokes all sounds of words. The aspirant is spellbound in ecstasy and awe. He trembles with love and awe, just as Arjuna did when he had the cosmic vision of Lord Krishna. So bright and glorious is the Light environing the Divine that the initiate is dazzled and bewildered.

This is a kind of vision one occasionally gets during meditation. You may behold a dazzling light with abrupt motion. You may behold a head of marvellous form, of the colour of a flame, red as fire, and very awful to look at. It has three wings of marvellous length and breadth, white as a dazzling cloud. At times they would beat terribly and again would be still. The head never utters a word, but remains altogether still. Now and again there is beating with its extended wings.

During meditation the colour of lights that you see varies according to the nature of the Tattva that flows through the nostrils. If there is Agni Tattva you will see red-coloured lights. You can change the Tattva by various ways. But the best way is by thought. 'As you think, so, you also become'. When the Agni Tattva flows, think intensely of Apas Tattva. Apas Tattva will begin to flow soon.

If you get experiences of the glimpses of Self during intense meditation, if you see a blazing light during meditation, and if you get spiritual visions of angels, archangels, Sages, Gods and any other extraordinary spiritual experiences, do not fall back in terror. Do not mistake them for phantoms. Do not give up the Sadhana. Plod on diligently. Break veil after veil.

March on boldly. Do not look back. Cross the intense void and darkness. Pierce the layer of attachment. Melt the subtle Egoism now. Truth will shine by itself. You will experience the Turiya (Arudha state).

Sometimes bad spirits will trouble you. They may have ugly fierce faces with long teeth. Drive them with your strong will. Give the word of command 'Get out'. They will go away. They are vampires. They are elementals. They will not do any harm to the Sadhakas. Your courage will be tested here. If you are timid you cannot march further. Draw power and courage from *Atman* within, the inexhaustible source (Avyaya). You will come across very good spirits also. They will help you a lot in your onward march. These are all Vighnas or obstacles in the way.

Aspirants are eager to get spiritual experience soon. As soon as they get them, they are afraid. They are awfully alarmed when they go above the body-consciousness. They entertain a passing wonder whether they will come back again or not. Why should they be afraid at all? It does not matter much whether they return to body-consciousness or not. All our attempts are mainly directed toward getting over this body-consciousness and being one with the higher spiritual consciousness. We are used to certain limitations. When these limitations suddenly drop away we feel that there is no definite base left to stand upon. That is the reason why we are afraid when we go above the body-consciousness. That is a novel experience. Courage is needed. Courage is an indispensable requisite. Scriptures say: '*This Atman can hardly be attained by weak (timid) persons.*' All sorts of forces have to be encountered on the way. A dacoit or an anarchist can easily realise God because he is fearless. A push in the right direction is only necessary for him. How did Jagai and Madhai, rogues of the first water, become very good saints? They pelted stones at Nityananda, the disciple of Lord Gauranga. Nityananda won them by pure divine love. Dacoit Ratnakara became sage Valmiki.

Jyotirmaya Darshan

When you advance in meditation you can see your Ishta Devata in physical form. Lord Vishnu will give you darshan with four hands; Lord Krishna will appear before you with flute in his hands; Rama with bow and arrow in his hands; Lord Siva with trident.

Sometimes the Lord will come before you in the form of a beggar or sick man with dirty rags. He may appear before you in the form of a coolie or a man of low caste. You must have the keen sense to detect him. Your hair will stand on end when you meet him.

He appears in your dreams. Lord Ganesha comes in the form of an elephant in dreams. Devi appears in the form of a girl in your dreams.

During deep meditation you will have Jyotirmaya Darshan. You will behold a huge pillar of light. You will see infinite light and you will merge yourself in it. You will be struck with awe and wonder.

If you worship Lord Krishna intensely and constantly, you will see only Lord Krishna everywhere.

A Yogi should always avoid fear, anger, laziness, too much sleep or waking and too much food and fasting. If the above rule be well and strictly practised each day, spiritual wisdom will arise of itself in three months without doubt. In four months, he sees the Gods; in five months, he knows (or becomes) Brahmanishtha and truly in six months attains liberation at will. There is no doubt.

International Sivananda Yoga Vedanta Centres

Ashrams

Sivananda Ashram Yoga Camp
673 Eighth Avenue, Val Morin
Quebec, J0T 2R0, CANADA
Tel.: +1 819 322 32 26
Fax: +1 819 322 58 76
E-mail: hq@sivananda.org
Web: www.sivananda.org/camp

Sivananda Yoga Dhanwantari Ashram
P.O. Neyyar Dam, Dt.
Thiruvananthapuram
Kerala 695 572, INDIA
Tel.: +91 471 227 30 93
Fax: +91 471 227 27 03
Mob.: (00.91) 949 563 09 51
E-mail: guestindia@sivananda.org
Web: www.sivananda.org/neyyardam

Sivananda Yoga Vedanta Minakshi Ashram
Kalloothu, Saramthangi Village
Vellayampatti P.O., Palamedu (via)
Vadippatti Taluk, Madurai district
625 503 Tamil Nadu, INDIA
Tel.: +91 452 209 06 62
E-mail: madurai@sivananda.org
Web: www.sivananda.org/madurai

Sivananda Kutir (near Siror Bridge)
P.O. Netala, Uttara Kashi District
Uttaranchal, Himalayas 249193, INDIA
Tel.: +91 90 12 78 94 28
Tel.: +91 99 27 09 97 26
E-mail: himlayas@sivananda.org
Web: www.sivananda.org/netala

Sivananda Ashram Yoga Ranch
P.O. Box 195, Budd Road
Woodbourne, NY 12788, U.S.A.
Tel.: +1 845 436 64 92
Fax: +1 845 363 46 31
E-mail: yogaranch@sivananda.org
Web: www.sivanandayogaranch.org

Sivananda Ashram Yoga Retreat
P.O. Box N 7550
Paradise Island, Nassau,
BAHAMAS
Tel.: +1 866 559 51 67 (from USA)
Tel.: +1 416 479 01 99 (from Canada)
Tel.: +1 242 363 2902 (from all other countries)
Fax: (00.1) 242 363 37 83
E-mail: nassau@sivananda.org
Web: www.sivanandabahamas.org

Sivananda Ashram Yoga Farm
14651 Ballantree Lane, Comp. 8
Grass Valley, CA 95949, U.S.A.
Tel.: +1 530 272 93 22
Tel. (USA): 1 800 469 9642
Fax: +1 530 477 60 54
E-mail: yogafarm@sivananda.org
Web: www.sivanandayogafarm.org

Sivananda Yoga Retreat House
Bichlach, 40
6370, Reith near Kitzbühel,
AUSTRIA
Tel.: +43 (0)53 56 67 404
Fax: +43 (0)53 56 67 4044
E-mail: tyrol@sivananda.net
Web: www.sivananda.org/tyrol

Ashram de Yoga Sivananda
26 impasse du Bignon,
45170 Neuville aux bois,
FRANCE
Tel.: +33 (0)2 38 91 88 82
Fax: +33 (0)2 38 91 18 09
E-mail: orleans@sivananda.net
Web: www.sivananda.org/orleans

Centres

ARGENTINA

Centro Internacional Yoga Sivananda
Sánchez de Bustamante 2372
Capital Federal – Buenos Aires 1425
Tel.: +54 11 48 04 78 13
Fax: +54 11 48 05 42 70
E-mail: buenosaires@sivananda.org
Web: www.sivananda.org/buenosaires

Centro de Yoga Sivananda
Rioja 425
Neuquén 8300
Tel.: +54 29 94 42 55 65
E-mail: neuquen@sivananda.org
Web: www.sivananda.org/neuquen

AUSTRALIA

Sivananda Yoga Vedanta Centre
86 Tope street, South Melbourne, Victoria 3205
Tel.: +61 (0) 42 99 27 312
E-mail: melbourne@sivananda.net
Web: www.sivananda.com.au

AUSTRIA

Sivananda Yoga Vedanta Zentrum
Prinz-Eugenstrasse 18
Vienne 1040
Tel.: +43 01 586 34 53
Fax: +43 01 586 3453 40
E-mail: vienna@sivananda.net
Web: www.sivananda.org/viena

BRAZIL

Centro Sivananda de Yoga Vedanta
Rua Santo Antônio 374
Bairro Independência
Porto Alegre 90 220 - 010 – RS
Tel.: +55 51 30 24 77 17
E-mail: portoalegre@sivananda.org
Web: www.sivananda.org/portoalegre

CANADA

Sivananda Yoga Vedanta Centre
5178, Saint Laurent boulevard
Montreal, Qu.bec, H2T 1R8
Tel.: +1 514 279 35 45
Fax: +1 514 279 35 27
E-mail: montreal@sivananda.org
Web: www.sivananda.org/montreal

Sivananda Yoga Vedanta Centre
77 Harbord Street
Toronto, Ontario, M5S 1G4
Tel.: +1 416 966 96 42
Fax: +1 416 966 13 78
E-mail: toronto@sivananda.org
Web: www.sivananda.org/toronto

FRANCE

Centre Sivananda de Yoga Vedanta
140 rue du faubourg Saint-Martin
75010 Paris
Tel.: +33 (0)1 40 26 77 49
Fax: +33 (0)1 42 33 51 97
E-mail: paris@sivananda.net
Web: www.sivananda.org/paris

GERMANY

Sivananda Yoga Vedanta Zentrum
Steinheilstrasse 1
München 80333
Tel.: +49 089 700 9669 0
Fax: +49 089 700 9669 69
E-mail: munich@sivananda.net
Web: www.sivananda.org/munich

Sivananda Yoga Vedanta Zentrum
Schmiljanstrasse 24
D-12161 Berlin, GERMANY
Tel: +49.30.8599.9798
Fax: +49.30.8599.9797
e-mail: Berlin@sivananda.net
Web: www.sivananda.org/berlin

INDIA

Sivananda Yoga Vedanta Nataraja Centre
A-41, Kailash Colony
New Delhi 110 048
Tel.: +91.11 32 06 90 70 or 29 23 09 62
E-mail: delhi@sivananda.org
Web: www.sivananda.org/delhi/home.php

Sivananda Yoga Vedanta Dwarka Centre
PSP Pocket, Sector – 6
(near DAV school and next to Kamakshi Apts)
Swami Sivananda Marg, Dwarka
New Delhi 110 075
Tel.: +91.11 64 56 85 26
or 45 56 60 16
E-mail: dwarka@sivananda.org
Web: www.sivananda.org/dwarka/home.php

Sivananda Yoga Vedanta Centre
TC 37/1927 (5), Airport Road,
West Fort P.O.
695 023 Thiruvananthapuram.
Kerala
Tel.: +91.471 245 09 42 or 246 53 68
Mob.: +91.94 97 00 84 32
E-mail: trivandrum@sivananda.org
Web: www.sivananda.org/trivandrum

Sivananda Yoga Vedanta Centre
3/655 Kuppam Road, Kaveri Nagar, Kottivakkam
600 041 Chennai (Madras). Tamil Nadu
Tel.: +91.44 24 51 16 26 / 25 46
Mob.: +91 761 06 790
E-mail: chennai@sivananda.org
Web: www.sivananda.org/chennai

Sivananda Yoga Vedanta Centre
444, K.K. Nagar. East 9th Street
625 020 Madurai. Tamil Nadu
Tel.: +91.452 252 11 70 or 252 26 34
Mob.: +91.909 224 07 02
E-mail: maduraicentre@sivananda.org
Web: www.sivananda.org/maduraicentre

ISRAEL

Sivananda Yoga Vedanta Centre
6 Lateris Street
Tel Aviv 64166
Tel.: +972) 03 691 67 93
Fax: +972) 03 696 39 39
E-mail: telaviv@sivananda.org
Web: www.sivananda.org/telaviv

ITALY

Centro Yoga Vedanta Sivananda
Roma
via Oreste Tommasini, 7
Roma 00162
Tel.: +39 06 45 49 65 29
Mob.: +39 347 426 1345
E-mail: roma@sivananda.org
Web: sivananda-yoga-roma.it

Centro Yoga Vedanta Sivananda
via Guercino 1
Milano 20154
Tel.: +39 02 36 70 86 47
Mobile: +39 33 47 60 53 76
E-mail: milano@sivananda.org
Web: www.sivananda.org/milano

JAPAN

Sivananda Yoga Vedanta Center
4-15-3 Koenji-kita, Suginami-ku
Tokyo 1660002
Tel.: +81 03 53 56 77 91
E-mail: tokyo@sivananda.org
Web: www.sivananda.jp

LITHUANIA

Sivananda Jogos Vedantos Centras
M.K. Ciurlionio g. 66
Vilnius 03100
Tel.: +370) 8 64 87 28 64
E-mail: vilnius@sivananda.net
Web: www.sivananda.org/vilnius

SPAIN

Centro de Yoga Sivananda Vedanta
Calle Eraso 4
Madrid 28028
Tel.: +34.91 361 51 50
Fax: +34.91 361 51 94
E-mail: madrid@sivananda.net
Web: www.sivananda.org/madrid

SWITZERLAND

Centre Sivananda de Yoga Vedanta
1 rue des Minoteries
Geneva 1205
Tel.: +41 022 328 03 28
Fax: +41 022 328 03 59
E-mail: geneva@sivananda.net
Web: www.sivananda.org/geneva

THAILAND

Sivananda Yoga Vedanta Centre
3 Soi Prapinit – Suan Phlu
South Sathorn Road,
Thungmahamek
Bangkok 10120
Tel.: +66 (0) 2 287 17 14 /15
Mob.: +66 81 91 56 195
E-mail: bangkok@sivananda.org
Web: www.sivananda.org/thailand/home.php

UNITED KINGDOM

Sivananda Yoga Vedanta Centre
45 – 51 Felsham Road
London SW15 1AZ
Tel.: +44 020 87 80 01 60
Fax: +44 020 87 80 01 28
E-mail: london@sivananda.net
Web: www.sivananda.co.uk

UNITED STATES OF AMERICA

Sivananda Yoga Vedanta Center
1246 West Bryn Mawr
Chicago, IL 60660
Tel.: (00.1) 773 878 77 71
E-mail: chicago@sivananda.org
Web: www.sivananda.org/chicago

Sivananda Yoga Vedanta Center
243 West 24th Street
New York, NY 10011
Tel.: +1 212 255 45 60
Fax: +1 212 727 73 92
E-mail: newyork@sivananda.org
Web: www.sivananda.org/ny

Sivananda Yoga Vedanta Center
1200 Arguello Boulevard
San Francisco, CA 94122
Tel.: (00.1) 415 681 27 31
E-mail: sanfrancisco@sivananda.org
Web: www.sivananda.org/la

Sivananda Yoga Vedanta Center
13325 Beach Avenue
Marina del Rey, CA 90292
Tel.: +1 310 822 96 42
E-mail: losangeles@sivananda.org
Web: www.sivananda.org/la

URUGUAY

Asociación de Yoga Sivananda
Acevedo Díaz 1523
Montevideo 11200
Tel.: +598 24 01 09 29 / 66 85
Fax: +598 24 00 73 88
E-mail: montevideo@sivananda.org
Web: www.sivananda.org/montevideo

VIETNAM
Sivananda Yoga Vedanta Centre
25 Tran Quy Khoach Street,
District 1
Ho Chi Minh City
Tel.: +84 08 66 80 54 27 / 28
E-mail: hochiminh@sivananda.org
Web: www.sivanandayogavietnam.org